Keizersgracht 40-42-44
The *Groenland* (Greenland) warehouses; named like so many
warehouses, after places where the owners once did business. Built
in 1621, these three were once part of five identical step-gables. Goods
were conveniently loaded directly from building to boat.

Amsterdam Canal Guide

Tim Killiam

and Marieke van der Zeijden

text: Hans Tulleners

Uitgeverij Het Spectrum ⚡ Utrecht/Antwerpen

Illustrated by Tim Killiam
Layout and cover: Studio Spectrum/Tim Killiam
Cover drawings: Tim Killiam, coloring by Frans Vonno
First printing 1978

20-1001.01 D 1978/0265/184 ISBN 90 274 5977 0

Contents

Preface

Drawings of every one of the approximately 3000 houses along Amsterdams four major canals are to be found in this book, each accompanied by a short, written description. For those already familiar with the city, the 'Amsterdam Canal Guide' is the most complete and up-to-date document on the façades along the Singel, Herengracht, Keizersgracht, and Prinsengracht. For those new to the city, it is an introduction to an unique urban experience.

The drawings are based on the façades as seen from the opposite side of the canal in 1977, while the text concentrates on historical and architectural information with emphasis on dates. To show the relationship of one side of the canal to the other, the drawings of the façades along either side are arranged up-side-down to each other. Thus, when the book is held right-side-up (with respect to the cover), the reader is facing *Centrum* and vice versa. The uneven numbers are always on the inside, the *Centrum* side. More detailed information and drawings about some 50 houses of characteristic type and style, follow the canal section along with an illustrated list of terms used within the text.

These four major canals and the façades that line them reflect an important part of Amsterdams history. Each façade is a story within itself representing one or more stages in a gradual development that took place over centuries. From a birdseye view, the façades along the four canals suggest the rings of a tree as they document the growth of the city. Traces of the influences that shaped the city are to be seen in the façades. Short texts and illustrations providing general background information have been included in the front and back of the canal section. These range from a geological history to how the piles are driven in the ground. Special attention has been paid to the development of the important gable types and their identification.

The façades of Amsterdams canal houses have already been the subject of two previous books which also contain line drawings of façades. The first was the 'Grachtenboek' (Canal Book) by Caspar Philips who made engravings of the façades along the Brouwersgracht, Herengracht, and Keizersgracht as they stood in about 1770. Two centuries later a new edition was brought out with text. Today, the drawings of Caspar Philips occasionally serve as models for reconstruction projects.

In 1977 a new book called 'Vier Eeuwen Herengracht', (Four Centuries Herengracht) was published. In it are drawings made by architectural students during World War II of the façades along the Herengracht. In a large and beautifully bound edition, it provides not only more information about the house behind the façade but also compares the 'new' drawings with those of Caspar Philips.

Both of the above books are valued today as documents as well as collector's items and both have been important references for this book. Nevertheless, the 'Amsterdam Canal Guide' goes further by covering *all* the houses on all four canals as they are *today*. And, by adapting a small, inexpensive and easy to use format, the 'Amsterdam Canal Guide' lets the city's heritage be taken out of the library and onto the canals themselves where it can be enjoyed by all.

Tim Killiam

Oudezijds Kolk (left)
The beginning of one of Amsterdams oldest canals where the Oudezijds Voorburgwal (coming from under) and the Oudezijds Achterburgwal (coming from right) meet to form the 'Kolk'. In the background, the cupola of the Sint Nicolaaskerk (St. Nicholas Church), built 1888.

Singel (overleaf)
The beginning of the Singel.

Introduction

Amsterdam is an old city. It is already mentioned in written records dating
from 1275 when it would have consisted of only a few rows of houses on
the east bank of the Amstel. The early origins of this district around the
Warmoesstraat is reflected in the names of canals like *Oudezijds
Voorburgwal* and *Oudezijds Achterburgwal* (literally translated 'old-side
front city-wall' and 'old-side rear city-wall' as opposed to the 'new-side
front (and rear) city-wall' on the west bank).

City expansions were accompanied by the digging of new canals which,
up until the 17th century were used for defence among other things, and
up until the 19th century, for transport.

Around 1300, the *Spui* (sluice), *Grimburgwal* and the two 'front city-walls'
were dug. The one on the 'new' side, *Nieuwe Zijds Voorburgwal* still shows
a bend in its course where the digging followed the course of the smaller
river that was there before.

A second expansion followed at the end of the 14th century when the two
'back city-wall's were dug (*Nieuwezijds* and *Oudezijds Achterburgwal*).
After it was filled in (see p. 363), the *Nieuwezijds Achterburgwal* became
the *Spuistraat*. Initially the city grew in an east-west movement, with *Spui*
and *Grimburgwal*. Bounding the southern side.

The *Singel* was dug around 1425 walling in the city in the south as well
as the west. Its bend initiated the concentric growth-ring pattern
developed by the expansions that followed. The 1425 expansion also
reached across the Amstel with the *Kloveniersburgwal* and back up to the
Nieuwemarkt where it became the *Geldersekade*. Later, in the 15th
century a somewhat more massive wall was built along the inside of the
outer canals of which some parts are still intact such as the lower part
of the *Munt* (mint). Also built in the same period was the *Waag* (weigh-
house) on the Nieuwmarkt which served as one of the city gates.

The next city expansion was caused partially by the fact that the city became a haven for many types of people. After the fall of Antwerp in 1585 (see list of dates p. 362) the city was flooded with refugees. Starting out from the beginning of the Singel and running west, a small canal was dug called the *Brouwersgracht*. At the corner, where the Herengracht is now, it turned southward to bend around the town. In the 17th century it was extended further westward from the corner. Today the difference between the 16th and the 17th century parts is seen in the narrowness of the earlier section between the Singel and the Herengracht (see map p. 366/367.)

The most important expansion, which would quadruple the size of the city, began in 1613: the *Herengracht*, *Keizersgracht* and *Prinsengracht* were dug beginning with the Brouwersgracht and running in concentric form to the Leidsegracht.

Aesthetic considerations played a major role in this latest expansion. The Keizersgracht was planned as the widest canal: 28 meters. The other two: 25 meters wide. The digging of the canals marked the beginning of the area just outside the Prinsengracht - the Jordaan. In 1658, the second phase of the expansion, the canals were extended from the Leidsegracht to the Amstel. Forming the boundry of the city was the (outer) Singelgracht with its 26 bastions upon which stood windmills. The city kept this form for almost two more centuries.

The total remaining number of 17th century houses is limited. Most of the houses date from the 18th and were often rebuilt in the 19th century. Only third of the buildings of the inner city are old (built before ± 1850). In spite of some 'break-through'streets and a few large-scale (office-) buildings the city has managed to keep its unique character through its unique combination of private houses and tree-lined canals with hundreds of bridges. Though not seen from the outside, the trees are to be found within the open space behind the houses as well where a 17th century ordinance required that the grounds be used as gardens.

A lot of the old and valuable has been preserved in Amsterdam. Let's hope that later generations will also be able to enjoy it.

Time chart

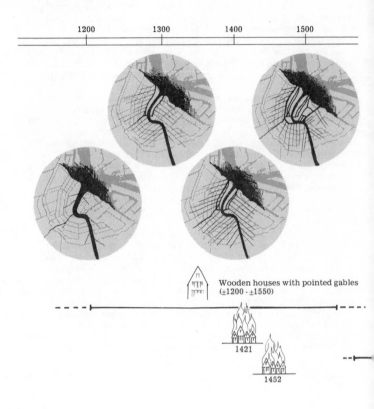

Wooden houses with pointed gables
(±1200 - ±1550)

1421

1452

Various stages in the
development of Amsterdam's
canals are shown here in
chronological order. The right-
hand plan is 'today'. The canal
system of any earlier period is
printed black on top of this
'today' situation, printed darker
grey.

The building periods of the
various gable types show how
the development from step- to
bell-gable in the so-called 'Golden
Age' coincided with the 17th
century expansions seen in the
plans directly above (2nd and
3rd from right).

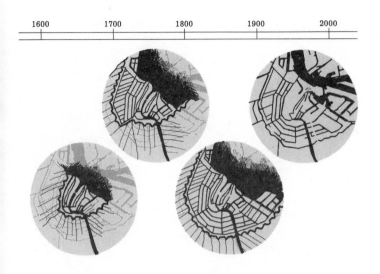

| 1600 | 1700 | 1800 | 1900 | 2000 |

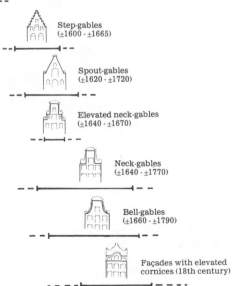

 Gables with roll ornaments
(±1570 - ±1600)

Step-gables
(±1600 - ±1665)

Spout-gables
(±1620 - ±1720)

Elevated neck-gables
(±1640 - ±1670)

Neck-gables
(±1640 - ±1770)

Bell-gables
(±1660 - ±1790)

Façades with elevated
cornices (18th century)

Façades with cornices (17th, 18th
and esp. 19th century)

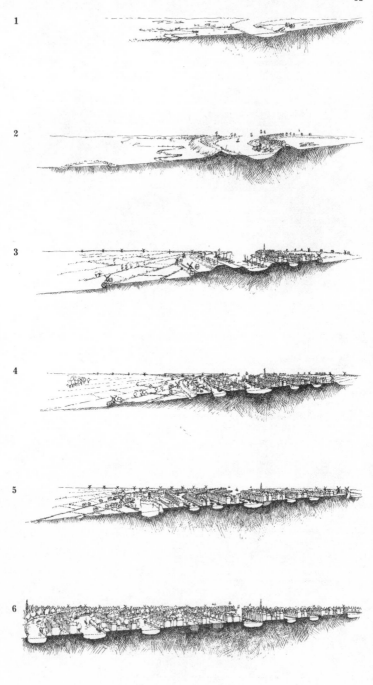

After an idea from Wim Timp, Municipal Bureau of Monument Care.

From polder to city

1. The natural watershed
A system of streams and tributaries gently drains excess water off the swamps and marshlands and, via the Amstel river, to the sea.

2. The dikes
Early inhabitants build their houses up on 'terps' (raised mounds of earth). When for some natural reason the sea level begins to rise, the settlers along the mouth of the Amstel construct the Zeedijk (sea-dike) and the Nieuwendijk (new-dike) as protection.

3. The windmill
The sea level keeps rising but a new innovation, using wind-power, allows the farmer to keep the water level in his fields artificially low. A side-effect however, since the peat shrinks as it dries, is that the level of the land sinks, thereby increasing the dependance on the dikes and windmills.

4. The city growth pattern
As the city grows the surrounding area must be filled in order to bring it up to the older parts. Canals are dug which provide drainage and sewage disposal as well as door-to-door transportation for commerce. The canals are flushed at low tide and re-filled with the high tide. To make the most use of the prevailing winds, the windmills are built on the southwest outskirts where they become the focal points for various industries. Traces of these industries are left in the names of streets and canals like Looiersgracht (tanners-canal) in the Jordaan area.

5. The city walls
Political and military considerations encouraged the building of walls (as well as canals), later to become fortified. The immovability of these walls in turn encourages maximum use of the space inside. Even so, developments spring up along the irrigation and transport canals outside the city walls. Sometimes a little extra space could be gained by making the waterways a little narrower.

6. Expansion
A thriving economy and a rapidly increasing population causes a period of tremendous growth in the 17th century. Although it was neither the first nor the last, it was certainly the most dramatic expansion. In about fifty years a huge additional area of land was enclosed within new, fortified city walls. Showing consideration for the value of the newly gained land, the area is planned in an orderly, concentric pattern. The map on pages 366-367 shows the difference between the old, closed spaces inside the Singel and the new, open spaces outside it. The form of the city acquired in this 17th century expansion changed very little until late in the 19th century.

The ground underneath

Three natural processes

The sea leaves deposits of clay

The rivers form a great sandy delta

Peat is left by the swamps that develop behind the wall of dunes formed by the action of the sea.

The ground under Amsterdam and much of Holland is made of three major ingredients: clay, sand and peat.
Layers of clay are left from periodical invasions by the sea. The sand is from the deltas formed by the Rhine, Maas and other smaller rivers. The peat layers are left by the swamps and marshes that developed behind the coastal dunes.

Over 250,000 years ago Holland was merely a bay in the North Sea. Then, over thousands of years the rivers built up sandy deltas. Later, along the coast, the action of the sea pushed the sand up to form a wall of dunes. Protected from the sea by the dunes, lagunes developed into plant-rich swamps and bogs. Repeats and various combinations of the above processes are responsible for the layer-cake formations underneath Amsterdam today. When Amsterdammers talk of the 'first and second layers', they mean the sand layers starting at ± 14 meters and ± 20 meters below the surface. Depending on when they were built and how heavy they are, most of the houses in Amsterdam stand on one of these two layers. Another layer, the so-called *boerenlaag* (farmers-layer), begins ± 7 meters below the surface, named probably after the fact that it is the same layer found closest to the surface out in the farmlands. Although better suited for the lighter weight wooden buildings, it was somtimes used for masonry buildings, especially if a recent fire had just left nothing but the old foundation. There are still buildings standing on the *boerenlaag* in Amsterdam, mostly in the Jordaan area.

Not very long ago the layer of peat presently found 4 to 5 meters below the surface, was once, not very long ago, top soil. The layer of sand and rubble above it is fill which originally would have come from canal dredgings. The big 17th century expansion required sand to be brought all the way from the coast. Since ±1945 sand has been used from dredgings from the IJsselmeer (the inland sea once called the Zuiderzee), the North Sea and from the digging of artificial lakes outside the city.

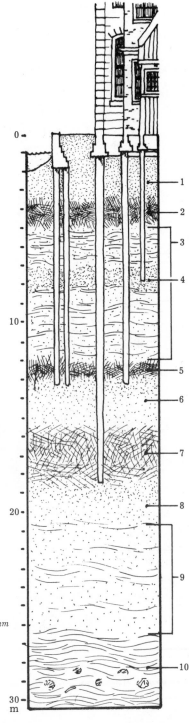

Section through the ground under Amsterdam
1. sand
2. peat
3. sand and clay
4. so-called *boerenlaag*
5. peat
6. first sand layer
7. sand and peat
8. second sand layer
9. sand with layers of clay
10. clay and shells

The Amsterdam canal house

1. crest
2. alliance shields
3. corner vases
4. loft-shutters
5. triglyph
6. console
7. fronton
8. hoist beam
9. cartouche
10. 17th century building height
11. claw piece
12. yearstone
13. oeil-de-boef (bull's eye)
14. relieving arch
15. 18th century sash work
16. 19th century sash work
17. festoon
18. wall anchor
19. 17th century cross-frame window
20. gable stone
21. *pui* cornice
22. *pui* beam
23. bottle baluster
24. harp piece
25. fan railing
26. pothouse
27. stoop
28. frontal stoop
29. 18th century building height
30. *attiek*
31. elevated cornice
32. attic loft
33. spout-gable
34. loft
35. fanlight
36. door lintel
37. cushion-door
38. pull bell
39. stoop bench
40. souterrain
41. sand and rubble
42. peat
43. first sand layer
44. second sand layer

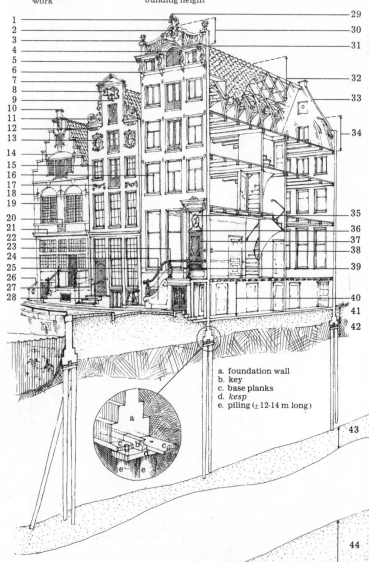

a. foundation wall
b. key
c. base planks
d. *kesp*
e. piling (± 12-14 m long)

Singel 410

17th century

18th century

19th century

The corner house shown here, Singel 410, was built in 1647. The upper
part, the elevated neck-gable and the house behind it have changed very
little since then. But the middle part is from an 18th century rebuilding
and the wooden *onderpui* (sub-structure) was built still later in the 19th
century.
Thus the façade may often be from a later period than the house behind
it. There are quite a few 17th century houses in Amsterdam with 18th or
19th century façade, and only a few with unaltered, older gables.

Gable types

Rather than large palaces and churches, Amsterdam is known for its houses which comprise so much of the inner city's 700 hectares (1729 acres). The total of approximately 7000 private homes now classified and protected as monuments is a testimony to the city's importance as a merchant center in the 17th and 18th centuries. The trademark of the city remains the private house, each with its own roof, door, and façade. The development of the latter is described in further below.

Wooden houses with pointed gables ($\pm$1200-$\pm$1550)
In the city's first three and a half centuries most houses were built of wood. The earliest type of houses were merely a single space defined by four wooden walls and a roof, but with the exception of a few places in North-Holland like Durgerdam, Broek in Waterland, and Edam, these houses have all either burned down or been torn down. In Amsterdam there are still two houses that would fall under the catagory of being wooden houses, even so they are both partly of brick. The oldest of the two, shown to the left, is Begijnhof 34 which dates from $\pm$ 1475. The pointed wooden gable is topped with a *makelaar* (the top piece that acts as a backbone joint). Earlier, this façade had steps leading up to what was once the front door on the left side. The upper part of the façade, supported by consoles, hangs slightly out over the lower part. Most of the weight of the house is supported by its wooden skeleton. Until the 16th century, the city stood full with this sort of house.
The second 'wooden' house is Zeedijk 1 dating from $\pm$ 1550. The danger of fire was always great with the wooden houses. All sorts of ordinances were passed to safeguard the city from fire, and by 1669 it was forbidden to build any more wooden façades.

Begijnhof 34

Singel 423

Façades with roll ornaments
(±1570-1600)

Very few of these old brick
façades were built in Amsterdam
and of them, only two are left.
One of them is no. 12 St.
Annenstraat (running off of the
city's oldest street, the
Warmoesstraat). Shown here
are the roll ornaments from the
other example, Singel 423. The
top of the façade has ball-shaped
pinnacles and a 1606 yearstone.
Until ±1700 the cross-frame
windows were filled with leaded
glass. Above the windows are
the so-called relieving arches
often found on step-gables which
perform a decorative as well as
structural function by carrying
the weight of the wall above to
either side of the window. Two
of the lion masks that ornament
the façade are visible in the
drawing.

Step-gables (±1600-±1665)

The step-gable, along with a
large number of wooden gables
filled the city prior to ± 1665.
The roof as shown here on
Herengracht no. 361, begins at
the ceiling level of the first floor.
Thus the step-gable is recognized
by its typical 17th century
building height as well as its
stepped profile. This façade
from ± 1655 has Renaissance
characteristics in the form of
horizontal, sandstone bands.
The relieving arches above the
windows include keystones (at
the top) and springers (the
sandstone blocks at the base of
the arch). The top of each of
the 'steps' is decked with a
sandstone coping block. In the
18th century the façade had
little ornamentation, and then
only on the top of the severe
brick façade.

Herengracht 361

Prinsengracht 771-773

Spout-gables (±1620-±1720)

This type of gable was rarely used for the front façade of a house, but it was often used on the rear façade, where, as opposed to the front façade, it usually remained relatively unaltered. The spout-gable as a front façade was more frequently used for warehouses. Many can be found lining the Prinsengracht which in the 1613 extension plan was designated a commercial area.

Today a lot of these warehouses, often as deep as 30 meters, are being converted to apartments or offices. In both cases, because of the depth, light-wells must often be built in the middle of the building. The example shown here, Prinsengracht 771-773, dates from ± 1665 and was converted to an office space in 1976.

The spout-gables are recognized by their upside-down funnel shape and their tops which are ornamented with a fronton or finished with a sandstone coping. The upper corners are also decked with a sandstone plate or volute. The loft-doors and window opening are often arched and the stone blocks around the loft-openings, as well as having a decorative function, serve to provide a stable base for the door hinges. The metal rollers above the openings protect both the brickwork and the rope from chafe as goods are swung in and out.

Elevated neck-gables (±1640-±1670)

This type of gable is sometimes seen as a cross between the step-gable and the 'normal' neck-gable. It has only two steps both of which are filled with sandstone claw pieces. (The 'normal' neck-gable has only one step on either side.) The example shown here, Prinsengracht 92, has typical 17th century ornamentation: fronton on top and 'oeils-de-boeuf' (bull's eyes). Often the façade is faced with pilasters.

On Prinsengracht 92, built in 1661, the upper pilasters are Ionic while those on the 1st and 2nd floors are Doric. Elevated neck-gables were built over a very short period especially compared to the 'normal' neck-gable.

Neck-gables (±1640-±1770)
The first *halsgevel* (Herengracht 168, p. 95) dating from 1638, was designed by Philip Vingboons. The top of most brick neck-gables is characterised by the single pair of 'steps' filled with sandstone claw pieces. The 17th century neck-gable as exemplified here by Keizersgracht 504 is recognizable by its fronton (sometimes rounded) and by the fruit and flower motif in the claw pieces. This motif appears again in the festoons (also called garlands) The 18th century neck-gable is somewhat taller and its claw pieces more richly ornamented than its 17th century predecessor. All sorts of variations can be found. Singel 116 shown here dates from 1752 and sports three heads with large noses. Although most neck-gable façades are brick, some were made entirely from sandstone, the most well-known being Herengracht nos. 364 to and including 370 (see pp. 112-113).

Prinsengracht 92

Keizersgracht 504

Singel 116

Bell-gables (±1660-±1790). Bell-gables and neck-gables are similar in that both are bell-shaped in silhouette. But instead of sandstone claw pieces the brick area is extended and finished with a sandstone trim. The example shown here on the left, Singel 92 dates from ± 1680. It is typical of the early, 17th century bell-gables with its fronton (here rounded) and cluster ornamentation along the sides of the top. A typical 18th century neck-gable, Herengracht 287, has been drawn along side the Singel house to illustrate the difference in height. The Herengracht house dates from ± 1750. It is ornamented with sandstone trim and topped with a Louis XV crest. Most bell-gables were built in this period and in this style.

Singel 97 (L), *Herengracht 287* (R)

Façades with elevated cornices
(18th century)

The majority of old houses in Amsterdam are 2 or 3 windows wide, have brick façades, and are topped with a straight cornice. In the 18th century the cornice was often arched (or 'elevated') in the middle to accommodate larger loft-shutters providing easier access to the hoist beam.

Singel 56, above, has a richly ornamented and bell-shaped *attiek* over the elevated cornice and four consoles. Note how the *attiek* covers and hides the end of the roof.

Singel 56

Herengracht 274, middle, dates from ± 1740 and also has an elevated cornice. Instead of the shutters there is a gable stone identifying the house as 'D'Witte Lelie' (the white lily). And above the cornice is an *attiek* in the form of an open balustrade. These elevated cornices, often highly ornamented, were all built in the 18th century. In the 19th century the amount of ornamentation declined and the elevated cornice became a straight cornice.

Herengracht 274

Cornice façades (17th, 18th, and esp. 19th century)

Most of the cornice façades were built in the 19th century. After ± 1790 no more step-, spout-, neck- and bell-gables were built. There was a sobering process in the architecture. The sculpture work, provided by the stone-cutters guild until 1798, disappeared from the tops. Keizersgracht 610 has a top that was 'modernised' into a cornice. Before the rebuilding it was an identical triplet of nos. 608 and 606. Many gables were rebuilt in the late 18th and 19th century as cornice façades. These 'sobered' tops, with considerably less ornamentation, seemed to reflect the deteriorating economic situation that developed in that period. Cornice façades were built in the city up until ± 1920.

Keizersgracht 610

Singel

Key to symbols

123 House number.
(44) Corner building whose front façade is on a side street or canal.

M. identifies a building on the Monument List.

C abbreviation for century (17thC).

* more information to be found in Appendix, pp. 332.

e.g. for example; among other things.

Dutch words are printed in *cursief*.

Relevant terms are defined in the List of terms, pp. 352-361.

Stromarkt

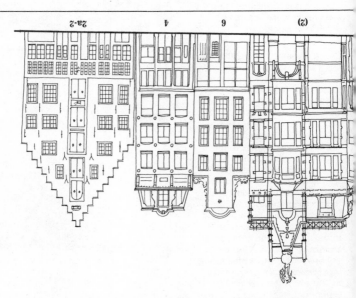

Singel 2-6

2-2a M. built ±1610; one of the oldest houses in Amsterdam and also one of the broadest step-gables; *gable stone*; combination home/warehouse.*
4 late 19thC façade with straight cornice and ornamented window.
6 M. early 18thC neck-gable with 19thC street front.
(Haarlemmerstraat 2) late 19thC building; railing on the flat roof, globe on the small gable topped by an angel, bay windows.

The canals are arranged in concentric order, starting counter-clockwise with the Singel. Uneven numbers are always in the inside, seen when 'facing' Centrum (right-side-up with respect to the cover).

Stromarkt

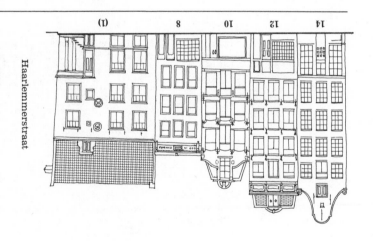

Haarlemmerstraat

(1)   8   10   12   14

Singel 8-14

(Haarlemmerstraat 1) M. 18thC side-façade with round windows that shed light on staircase well; saddle roof visible from side.

8 M. built ±1800; brick façade with Empire cornice and 2 consoles; shop front altered later; proverb added later to cornice.

10 late 19thC house with flat roof and balconies.

12 M. 18thC building with cornice façade. The top was changed in the 19thC when the saddle roof was removed.

14 M. 18thC building with bell-formed top with 2 volutes.

16 M. 18thC 6 window wide building with a hipped roof (most buildings are only 2-3 windows wide); the door is varnished rather than painted.
18 M. early 19thC building with Empire cornice and 2 consoles.
20 M. early 19thC building with Empire cornice; roof altered later; frontal stoop in place of the usual stoop (see no. 18).
22 M. building dates from 1712: original door frame and stoop, but what was the door itself is now a window; top altered later.

22   20   18   16

Brouwersgracht

Stromarkt

(Stromarkt 2) side façade, mainly 19thC.
1 M. late 18thC cornice façade; lower part altered early 20thC; wooden street front scheduled for restoration soon by owner 'Stadsherstel'. The rear façade of this building faces the Stromarkt.
3 M. rebuilt 19thC with cornice façade; the stoop is the oldest part.
5 19thC cornice facade; saddle roof is easily seen from the street.
7 known as the narrowest house in Amsterdam, no wider than a door. In fact, this is the back-side of a house on the Jeroenensteeg.
7a-9 newly built in early 20thC: accent is on the windows, specifically the vertical lines.

Singel 24-34

24 M. built ±1760: straight cornice and fine sandstone *attiek* with ship; street front and windows altered later.
26 18thC neck-gable but door framing is from later period.
28 18thC neck-gable; formerly a home/warehouse.
30 18thC building with straight cornice and *attiek*; the front of the souterrain is sculptured; large Amsterdam door has disappeared (compare nos. 28 and 32), and has been replaced by two separate entrances.
32 M. 18thC canal house with straight cornice from a later period.
34 M. 18thC façade with fanlight; hipped roof was added at a later date.

11 M. the Lutheran Church, built ±1670; designed by A. Dortsman; domeshape is rare in the Netherlands; rebuilt in 19thC after a fire and later fully restored.

The Sonesta Hotel uses it as a conference hall. There is an underground tunnel connecting the church to the hotel, 13 M. built ±1800 cornice façade with transverse roof; handsome entrance.

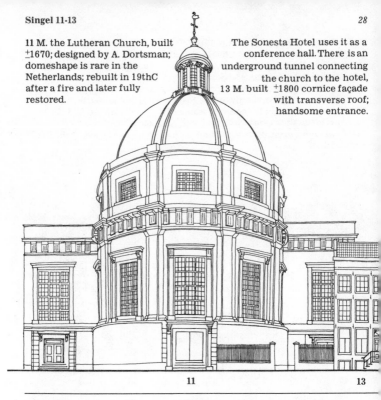

11   13

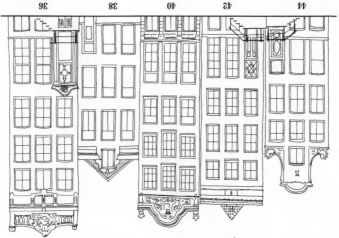

36   38   40   42   44

Singel 36-44

36 M. built in 1763: cornice with *attiek*. The top crest and door frame are Louis XV asymmetrical style.

38 late 19thC building with windows all of equal size; no stoop.

40 M. built ±1725; cornice with Louis XIV ornaments; 2 corner vases; stoop gone.

42 18thC building with early 19thC cornice; roof just top visible; door and entrance from early 19thC.

44 M. neck-gable from ±1750; slightly altered; cushion-door; stoop bench. recently been restored.

15 late 19thC façade with straight cornice and dormer; mansarde roof (compare no. 13); basement entrance since removed.

17 a very un-Amsterdam house from the 19thC; reminiscent of German half-timbered style; frontal stoop.

19-21 M. 17thC house; wider than it is deep, which is unusual in Amsterdam; bell-gable added – ±1760 providing a ware house function to what was earlier just a home; handsome entrance dates from late 17thC;

23-25 M. Beautiful twin cornice façades; both have a remarkably well preserved elevated cornice with *attiek* (± 1740); no. 25 still has a stoop bench.

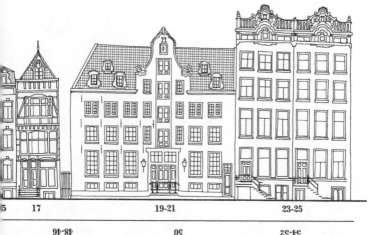

5   17   19-21   23-25

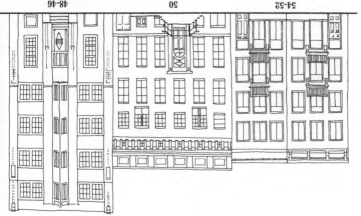

48-46   50   54-52

46-48 M. built in 1920; good example of Amsterdam school characteristics with brick ornamentation. Note width of the windows stressed rather than height.

50 M. predominantly 19thC façade with straight cornice and brick *attiek*; now 6 windows wide, however in former days probably 2 separate houses; door in three parts; double stoop.

52-54 M. late 19thC houses with straight cornices; balconies (rarely seen on canals); doors at street-level (compare no. 50).

27 M. 19thC cornice façade; stoop and entrance in the middle which is unusual; building does not lean forward (compare no. 25).

29 M. identified as 19thC by its stucco and straight cornice; top also altered in that period; house number also in same style.

31 neo-renaissance step-gable from ±1890; ground floor and stoop older; windows on the second floor relatively large; lion masks underneath the corner vases.

33 20thC building; flat roof and a beautiful tile tableau over the entrance.

66 M. 18thC elevated cornice with Louis XV ornamentation; corner vases combination).

64 M. 1638 step-gable and an 18thC under structure (an unusual date from ±1760; building forms a twin with no. 68.*

62 late 19thC neo-renaissance step-gable; stoop is older.

60 M. 18thC building with a sandstone elevated cornice. In spite of the cornices, nos. 56, 58 and 60 have a typical Amsterdam saddle roof.

58 M. 18thC building; cornice from early 19thC; door framing and stoop have Louis XV ornamentation, cellar front also ornamented.

56 M. 18thC building with sandstone cornice, crest and bust.

35 newly built in the 1920's; façade in outward bending relief.

37 newly built in the 1920's; semi-circular windows on 3rd floor. The façade is un-painted brick.

39 M. top converted about 1800 into a hipped roof; unusual 4 window wide cornice façade.

41 M. narrow house with elevated cornice façade dating back to ±1790.

No house number; 19thC cornice façade; altered roof; there is no street number and no door. It may actually be the rear of a building on the next street or an annex to one of the buildings on either side.

43 17thC corner building altered many times; straight cornice and hipped roof built ±1800; original wooden street front still present.

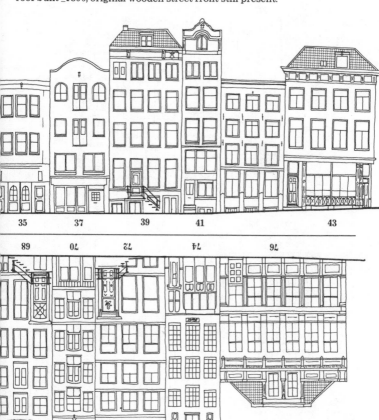

35   37   39   41   43

89   70   72   74   76

76 late 19thC house with straight cornice and a large dormer.

74 M. 18thC neck-gable with gable stone; two oval windows in sculptured sandstone frames. The stoop disappeared with the reconstruction of the lower structure in 1912.

72 M. 19thC building with straight cornice; stoop and door framing older.

70 late 18thC warehouse (still un-protected by monument classification); under one hipped roof with no. 72.

68 M. 18thC with elevated cornice; Louis XV ornamentation dating ±1760; a twin with no. 66; hardly altered.*

45 - (Korte Korsjespoortsteeg 11a) M. corner house built in 1725 (date inscribed on top): two corner vases; handsome sculptured sandstone and elevated cornice; ornamentation in stone.

47 M. largely 19thC façade with straight cornice and dormer.

49 newly built in early 20thC; flat roof.

51 M. early 19thC cornice façade; saddle roof easily seen; stoop gone.

53 M. identified as 17thC by its size and wooden front; much altered; the bell-gable was sobered and the windows enlarged in 19thC.

55 M. 19thC cornice façade; wooden street front much older.

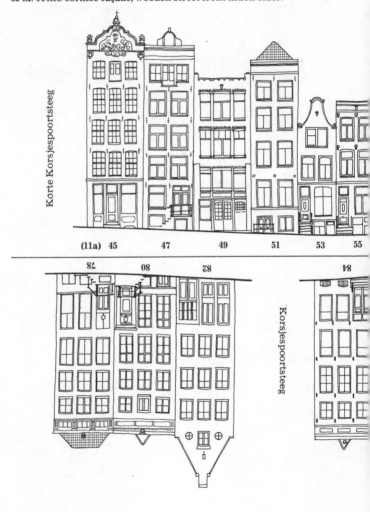

(11a)   45   47   49   51   53   55

78 M. built ±1800 with straight cornice and hipped roof.

80 M. late 18thC building with cornice; top of saddle roof just visible.

82 newly built in 1940; sort of a spout-gable; same size windows on all floors (compare with no. 80).

84 M. 19thC building; straight cornice, ornamented anchors and frontal stoop; top of roof just visible.

57-59 newly built in 1903; railing done in Jugendstil iron work.
61 M. late 18thC cornice façade with consoles and hipped roof; little changed.
63 M. 18thC bell-gable; top sobered later; cushion-door; fanlight.
65 M. bell-gable dating from ±1735; little changed; windows become smaller towards the top as in most old buildings.
67 M. neck-gable from 1724 (see top); corner vases; entrance altered.
69 late 19thC cornice façade (saddle roofs were hardly built anymore then).
71 M. sobered in 19thC into a small cornice façade; wooden street front.

| 57-59 | 61 | 63 | 65 | 67 | 69 | 71 |

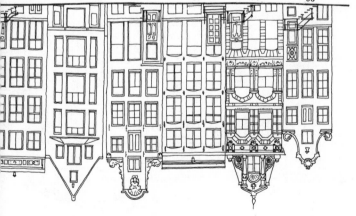

| 98 | 88 | 90 | 92 | 94 | 96 |

96 M. fine bell-gable from ±1755; high stoop; little else changed.
94 façade dates from 1876; lower structure and stoop older.
92 M. cornice façade; windows slightly arched; frontal stoop in place of the usual (see nos. 90 and 94).
90 M. early 18thC neck-gable; hoist beam ornamented with a cartouche.
88 adapted architecture from the 1940's; bay windows give outward relief to façade.
86 M. 19thC building with cornice; original sash work on first floor altered.

73 M. neck-gable ±1730; façade altered 19thC; wooden street-front also altered; frontal stoop.

75 M. neck-gable built in 1723 with 17thC elements including oval glass in sculptured sandstone frames; wooden street front; gable stone.

77 M. neck-gable from 1744 (see gable stone above hoist beam).

79 late 19thC façade with top in bell-shape; 18thC volutes.

81 altered around 1900; flat-topped roof; wooden street front; frontal stoop.

83-85 M. side façade dates to 1652 with pilasters and festoons; *pui* beam; pothouse: wooden street front; little changed.

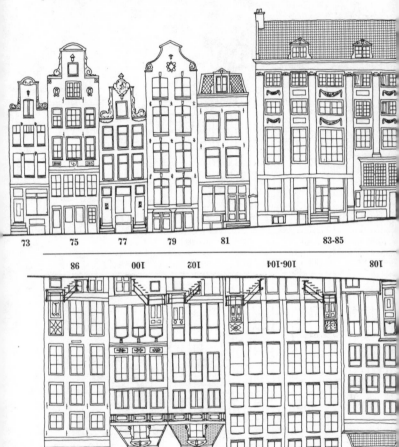

| 73 | 75 | 77 | 79 | 81 | 83-85 |

| 86 | 100 | 102 | 106-104 | 108 |

98 M. early 19thC cornice façade; on the street front is written 'Het Meerblad.'

100 M. façade converted completely into cornice façade ±1870.

102 M. 18thC façade with straight cornice and consoles (compare no. 100).

104-106 M. tallest twin bell-gables in Amsterdam dating back to ±1740; top ornamented with vases. No. 106 has a decorative fanlight. The windows get smaller towards the top as with most old houses.*

108 M. 18thC façade with hipped roof and cornice from ±1800; window railings on first floor; stoop posts.

87 M. tall neck-gable; corner vases and bust above hoist beam indicate house built ±1730; street front altered later.
89 late 19thC cornice façade; roof instead of saddle; flat-topped dormer.
91 early 20thC cornice façade; harmony of windows is completely disturbed (compare no. 93).
93 M. built ±1750; façade with elevated cornice including consoles and ornamentation in the middle; sometimes called a sunken bell-gable; little else has been changed.
95 M. hipped roof built around 1800; straight cornice; 4 windows wide instead of normal 2; 2 doors.

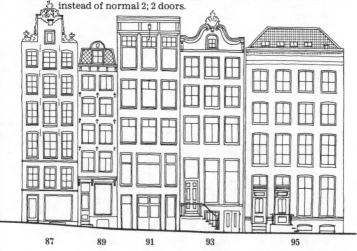

87   89   91   93   95

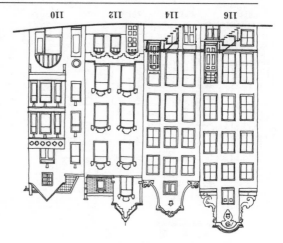

110   112   114   116

110 corner house dates from beginning of 20thC.
112 newly built early 20thC with small top gable; windows same size on all floors (compare no. 114).
114 M. bell-gable from ±1750; lower part altered 19thC; door dates from ±1900 and has Jugendstil wrought-iron railing.
116 M. neck-gable with nicely ornamented claw pieces from ±1750 from which comes name 'house of noses'; door and fanlight early 19thC.

97 M. late 17thC bell-gable with corner vases and fronton; ground floor and 1st floor altered in beginning of 19thC when stoop disappeared. The door can be opened in 2 parts.

99 M. 18thC building; altered and elevated in beginning of 19thC when straight cornice was built; large door was replaced by small entrance way and 2 smaller doors.

101 M. early 18thC neck-gable; much altered, stoop gone; façade is painted unusual color.

103 asymmetrical construction with bay windows from early 20thC.

105 newly built ±1910 with flat roof.

107 neo-Renaissance step-gable from ±1890; ground floor has semi-circular windows.

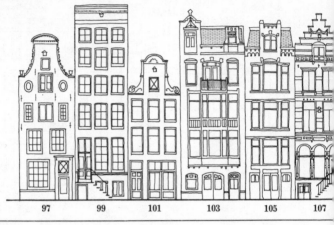

97   99   101   103   105   107

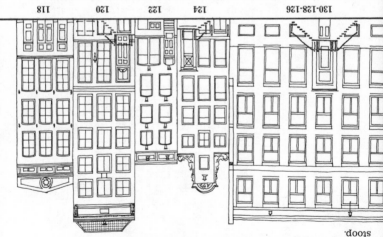

118   120   122   124   130·128·126

118 M. 19thC building with cornice with slightly peaked elevation; sun design of the wooden cornice identifies this auction hall as 'De Zon' (the sun).

120 M. cornice façade with hipped roof, ±1800; 17thC sandstone front.

122 late 19thC façade with straight cornice and 2 hoist beams; traditional large door was replaced by a portal and 2 doors.

124 M. neck-gable from 1st quarter of 18thC; house number and the name of the occupants inscribed in the same style.

126·128·130 newly built construction in historical style replaces 3 older houses that stood here until 1915; 6 windows wide; 2 hoist beams; double stoop.

109 façade altered before 1900; modern door with old lintel.
111 M. built ±1785; façade with straight cornice and consoles; since then much altered; door and stoop; no sash work on 3rd floor windows.
113 M. door and door frame dates from ±1750; double stoop; 4 windows wide façade with straight cornice; fine consoles.
115 M. ±1745 façade with ornamented, elevated cornice; door framing and doorway lintel from same period. The saddle roof was altered when the building height was increased.

109   111   113   115

132   134   136   138

132 M. 4 window wide, sandstone façade; door frame from ±1730; Empire stoop railing from ±1800; double stoop.
134 M. built ±1740; sandstone façade with elevated cornice, *attiek* and 3 Louis XVI bottle shaped balusters on stoop.
136 M. ±1800 cornice façade with sandstone corner lisenas.
138 M. 18thC building 19thC top, festoons under the straight cornice; fanlight and door early 19thC.

117 M. largely 19thC façade, cornice and hipped roof.
119 M. 18thC building; elevated in 19thC when straight cornice was fitted; 18thC *attiek* replaced on top; nice old door.
121 M. ±1730 transverse roof; façade with straight cornice, consoles and windows; brick façade is not painted.
123-125 M. these 2 houses were joined by a straight cornice and a sandstone façade beginning of the 18thC; door frame also 18thC.

117   119   121   123-125

142-140   144   146   148

148 M. 18thC bell-shaped top; the sandstone ornaments that go with an 18thC bell-gable are missing.
146 M. early 19thC façade with straight cornice and consoles; transverse roof. The door and frame date from the same period.
144 M. early 19thC cornice façade, slightly over 3 meters wide.
The step-gable was reconstructed with the 1967 restoration.*
altered into a cornice façade while the original lower part was retaind.
Hendrick de Keyser ±1605. In the course of the years no. 140 has been
140-142 M. early 17thC twin façade with roll ornaments, designed by

127 newly built in 1915: 3 identical floors, same size windows; lower structure runs back until the Spuistraat.

129 M. 19thC cornice façade; arched windows.

131 'doll'-size corner house with 17thC building height; façade altered early 19thC; roof changed later.

133 façade altered end 19thC but the building is older; cornice façade; frontal stoop; 2 doors in place of the unusual, large, single door.

135 M. handsome façade from ±1740; 2 corner vases; property of 'Stadsherstel'.

137 M. façade with cornice elevated for *attiek* shutters ±1740; ornamented cellar front; cushion door.

139 reconstructed early 20thC making use of an older, straight cornice from ±1800; windows of same size on all floors.

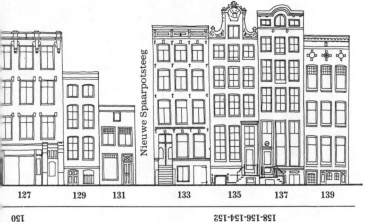

Nieuwe Spaarpotsteeg

127   129   131   133   135   137   139

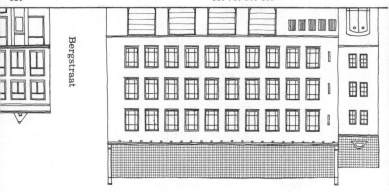

150   158-156-154-152

Bergstraat

130 M. 19thC cornice façade still with its 17thC building height; door in side façade retains 17thC width; front of saddle roof finished in wood.

152-154-156-158 overscaled (use of several plots for construction of one complex); newly built in 1939 with large transverse roof and windows; unusual sash work.

141 M. 19thC cornice façade; small window in cornice; frontal stoop.

143 M. 19thC cornice façade; window grouping differs from no. 141, result: no stoop; entrance is at street-level.

145 M. late 18thC bell gable with rare Louis XVI ornamentation on top; door dates from ±1790.

147 newly built ±1900 with an effort to reconstruct in the old style; top is spout-gable shaped; windows grow smaller towards top.

149 late 19thC façade; upper structure altered later; unusual hoist beam.

151-153 newly built with Amsterdam school features; oval-shaped windows on 1st, 2nd floor. No. 153 has inscription stones dating 1912.

155 M. ±1755 bell gable with Louis XV on top.

| 141 | 143 | 145 | 147 | 149 | 151-153 | 155 |

| 160 | 162 | 164 | 166 | 168 | 172-170 | 174 |

174 M. ±1730; cornice façade with ornamentation; elevated in middle.

170-172 M. 4 window wide cornice façade; straight cornice encloses 4 windows from late 18thC; ornate entrance.

168 early 19thC façade with straight cornice and hipped roof.

166 M. narrowest shop in Amsterdam (1.80 meters wide); late 18thC cornice façade.

164 M. late 18thC building with straight cornice and hipped roof.

162 M. 18thC building; top sobered in bell-gable shape in 19thC; handsome fanlight.

160 late 19thC straight cornice façade; dormer and flat roof; stoop may be older.

157 M. stucco neck-gable from 1717; about to be restored by 'Stadsherstel'; handsomely situated close to Amsterdam's widest bridge, where once stood a tower.

159 M. bell-gable from ±1760 (see 2nd part text no. 157).

159a - Torensteeg 8 M. side of neck-gable ±1745; sculptured window frames (note complete lack of function in top ornaments.

161 M. corner house with façade slanting into the Torensteeg; straight cornice fitted just before 1800; saddle roof easily visible.

163 M. 18thC building; straight cornice fitted early 19thC; sash work partially altered.

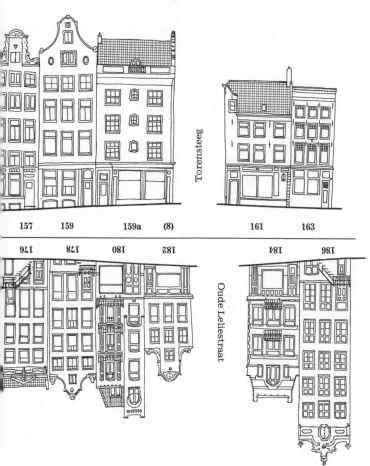

157   159   159a   (8)   161   163

Torensteeg

176   178   180   182   184   186

Oude Leliestraat

176 M. late 18thC façade with straight cornice, consoles and fronton; Louis XVI ornamentation on consoles and cornice; transverse roof; high stoop; building has undergone little change.

178 M. bell-gable from ±1760 with large ornaments on top.

180 newly built in 1905 with 3 identical flats; 'defense tower' on roof with semi-circular window; Jugendstil doors.

182 M. 17thC corner house with early 18thC neck-gable; lower shop front has been altered frequently.

184 newly built in the 20thC; trapezoidal shaped top.

186 M. sandstone façade with ornamented cornice and bust of Mercury dating ±1730; hoist beam with head; hardly changed.

Overscaled modern architecture from 1914 for which 6 old houses were torn down on the Singel, and still more on the Spuistraat. This building and the next (p. 43) continue through to the Spuistraat where they share the same number, 138.

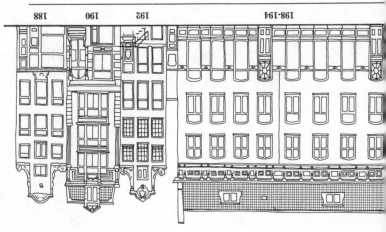

188 M. 1737 neck-gable with gable stone, 'De Roo Oly molen' (oil mill); lower street front has been altered.

190 late 19thC with flat roof and ashlar street front.

192 M. beautiful neck-gable from 1739; date of construction under claw pieces; cushion-door; house has undergone little change.

194-198 construction from 1879 with straight cornice and many consoles; transverse roof. The upper part of the windows have been arched.

Singel 202-210

202-208 newly built in 1921 with Amsterdam School features: much relief and brick ornamentation in the façade. On the side is the Driekoningenstraat. Through this alley is good view of the Bartolotti house, Herengracht 170-172 and behind it, the Westertoren.
210 M. most warehouses were built in the 17thC; here an example from ±1790 with straight cornice and hipped roof. It has an ashlar street front with 2 entrances and semi-circular fanlights.

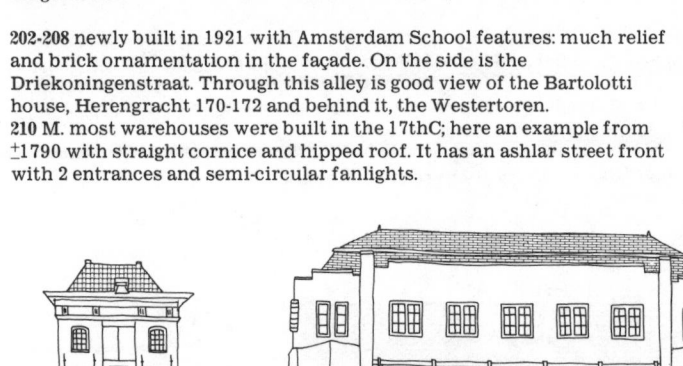

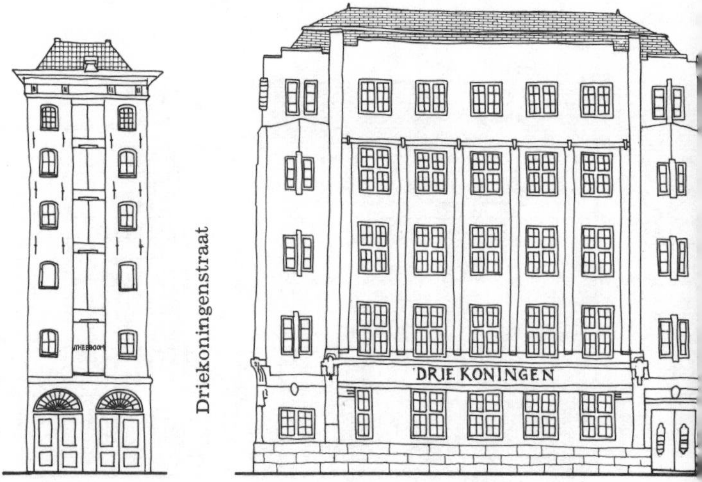

210   Driekoningenstraat   DRIE KONINGEN   208-202

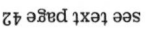

see text page 42

183 1925 with Amsterdam school features; relief and brick ornamentation; wooden elements in façade.

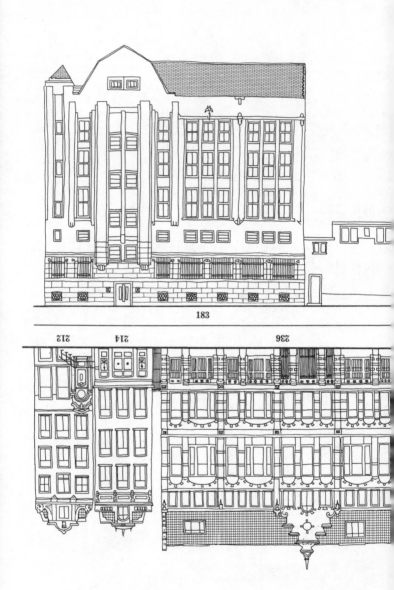

183

212   214   236

212 M. 18thC building with sandstone bell-shaped top; saddle roof was replaced by a flat roof in the 19thC; ashlar street front also from 19thC; circular fanlight.
214 19thC façade with straight cornice, balustrade and ornamented dormer; entrance at street-level (compare no. 212).
236 ±1890; 5 buildings were demolished for this one constructed in neo-renaissance style (see, for example, the step-gable and arches above the windows).

187 M. Witte Huis (white house); a 'young' momument designed by the Verheul Brothers in 1899; Jugendstil, especially ashlar street front; white tiles. The University of Amsterdam wanted to pull this building down in 1974, but numerous protests managed to save it.

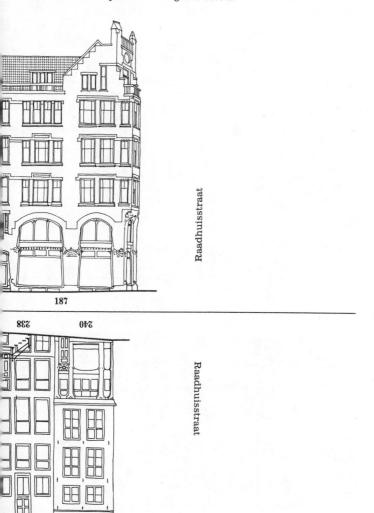

187

Raadhuisstraat

Raadhuisstraat

238   240

238 M. 17thC bell-gable with festoons around the hoist beam and fronton on top; 2 pinnacles.
240 M. early 19thC façade with straight cornice and 2 small windows; saddle roof just visible; shop front with Jugendstil motif ±1900.

207 over-scaled construction newly built in 1900; bay window on the corner of the Raadhuisstraat. In 1894 8 houses were demolished for this building. Earlier the Warmoesgracht ran through the N.Z. Voorburgwal and the Herengracht. It was filled in 1896 when the Raadhuisstraat was laid out.

Raadhuisstraat

207

250

250 5 old buildings stood here until 1911. Then in 1912, this over-scaled construction was newly built in a historical style making use of stone, pilasters, festoons and a balustrade. The complex was enlarged in 1927 when another 3 houses were torn down.

213 8 houses were demolished for this over-scaled construction newly built in 1908. Still more houses on the backside, along Spuistraat, were also torn down. In 1932 a piece was added (see page 48).

213

258 M. ±1660 painted sandstone neck-gable with festoons and an eagle on top; 19thC entrance.

260 M. 17thC neck-gable. The slope of the wooden roof is visible in the upper windows.

262 M. neck-gable from ±1750; sculptured stoop.

264 M. 18thC building with ornamented cornice; doorway lintel.

266 M. late 17thC neck-gable; door frame is from ±1800.

268 M. cornice façade from ±1800 as well as street front.

233 M. bell-gable from ±1750; lower part altered late 19thC when balconies were also fitted; stoop has a turning approach.

235 M. 19thC cornice façade with wooden wainscoting covering the saddle roof; 2 frontal stoops.

237 late 19thC corner house with window frames. The building does not lean (compare nos. 233 and 235).

233   235   237

Paleisstraat

270   272   274   276   278   280

Gasthuismolensteeg

280 M. 18thC building with straight cornice from early 19thC.

278 M. cornice façade with late 19thC shopfront; name of bar handsomely painted on window.

276 M. 18thC building with altered 19thC top; 18thC door frame.

274 M. late 18thC house with cornice and 19thC roof.

272 M. cornice façade; rebuilt in 19thC with original cornice from ±1800; door larger than usual; minimal stoop.

270 M. ±1800 corner façade; saddle roof has disappeared (compare no. 268).

239 20 houses were demolished for the 'Bungehuis' built 1932-34; ashlar façade; windows and doors in bronze; nothing painted.

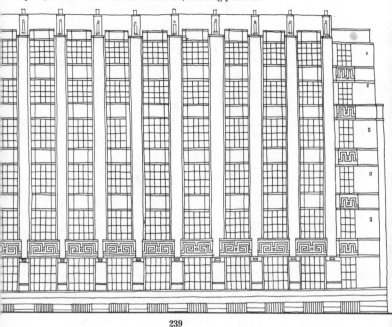

239

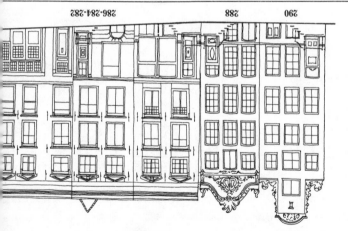

286-284-282   288   290

Singel 282-290

282-284-286 M. 3 houses all built in 1639 by one of the well known 17thC architects, Philip Vingboons. The tops were altered later but the houses still carry their 17thC window frontons; lisena façade. No. 284 has an Empire door; the door of no. 286 is varnished instead of painted the usual canal-green.

288 M. ±1755 sandstone façade with sculptured, elevated cornice; 3 Louis XIV bottle shaped balusters on the stoop and Empire cushion door; stoop bench; unusual *attiek* shutter in the shape of a clover.*

290 M. neck-gable, upper part early 18thC, lower part rebuilt 19thC; at restoration in 1974, the 19thC elements were removed (white blocks); the house number is in an unusual place over the door.

259 M. neck-gable from ±1740; lower part of façade has been altared; stoop gone; building leans (compare no. 239).

261 M. early 19thC cornice façade; wooden street front looks older; 'Aristoteles'.

263 M. early 18thC neck-gable; lower part compares with no. 259.

265 M. early 17thC double house with transverse roof; altered considerably; stuccoed in 19thC; ± 1790 door frames with Louis XVI ornamentation.

267 M. 18thC façade with straight cornice; roof and street front altered.

259   261   263   265   267

292   294   296   298   300   302

302 M. late 18thC building with cornice and hipped roof; stoop gone.

300 M. 18thC warehouse; above the large door is an ornament from ±1750.

298 M. late 18thC house with ornamented cornice and transverse roof.

296 M. 18thC house with early 19thC top and roof.

292 and 294). A monstrosity from 1918 was torn down for this purpose.

294 M. 18thC neck-gable rebuilt in 1974 on commission from a hotel (nos.

±1740; fine fanlight.

292 M. 18thC; crested *attiek*, two exceptional chimneys, door framing from

Singel 292-302

269 M. 17thC neck-gable with fronton pilasters and fine cushion door; old wooden shop front was rebuilt with brick in the 18thC, though the *pui* beam has been retained.

272 M. early 19thC cornice façade; street front recently restored.

273 M. little brother of no. 271 (see above); windows on 2nd and 3rd floor altered; street front spoiled.

277-279 end 19thC neo-Renaissance step-gable; ashlar street front.

281 4 window wide cornice façade; straight cornice with consoles; stuccoed and drastically rebuilt 19thC; street front spoiled 20thC.

269   271   273   277-279   281

304   306   308   310   (2)-312

Treeftsteeg

Romeinsarmsteeg

304 M. 17thC house with cornice dating from ±1800; street front altered.

On the left runs an alley to the Herengracht.

306 M. tall, detached neck-gable; date of construction, 1735, is above hoist beam; considerably altered in 19thC; stoop gone.

308 M. cornice façade with 19thC stucco over previous brick; saddle roof just visible.

310 M. 17thC house with 19thC cornice and flat-topped roof; wooden street front.

312 - (**Romeinsarmsteeg 2**) M. early 18thC neck-gable; wooden street front early 19thC; almost 20 meters deep; to its right, a small warehouse.

283 M. façade with straight cornice and consoles; door frame from building period ±1740; *attiek* disappeared in 19thC.
285 M. bell-gable from ±1755; behind its façade the house slants off to the side (see hoist beam); sash work of larger window removed later; ornamented stoop.
287 M. early 19thC cornice façade; street front above 1st floor drastically altered; misleading gable stone dating 1632.
289-291-293 over-scaled construction newly built in 1923 Amsterdam School features; replaces 3 earlier houses.

283   285   287   289-291-293

Romeinsarmsteeg

320   318   316   314

314 until 1964 a cornice façade stood here; replaced in 1977 by an example of adapted architecture.
316 M. neck-gable from ±1740; fronton is gone.
318 M. rare bell-shaped top of sandstone ±1750; ornamented stoop.
320 M. 18thC building with Louis XVI ornamentation on top of an elevated cornice; door enlarged in later period (compare no. 318).

295 M. 18thC façade with straight cornice and *attiek*; rebuilt in 1963 after fire; door frame with Louis XVI ornamentation from ±1790.

297 newly built in historical style; looks older than it is.

299 M. 18thC façade with elevated, straight cornice; beautiful door in 2 parts with early 18thC door frame.

301 M. façade predominantly 19thC; the cornice of this house is too small for the top.

303 built in 1961 in historical style; unusual combination of 4 windows below and rows of 3 windows above; no house number.

295   297   299   301   303

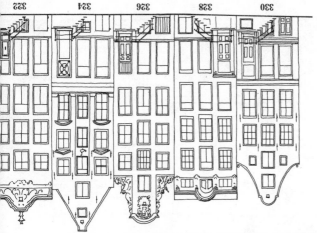

322   324   326   328   330

330 M. 19thC bell-shaped top on 17thC lisena façade; wooden street front replaced by brick 18thC; house leans (compare no. 340).

328 M. façade with elevated cornice; consoles with Louis XV ornaments; beautiful balusters on sculptured stoop; door frame from building period ±1750, door ±1800.

326 M. early 18thC neck-gable with fine, ornate claw pieces.

324 M. middle structure 17thC with window frontons and gable stone; top vase on top; 2 doors instead of the usual large door (see no. 324); 'Aristoteles'.

322 M. 18thC building with fine ornamentation on the elevated cornice; later altered into spout-gable; street front and stoop 18thC.

305 M. This neck-gable lost its late 17thC character during a restoration in the 60's when an extra floor was added.
307 M. door is suspended in the façade; restored in the same period as 305 but here the sash work is out of place as are the windows on the first 3 floors; straight cornice is early 19thC.
309 newly built in 1884 with flat roof instead of saddle roof.
311 M. early 19thC cornice façade; street front is more recent.
313 M. early 19thC cornice façade; brother of no. 311; older street front.

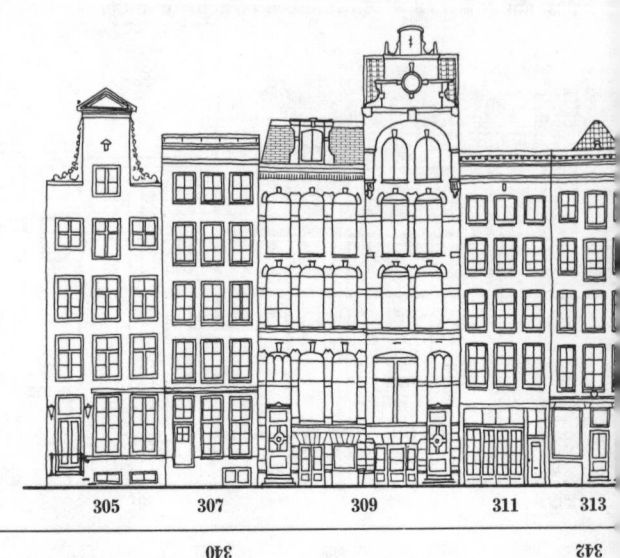

305   307   309   311   313

340   342

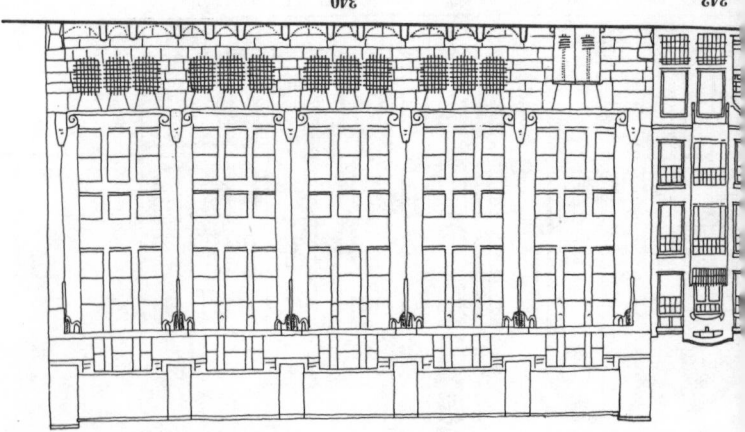

340 actually an unacceptable example of over-scaling from 1919; runs through to Herengracht 295-293; houses had to be torn down on both canals.
342 built ±1910; eye-catching bay windows.

315 M. 18thC building with rare transverse roof; street front changed.
317 M. the top of this building, an elevated straight cornice, is still genuine 18thC; during a recent restoration the height was increased and parts of the façade altered; frontal stoop.
319 M. corner house under straight cornice; during recent restoration the late 18thC sash work was restored; roof was altered much later when the height was increased.
321 M. 18thC house; probably carried a neck- or bell-gable in the past; now sobered into a kind of 19thC spout-gable.

315   317   319   321

Raamsteeg

Oude Spiegelstraat

344   346   348   350   352   354

Singel 344-354

344 M. 17thC house with early 18thC bell-gable.
346 M. house has 17thC wooden street front, 18thC façade and 19thC cornice with dormer; property of 'Stadsherstel'.
348 M. ±1760 bell-gable; top has Louis XV 19thC asymmetrical ornamentation; shop front has been altered.
350 M. 17thC house (seen by its height); wooden gable top; 19thC reconstructed side façade with pothouse; will soon be restored by 'Stadsherstel'.
352 M. 18thC façade with straight cornice and consoles from 19thC.
354 M. 17thC bell-gable; festoons and 1679 date stone; much altered later including street front; stoop bench. Advertising was adopted in the form of a wrought-iron signboard.

323-347 13 houses were demolished for this over-scaled construction newly built in 1923 also torn down in Spuistraat (backside).

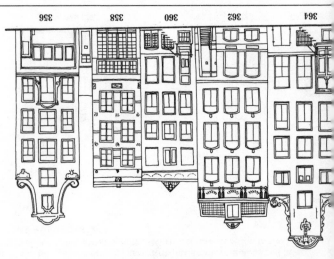

Singel 356-364

356 M. bell-gable built ±1740 with sculptured window frames; street front altered many times and the stoop is gone.

358 M. 17thC house includes beautiful gable stone and sculptured heads; stuccoed and painted later; straight cornice fitted early 19thC; street front altered often, house leans a lot (compare no. 360).

360 late 19thC cornice façade; saddle roof just visible.

362 late 19thC façade with straight cornice and flat-topped roof.

364 M. neck-gable from 1702; date above hoist beam; little changed. In the 19thC the large door was replaced by the present 2 doors.

A walk into the Vliegendesteeg reveals a small bell-gable, no. 5, with a handsome street front from ±1770.

349-351-353 M. 17thC wooden street fronts still intact; height raised by one floor in the 19thC; transverse roof; quite an unusual complex.

323-347   Vliegendesteeg   349-351-353

366   368   370   372   374   376   378

Singel 366-378

366 M. late 18thC façade with ornamented straight cornice enclosing small windows; early 19thC cut-stone street front with frontal stoop.

368 M. 18thC building with straight cornice and 2 hoist beams that were fitted early 19thC; wooden street front; handsome fanlight. The house will soon be restored by 'Stadsherstel'.

370 M. top and 2nd floor still 17thC; bell-gable; festoon around hoist beam; fronton on top gone, now a straight cornice.

372 M. 18thC with top altered 19thC; now cornice façade: dormer.

374 M. mainly 19thC façade with 'broken' cornice and loft-shutter.

376 M. 17thC bell-gable; several alterations; upper window group 17thC.

378 M. façade, just before 1800; straight cornice; transverse roof.

355 M. early 18thC cornice façade; street front and door hardly altered.
357 M. cornice façade with altered top; older saddle roof replaced by present mansarde roof with dormer; building height slightly increased.
359 M. predominantly 19thC building; called a bell-gable despite typical 19thC sobering (no ornaments).
361 building from 1907; windows same size on all floors; flat roof; tile tableau in front portal.
363 building from 1913; 3 identical flats with balconies.
367 M. identified 17thC by building height and Adam and Eve gable stone; rebuilt many times; 19thC cornice façade.

355   357   359   361   363   367

380   382   384   386   388   390

380 late 19thC façade with windows of same size on all floors (compare nos. 386 and 378); ashlar street front with entrance on street-level.
382 M. 19thC façade with straight cornice and dormer.
384 M. early 18thC neck-gable; the traditional large door has disappeared, now small portal with 2 doors (compare no. 386).
386 M. early 18thC façade with ornate, elevated cornice and 2 corner vases; hardly changed.
388 M. early 18thC neck-gable; beautiful entrance from ±1800.
390 M. early 18thC façade with ornate, elevated cornice and 2 semi-reclining statues; perhaps one of the most beautiful entrances of this period.

369 M. 18thC building; top sobered into a simple bell-gable in the 19thC with no ornaments.

371 M. 18thC building; much rebuilt; top drastically altered into a cornice façade in 19thC; 20thC wooden street front.

373-375 newly built in 1913; runs through to the Spuistraat; gable stone; flat roof.

377-379 M. handsome twin neck-gable built 1730; claw pieces ornamented with vases and date; restored 1976.*

381 M. 18thC building with a straight cornice and dormer fitted onto the top (rare); traditional large door gone; frontal stoop.

| 369 | 371 | 373-375 | 377-379 | 381 |

392 façade from 1892 (see bay window); house does not lean (compare no. 390).

396 early 19thC façade; stoop bench. (Few stoops were built after 1800); stoop gone.

398 M. 18thC house with straight but early 19thC cornice; stoop gone.

400 M. neck-gable from ±1730; 19thC ashlar street front; cushion-door.

402 M. bell-gable from ±1760, top probably sobered in 19thC.

404 late 19thC façade with straight cornice, dormer and flat-topped roof.

406 M. a 1940 restoration spoiled façade; only the top part remains genuine.

383-385 20thC building; replaces 2 old houses.
387 late 19thC corner house; on 2nd floor half-circle fanlights.
389-391 M. 17thC houses; changes over the years but not the height;
stuccoed in 19thC and fitted with simple bell-gables.
393 M. neck-gable from ±1750; radically reconstructed in 19thC; fanlight
has 'family-tree' motif; stoop bench.

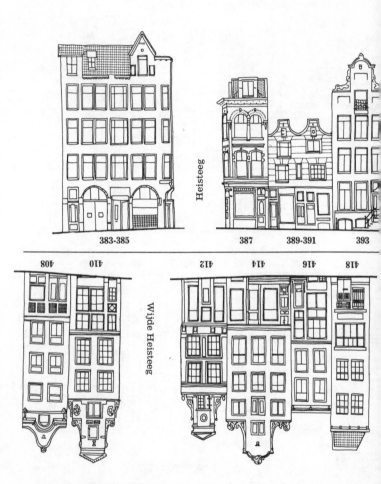

383-385   Heisteeg   387   389-391   393

Wijde Heisteeg

408   410   412   414   416   418

408 M. ±1730 façade with ornate, elevated, wooden cornice (sometimes
called a sunken bell-gable); street front has been changed often.
410 M. rare elevated neck-gable from 1647 (see top); in place of 2 90 degree
corners, there are now 4 filled with claw pieces; much altered; early 19thC
street front; note nets in top against pigeons.
412 M. 17thC neck-gable with fronton and 2 pinnacles; several rebuildings.
414 M. neck-gable with Louis XV ornamentation (asymmetrical) in the
claw pieces from ±1770; shop front altered repeatedly.
416 M. 17thC wooden street front is oldest part; 19thC cornice and
brickwork.
418 narrow corner house; early 20thC; built through to the Herengracht.

395 M. early 19thC cornice façade; stoop older; windows of the same size on all floors; flat roof instead of saddle roof.

397 M. 18thC building; top sobered into cornice façade in 19thC; door frame from ±1750.

399 M. cornice façade from ±1800; a century later saddle roof changed to flat roof.

401 M. predominantly 19thC building; arched windows; stoop older.

403 M. 17thC house; top raised in beginning of 19thC and finished with straight cornice and *attiek*; until 1928 there were 3 houses next door.

395   397   399   401   403

420   422   424   426   428   430

Beulingsloot

420 M. 18thC corner house with 19thC straight cornice and dormer.

422 M. 19thC façade with bell-shaped top; no house number, and the door can no longer be opened.

424 19thC façade with straight cornice and dormer; street front altered.

426 M. brick structure; early 19thC; covered with straight cornice.

428 perhaps this will become a monument someday; one of the best known examples of adapted architecture in Amsterdam. The façade with its concrete elements was designed by A. Cahen and J. Girod in 1970.

430 M. ±1795 façade with straight cornice and hipped roof; the building used to share a street front with 432 but they did not fit well together. At the restoration in 1973, the lower part was rebuilt.*

411 M. Old Lutheran Church dating back to 1633; constructed on an unusually shaped piece of land. The church is now used by the University of Amsterdam.

413 M. the 19thC corner façade that stood here before was replaced in 1969 by 'Stadsherstel's reconstruction of the original façade and bell-gable from ±1750.

415 M. 18thC façade with straight cornice, consoles and hoist beam; saddle roof visible. It was restored by 'Stadsherstel' in 1969.

417 M. early 19thC cornice façade; restored by 'Stadsherstel' in 1969.

419 M. early 18thC neck-gable with ashlar street front; restored by 'Stadsherstel' in 1968; see below window.

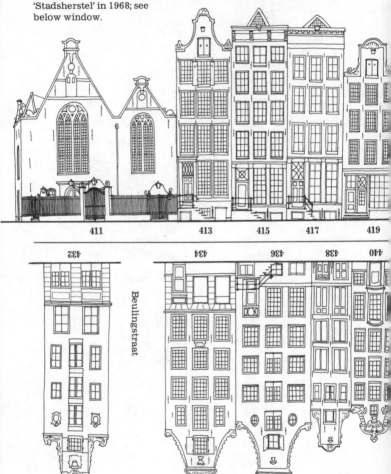

411   413   415   417   419

432   434   436   438   440

Beulingstraat

432 M. early 18thC neck-gable; until recently used as a warehouse; oval windows with sculptured frames with the hoist beam passing through a third frame; lower structure (see no. 430) rebuilt in same style.*

434 M. 17thC bell-gable; altered considerably; gable stone recent.

436 M. 17thC bell-gable; little altered; stoop bench.

438 M. top still has some 17thC elements including claw pieces; window grouping altered considerably; stoop gone.

440 M. bell-gable from ±1740; rare entrance at the middle of the house on street-level; fine top has been excessively ornamented.

446

Singel 446

446 M. in 1881 the neo-Gothic 'Krijtberg' (chalk-mountain) was built here replacing 3 houses. 2 years of labor went into this enormous building with 2 towers on the Singel side; interior is worth seeing; recently added to the Monuments list.

421 M. façade from 1733 with straight cornice; 2 dormers on transverse roof; the straight cornice was arched in the middle for the Amsterdam Arms; used to be a lodging, but since 1881 used by the University Library.
423 M. this beautiful house has served many functions over the years, e.g. for the militia; the 1606 façade has been decorated with roll ornaments and pinnacles; until 1972 there was still a simple entrance between the 2 large doors but it was removed during the restoration that year; house still has cross frame windows, the leaded glass however, is gone.

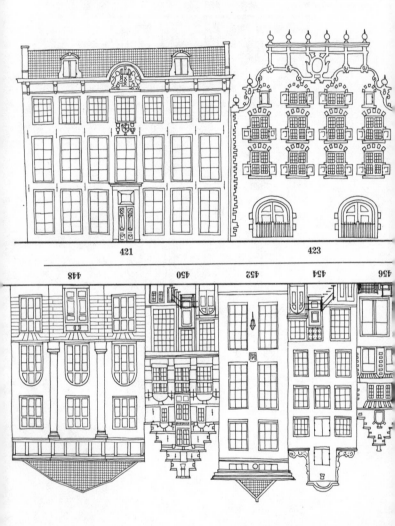

421   423

448   450   452   454   456

448 M. 19thC cornice façade with 2 sandstone pilasters and sandstone street front; 1st floor semi-circular arched windows, now a rectory.
450 M. step-gable from 1642 remarkably good shape; handsomely ornamented *pui* beam from later period, street front changed.
452 M. this 19thC cornice façade is part of the church situated behind it.
454 M. ±1725 neck-gable; the small gate gives access to the church behind it. this step-gable from 1607 was a twin to no. 454 a long time ago; lion heads; street front altered in 18thC.

425 St. Catherine's Church was built here in 1816 and stood until 1939; alongside was a 4 window wide cornice gable. In 1966 this over-scaled University Library was built with its modern front and plate glass that consequently loosened a few tongues.

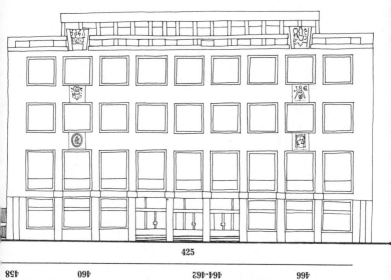

425

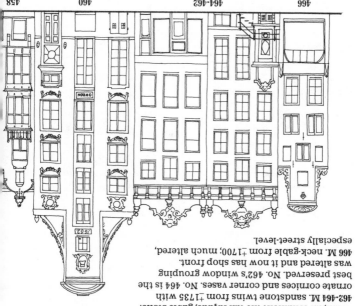

Singel 458-466

458 newly built in the early 20thC; a bit out of place in this row.
460 M. beautiful neck-gable of 1662 from a Philip Vingboons design: festoons, 2 pinnacles, 2 oval windows, and a cartouche around the hoist beam, all ornament the tall façade; gable stone.*
462-464 M. sandstone twins from ±1735 with ornate cornices and corner vases. No. 464 is the best preserved. No. 462's window grouping was altered and it now has shop front.
466 M. neck-gable from ±1700; much altered, especially street-level.

429-435 newly built in 1904; designed by D. van Ort with stone façade; a sort of loggia up on the corner. Until 1903 3 homes stood on this spot.

Heiligeweg

429-435

468

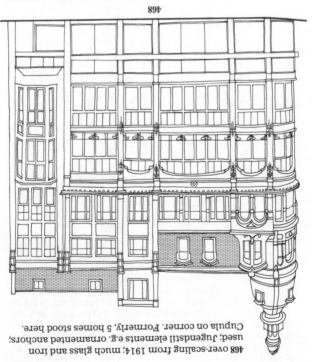

Leidsestraat

468 over-scaling from 1914; much glass and iron used; Jugendstil elements e.g. ornamented anchors; Cupula on corner. Formerly, 5 homes stood here.

Singel 468

437 corner house from end of 19thC; flat roof; small tower on the corner.
439-441-443 M. beautiful complex under one hipped roof; 17thC wooden street fronts; handsome doors; frontal stoop; no. 443 still has a pothouse.
445 newly built in 1915; window grouping is good; natural stone street front, brick above. This house does not lean like no. 443.

437   439-441-443   445

480   482   484   486   488   490

480 19thC building with small domes on the corner (see opposite side); much ornamentation on façade; street front altered later.
482 2 cornice façades; cornice on left is 18thC; rebuilt many times.
484 M. 17thC neck-gable with fronton; window grouping on 3rd floor 17thC; door frame 18thC; rebuilt several times.
486 M. early 18thC neck-gable; lower structure spoiled; wooden shop front from ±1920.
488 19thC façade with straight cornice; shop front altered in 1955.
490 neo-Renaissance step-gable from 1882 (date inscribed in top) with only 4 steps; shop front is from later period.

447 straight cornice and upper part of façade early 19thC; street front altered much later.
449 façade predominantly 19thC; street front changed in 20thC.
451-453 built 1897 in 17thC style (see top of façade); similar to a step-gable with relieving arches above the windows. The city registration office was once here (see inscription above entrance).

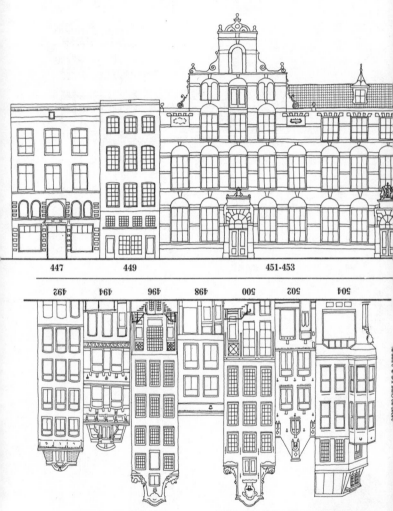

447   449   451-453

492 494 496 498 500 502 504

Singel 492-504

492 19thC façade with ornate straight cornice, dormer and flat-topped roof.
494 late 19thC façade with straight cornice, dormer and flat roof.
496 M. tall beautiful, bell-gable: 'De Berg' (the mountain) (see front on from 1739), with street front and 2 stoops (quite rare); late 18thC sash work in the windows.
498 M. early 19thC façade with straight cornice; building height 17thC.
500 M. neck-gable from ±1735 little changed; wooden street front altered later; the name of the house: 'D'Oude Schelvis' (the old haddock) below hoist beam.
502 late 19thC; similar to a spout-gable.
504 corner house from 1916 with flat roof and brick bay windows.

455-457 built in 1905; same style as no. 451-453.

455-457

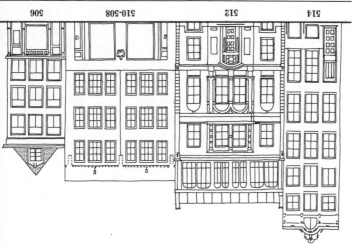

506   510-508   512   514

Singel 506-514

506 M. early 19thC corner house with straight cornice and dormer; saddle roof easily visible; shop front same period but altered later.
508-510 adapted architecture from 1920; brick ornamentation on top; flat roof; shop front altered later.
512 built 1865 with pilasters; a kind of glass-house built on top.
514 M. 18thC façade with straight, elevated cornice and shuttered loft opening in *attiek*; consoles and hoist beam; little else changed.

465-467 backside of a cinema built in 1913.

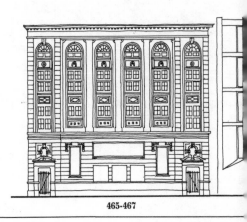

465-467

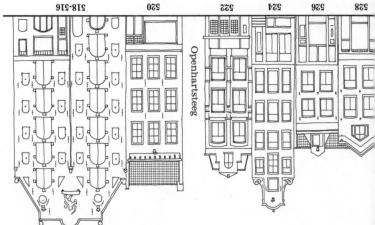

Singel 516-528

516-528 M. early 17thC double warehouse; trapezoidal façade with 2 volutes and 2 pinnacles; gable stone with name of building 'D'Eendragt' inscribed.
Unfortunately the lower part of no. 516 was changed.
520 in 1940 this building was restored into a house with 3 identical flats (see size of windows); transverse roof.
522 late 19thC façade with window railings on 1st and 2nd floor.
524 M. early 18thC tall neck-gable with wooden street front; frontal stoop and narrow door.
526 M. house predominantly 19thC because of stucco and straight cornice.
528 M. 19thC corner house identified by stucco and unique 'bent' cornice.

469-483 newly built in 1976 facing the Kalverstraat behind as well as the Singel; brick façade.

469-483

540

Singel 540

540 over-scaled building from 1966 with terrace. When the Vijzelstraat was widened in 1917 this type of 'city-forming' was employed.

542-544 this over-scaled building was completed in 1961 from a design by
K.L. Sijmons. The maximum building height on the canals is 16 meters
(51 feet). This building is overall 20 meters (64 feet) high and 37 meters
(118 feet) wide. Until the 50's there stood here a beautiful house from 1639
which was damaged by a bomber that crashed in 1943.
The *Munt* stands here (see page 75).

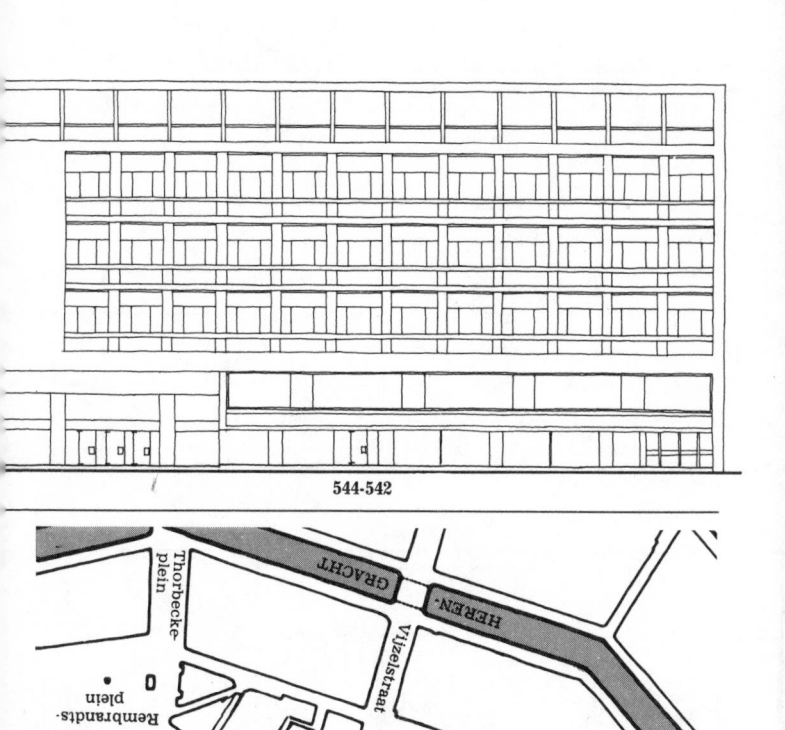

544-542

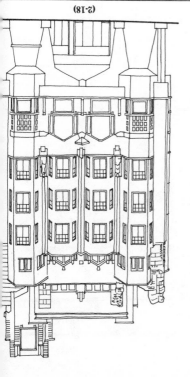

73

Vijzelstraat

(Vijzelstraat 2-18) hotel designed
by G.J. Rutgers and built in 1928.
On the left there were once 3 old
houses but they were torn down
in 1917 for the widening of the
Vijzelstraat.

(2-18)

The Munt
The 36 meter (118 feet) tower was built in 1480 on what was then the Regulierspoort. The design is from Hendrick de Keyser. The name which means 'coin' comes from the fact that during a period of war in 1672, money was temporarily stored here. In the foreground is the end of the flower market which has lined the last part of the Singel 'even' side since 1862.

Herengracht

1 M. 18thC neck gable with *pui* beam and pothouse from earlier date: sash work changed later; frontal stoop.
3 façade from 1889 with cornice and ornamented dormer; older stoop retained.

Brouwersgracht

1   3

Brouwersgracht

5 radically rebuilt in 1886 with use of the old fronton.
7 M. 17thC bell-gable from ± 1760; this 3.12 m wide building still has its 17thC height.
13 newly built in 1924, but a 17thC house had to be removed first.
15 early 18thC building with a 19thC cornice with consoles.
19 M. early 18thC neck-gable with a plastered street front; now a hotel with, considering the size of the house, the remarkable name 'New-York'.
21 M. late 17thC neck-gable. ± 1880 stoop gone and the entrance moved to basement; the original door is now a window.
23 ± 1875; the building height, however, has not changed in ± 350 years.

| 5 | 7 | 13 | 15 | 19 | 21 | 23 |

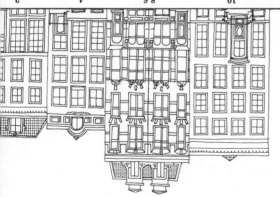

| 2 | 4 | 6-8 | 10 |

Herengracht 2-10

2 M. 17thC corner house, rebuilt several times in the 18th, and especially in the 19thC; now cornice façade with hipped roof; one of the nicest details of the house is the inscription in style on the *put* beam over the street front (note Heerengracht spelled with double 'e').
4 M. built in 1740; façade with elevated cornice; 18thC features well preserved.
6-8 late 19thC houses with cornice and dormer window.
10 M. 4 window wide façade with an early 19thC cornice; original door frame; low double stoop. (Most houses are 2 or 3 window wide.)

25 M. typical 19thC façade with cornice and consoles; arched windows; behind the façade a much older house.
27 M. building from 1890 with an imitation 17thC step-gable.
31 M. 18thC neck-gable; street front rebuilt; stoop gone and entrance moved to basement.
33 M. 17thC bell-gable with an unique top (horn of plenty) instead of fronton; pothouse; very little has been rebuilt.
35 M. house from 1720 with neck-gable; renovated by 'Stadsherstel' in 1964.

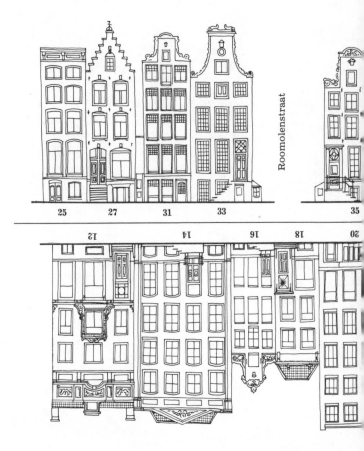

Herengracht 12-20

12 M. early 18thC cornice with 'closed' *attiek* and sandstone window front; framing around the middle window is unusual with 3 window wide houses; managed to get through the 19thC with very little damage.
14 M. 18thC; 4 window wide, sandstone façade; cornice and fronton; arched windows.
16 M. neck-gable from 1735 with claw pieces in unusual form; well preserved; sash work of the windows changed.
18 M. just before 1800 the façade was renovated; cornice with consoles; 2 hoist beams and hipped roof incorporated; frontal stoop.
20 M. 18thC building; building height was increased and the roof flattened in ± 1920; stoop gone.

37 M. unusual warehouse with bell gable from ± 1750; original loft doors in 1st floor removed when lower part was rebuilt.
39 M. warehouse with bell-gable from 1733 (see 'shoulder' ornaments); little changed; renovated in 1966 by 'Hendrick de Keyser'.
41 rebuilt in 1889; street front hardly changed.
43-45 M. warehouses with pointed gables; oldest houses on the Herengracht (possibly from before 1600). Renovated in 1975 by 'Stichting Aristoteles' who now occupies no. 43. The street front of no. 45 was slightly altered later.
47 cornice façade; previous 17thC warehouse demolished 1875.

37   39   41   43-45   47

24-22   26   28   30   32

Herengracht 22-32

22-24 M. used to be one big house before 1870; conversion into cornice façades.
26 M. ± 1800 building with cornice, oval windows and consoles; door frame shaped in half circle; very little has been rebuilt.
28 M. early 18thC neck-gable; the characteristic large door has been replaced by an entrance way with two small doors in this century.
30 newly built round ± 1900; handsome tile tableau below the windows of the ground floor.
32 M. early 19thC cornice façade with transverse roof; two small doors in place of one large door in the façade.

49 M. 17thC building; top altered in the 19thC; 17thC stoop and *pui* beam over ground floor.
51 M. 18thC elevated cornice façade; corner vases; little alteration.
53 M. 17thC building converted to cornice façade ± 1850; fine fanlight.
55 M. early 18thC neck-gable; half circle fanlight from ± 1800.
57 M. neck-gable from ± 1730; unusual frontal stoop; windows and entrance altered ± 1910.
59 M. elevated neck-gable with pilasters, built in 1659 (see top inscription); renovated in 1964 on commission from 'Hendrick de Keyser'.

49   51   53   55   57   59

34   36   38   40

40 M. late 18thC sandstone façade with cornice and hipped roof; consoles and rosettes; unusual half-circle fanlights over the ground floor windows.
38 M. early 17thC step-gable with only 2 steps; claw pieces and 2 pinnacles street front altered ± 1800; original construction.
36 cornice façade with dormer; no. 38's twin brother used to be here; old stoop preserved.
34 newly built in the 60's with a terrace.

61 M. 17thC neck-gable with festoon around hoist beam; street front altered ± 1900; restored in 1975; twin brother of no. 63.

63 M. Twin with no. 61, but not so much altered; street front changed in the 18thC; note the oeils-de-boeuf.

65 M. built in the 18thC; top converted into a cornice in the 19thC.

67 M. built in the 18thC; elevated cornice; balcony added in the 19thC.

69 M. bell-gable built ± 1750; altered in the 20thC; now has one floor less.

71 M. warehouse with spout-gable ± 1720; understructure altered.

61   63   65   67   69   71

52   50   48   46   44   42

52 double house built in early 19thC with windows worked into cornice; hipped roof; double stoop.

50 converted into cornice façade in 1870; ornaments under windows of 1st and 2nd floor.

48 M. sandstone façade ± 1760 with cornice balustrade and vases; very little changed in both interior and exterior.

46 M. early 18thC neck-gable; slight alteration; restored in 1969.

44 M. early 18thC neck-gable, very little has been changed.

42 built in 1870 with cornice arched in the middle; arched windows.

Herengracht 42-52

73 M. 17thC façade with pilasters; top converted into a spout-gable in the early 19thC; street front restored.

75 M. stuccoed façade with cornice and hipped roof; built in late 18thC; ornamented with festoons and consoles.

77 M. step-gable from ± 1630; 2 pothouses on side and front façade; door and windows renovated ± 1800; restored in 1966 by 'Hendrick de Keyser'.

79 M. well preserved neck-gable built in ± 1700 with pothouse on side.

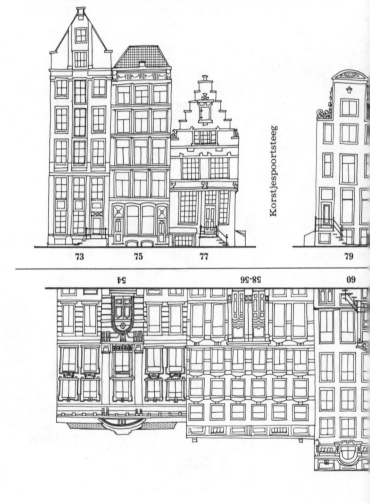

Korstjespoortsteeg

73   75   77   79

54   58-56   60

Herengracht 54-60

54 M. double house with a late 19thC façade; ornamented entrance with frontal stoop.

56-58 M. façade still has some early 17thC elements (e.g. relieving arches over the windows); uppermost floor and cornice added later, ± 1975; doors changed still later when the stoop was removed.

60 M. 18thC building with 19thC elevated cornice and *attiek* with 2 hoistbeams.

81 M. early 17thC step gable with handsome 18thC door; during its last renovation in 1977 the loft doors, stoop and cross-fame windows, among other things, were restored; original construction.
83 M. late 18thC cornice façade with hipped roof; 2nd entrance under stoop.
85 M. simple 18thC bell-gable; small windows next to *attiek* window now gone.
87 M. early 18thC neck-gable; altered in the 19thC; restored in 1975.
89 reconstruction of 17thC neck-gable following drawing from Caspar Philips' 1768 Canal Book; 1902 building since demolished.
91 M. elevated neck-gable with pilasters, built in 1657; little alteration.
93 M. 18thC building with 19thC cornice and dormer; door frame ± 1750.

| 81 | 83 | 85 | 87 | 89 | 91 | 93 |

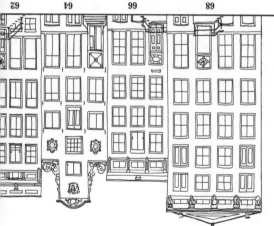

| 62 | 64 | 66 | 68 |

Herengracht 62-68

62 M. built in ± 1740; sobered 19thC cornice sculptured stoop; once a twin brother of no. 60.
64 M. early 18thC neck-façade with claw pieces and oeils-de-boeuf; older stoop changed to a frontal stoop in the 19thC.
66 M. late 18thC façade; recently a stone was installed with the name of the first owner ± 1600.
68 M. 4 window wide building, 1770; top changed later, *attiek* disappeared in the 19thC; new gable stone.

95 M. façade with ornamented cornice and hipped roof built in ± 1800.
97 M. house with unusual top built in ± 1860; equal high windows on all floors; window frames; two doors.
99 M. 18thC façade converted into a cornice façade in ± 1850; frontal stoop.
101 cornice façade built in ± 1870 with dormer window and equally sized windows.
103 M. cornice façade from ± 1870 with frontal stoop.
(Blauwburgwal 22) M. a so-called elevated bell-gable built ± 1670. Side façade has projecting beam ends; oval windows light the staircase; owned by 'Hendrick de Keyser' since 1977.

95   97   99   101   103   (22)

(2)   80   78   76   74   72-70

(Herenstraat 2) recent building from the 20thC with bay windows. There used to be a handsome neck-gable here.
80 old neck-gable from ± 1730, reconstructed in 1975.
78 M. early 18thC. neck-gable with a street-level entrance.
76 M. 18thC bell-gable; restored in 1975.
74 building radically altered ± 1900; Jugendstil elements (e.g. asymmetric top); natural stone lintels over the windows.
4 oeils-de-boeuf; stoop of no. 70 now gone.
70-72 M. façade with pilasters and fronton built ± 1640 (see date in façade);

105-107 newly built 1952 in adapted style (the previous building was
bombed during World War II); windows get smaller towards the top;
terrace on roof.

Blauwburgwal

105-107

Herenstraat

82   84   86   88

Herengracht 82-88

82 M. built in 17thC; the stone street front is probably 18thC; 19thC stucco
work on façade; restored in 1970.

84 M. early 17thC step-gable; wooden street front converted to brick 18thC;
lion masks visible over the substructure; no. 84 used to be a twin of no.
86; they still are identical at the bottom; original construction.

86 M. (see no. 84) 17thC building with large 18thC bell-gable; lion masks
over the street front.

88 newly built in 1880; used for student housing.

109 M. double house; ± 1775 façade with cornice and fronton; restored by
'Diogenes' in 1972. The door between no. 109 and no. 111 gives access to
a building on Singel.

111 M. double house with frontal stoop; radically rebuilt ± 1800.

113 asymmetric house with bay windows; built in 1902, when 17thC house
was torn down.

115 M. built in 1890; this early design of H.P. Berlage, who later was known
for his architectural innovations, is still traditional, with its neo-
renaissance step-gable, ornamented door frame and arched entranceway;
recently classified a monument.

| 109 | 111 | 113 | 115 |

| 90 | 92 | 94 | 96 | 98 |

90 M. 18thC façade with cornice, locally raised for a window; 19thC street
front is ashlar.

92 M. beautiful building from ± 1740 with cornice, consoles and
ornamented *attiek*; both interior and exterior are little changed.

94 M. used to be a twin with 92, the handsome *attiek* was replaced ± 1800
by what is there now; previous roof became a hipped roof.

96 M. late 17thC façade; cornice was changed in the 18thC; window frames
and dormers were added ± 1870.

98 M. 18thC cornice façade; one floor was added and roof changed in the
beginning of the 20thC.

117 built in 1940 with traditional top and 1940's style tower.
119 M. this rather classical structure with hipped roof and pilasters was
built in 1870.
121 converted into a cornice façade in 1870; looks older than it really is.

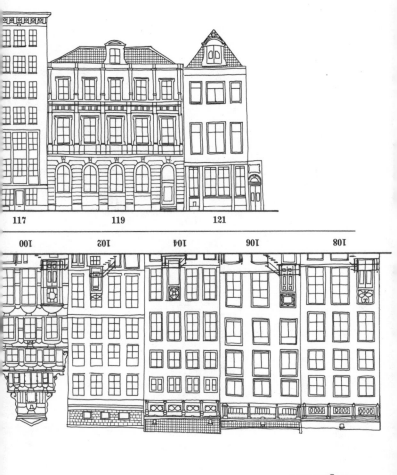

117   119   121

100   102   104   106   108

100 M. wide step-gable ± 1620 with only 3 steps filled in with claw pieces;
the top was restored in a 18thC restoration, only the entrance and windows
have been altered.
102 M. used to be a twin with no. 100 but was radically rebuilt in the 19thC;
floor added and top changed in the 20thC.
104 M. 18thC cornice façade with transverse roof; 4 windows wide. The
ornamented cornice with windows was added in beginning 19thC.
106 M. 18thC façade with cornice, consoles and (cornice) windows.
108 M. 18thC façade with cornice; the cornice was sobered ± 1800; little
changed since.

110 M. façade with cornice and consoles, ± 1750; original door frame; cornice sobered later.

112 M. 17thC building height; much alteration; top radically converted to unusual sort of cornice with balustrade.

114 M. handsome, well preserved cornice façade, 1750, with an almost bell-shaped top (so-called sunken-bell-gable); original door and framing; ornamented stoop.

116 M. 18thC façade with 19thC 'sobered' cornice. The door framing was restored in 1965.

118 M. 18thC; the sobered cornice and an extra floor were added in ± 1890 (compare no. 116).

118   116   114   112   110

127   125   123

123 façade altered in 1908; older, 19thC, street front.

125 M. early 17thC double house with 18thC elements (e.g. the double stoop with 2nd entrance). The façade was stuccoed and the cornice added in the 19thC.

127 M. 17thC double house; radically rebuilt in the 19thC with stucco work on the façade; cornice also 19thC.

129 building radically changed ± 1890; stoop from later date.
131 M. 17thC corner house with a bell-gable from later date. The house has retained its original height.
133 newly built in 1924; street level door.
135 M. late 18thC cornice façade; used to be a neck-gable, for the rest very little changed.
137 M. early 18thC neck-gable; street front altered in 19thC; stoop gone.

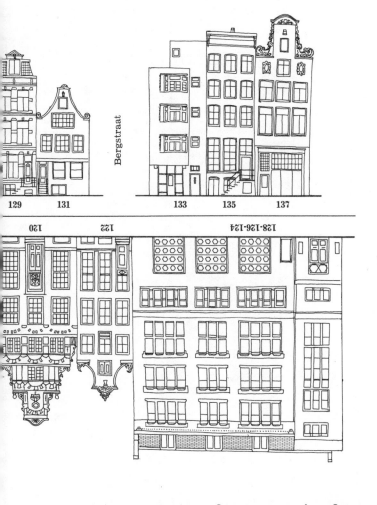

129   131   Bergstraat   133   135   137

120   122   128-126-124

Herengracht 120-128

120 M. remarkable building in two parts: the top with its step-gable, relieving arches and pinnacles still early 17thC, the rest was rebuilt ± 1800; frontal stoop.
122 M. ± 1760 bell-gable with Louis XV ornaments; little alteration.
124-126-128 3 houses had to be torn down for this over-scaled building, designed by architect Ouёndag in 1916; street front 'modernised' in 1960.

139 M. 17thC. neck-gable with very thin neck; street front altered and stoop removed just before 1900.

141-143-145 newly built in 1906 with horizontal emphasis in stone; over balcony are 2 gable stones with the images of the old church and the stock exchange building. There used to be 3 houses on this place.

147 M. largely 19thC cornice façade with arched door lintel.

149 building converted into a cornice façade in 1870; cornice interrupted by dormer window.

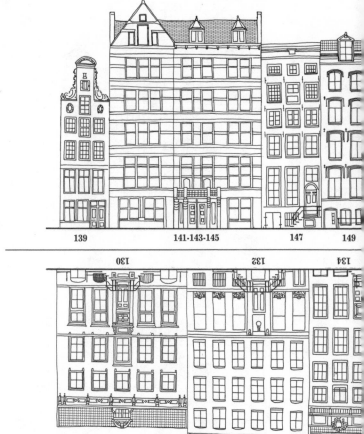

139   141-143-145   147   149

134   132   130

130 M. 17thC double house with double stoop; the cornice, dormer window and window frames were added in the 19thC.

132 M. used to be 2 buildings; now joined by cornice and transverse roof.

134 M. early 18thC sandstone façade with cornice and *attiek*; inscription 'd'Beeck' above middle 1st floor window; little alteration.

Herengracht 130-134

151 cornice façade with arched windows built ± 1880.
155 M. unusual warehouse with bell-gable, built ± 1760; named 'Engeland'.
Little has been changed, loft-doors on 1st and 2nd floor gone; its neighbour,
no. 157, has been better preserved.
157 M. ± 1725 warehouse with bell-gable; little alteration.
159 M. 18thC house; top and façade greatly altered in the 19thC, when
balustrade was added.
161 M. bell-gable from ± 1750; lower part rebuilt ± 1885.
163 M. early 18thC neck-gable with a barrel in the top; little alteration.

151   155   157   159   161   163

146   144   142   140   138   136

136 M. 18thC cornice façade; top sobered by a cornice ± 1800; fine cut-glass
fanlight; restored in 1966.
138 ± 1890 façade with street-level entrance (compare no. 136).
140 M. early 18thC neck-gable; sash work changed except on the 3rd floor.
142 cornice façade built ± just before 1900; street front looks older.
144 building converted into a cornice façade ± 1900; windows equally sized
on all floors; street front looks older.
146 M. elevated cornice façade built ± 1770; little alteration.

165 M. the top still has some old elements, ± 1760; radically rebuilt in the thirties; windows on all floors equally sized.
167 newly built ± 1910 with 2 bay windows; stuccoed façade.
169 radically rebuilt ± 1880, in 350 years the construction height hasn't changed; cornice runs over front and side façade.
169a built just in the beginning of the 20thC; top-gable, bay windows; balcony; door on street-level.

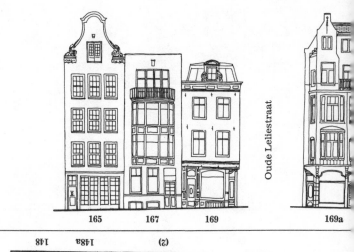

Oude Leliestraat

165   167   169   169a

Leliegracht

148   148a   (2)

148 M. early 18thC neck-gable; street front changed just before 1900.
148a - (Leliegracht 2) newly built ±1900, three bay windows over the corner.

Herengracht 148-148a

171 M. early 18thC neck-gable; not much alteration; nicely situated with view on the Leliegracht; restored in 1968.

173 M. 18thC building (or even older); height increased in the 19thC and topped with a cornice.

175 M. 17thC house; many visible signs of later restorations; possible 17thC stoop, 18thC street front, simple 19thC bell-gable.

177 M. 17thC house; much has been rebuilt; in the 19thC the rare 'bent' cornice was added.

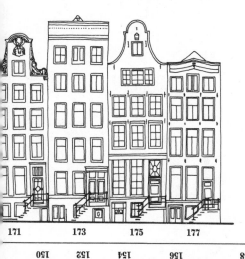

171   173   175   177

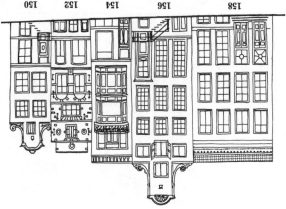

150   152   154   156   158

Herengracht 150-158

130 M. ± 1750 neck-gable with little alteration on the front façade; not so on the side façade where a photography studio has made much use of glass; pothouse also around to the side.

152 M. reminiscent of 17thC step-gable despite various rebuildings; one floor added in the 18thC; radically altered below the gable stone where the stoop has been removed and the entrance moved.

154 newly built ± 1910; flat roof and bay windows.

156 M. early 18thC neck-gable; very little alteration; restored 1956; but the 18thC sash work was not brought back in the upper windows.

158 M. 4 window wide cornice façade with transverse roof and 2 doors, ± 1810; before the last rebuilding it would have had 1 door; 'minimal' stoop.

179-197 newly built ± 1900; asymmetrical ashlar façade; 9 older houses were broken down for this over-scaled construction (see also no. 197).

179-197

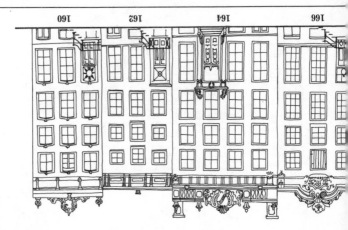

160 162 164 166

Herengracht 160-166

160 M. rare, ashlar façade ± 1760 with cornice, ornamentation and 2 corner vases, window framing (usually a 19thC tecture).

162 M. 18thC building, fine old top sobered in 19thC into a cornice with 4 consoles; restored in 1972.

164 M. 4 window wide sandstone cornice façade with 'open' *attiek* and 4 vases; door framing from the ± 1750 construction date; slight alterations.

166 M. handsome façade with elevated sandstone cornice, motto and hoist beam ornamented at the end with a woman's head; restored in 1960.

197 building from ± 1900 in older style with cross-frame windows and hipped roof.

199-201 newly built, in 1917, when 2 older houses, like no. 203, were demolished; unusual hipped roof with two chimneys.

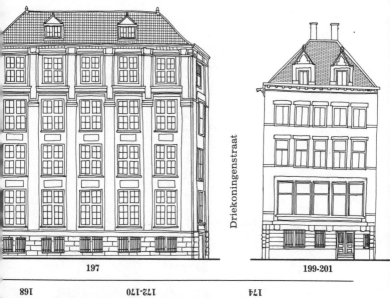

Driekoningenstraat

197   199-201

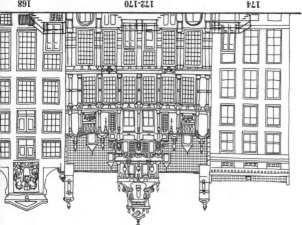

168   172-170   174

Herengracht 168-174

168 M. sandstone neck-gable from Philip Vingboons, ± 1638; first neck-gable in Amsterdam; façade altered ± 1730, when e.g. frontons above the windows were removed; few changes since. Is for over 200 years from the same owner (church society). Since 1960, a theatrical museum; interior worth a visit.

170-172 M. exceptionally fine double house from 1622, designed by Hendrick de Keyser and named the 'Bartolotti' house after the man who commissioned it, owned by 'Hendrick de Keyser'; the date of reconstruction is inscribed in the (rebuilt) top.

174 M. ashlar façade with cornice and transverse roof, ± 1800.

203 M. one of the few remaining old houses in this row; 17thC step-gable; the (few) steps are filled with claw-pieces; renovated in 1920 for the 1st time; little alteration.

205-207 newly built 1955 with too much glass; mis-placed next to the handsome no. 203.

209 M. 4 window wide 19thC façade with cornice; *attiek* gone; window front recently rebuilt.

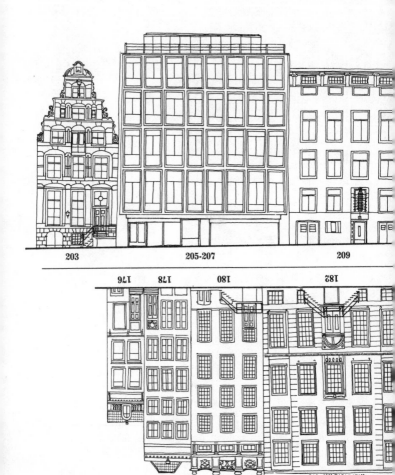

203   205-207   209

176   178   180   182

double stoop restored in 1972.

182 M. double house from 1772 with sandstone façade, cornice and *attiek*;
late 18thC sash work brought back by renovation.

180 M. façade from ± 1780 with cornice, *attiek* and vases; little changed;
stoop; little changed since.

178 M. cornice façade from just before 1800 with hipped roof; frontal
with cornice, balustrade and window framing.

176 M. 17thC 'baby' house amoung its larger neighbours; 19thC façade

211 M. 18thC neck-gable with ornamental vases; well preserved corner house. (In 1896 it was bordered on two sides by water. The Warmoesgracht, a canal between Singel and Herengracht, had not yet been filled-in to become the Raadhuisstraat.) The house was restored in 1959.

211

Raadhuisstraat

Herengracht 184-192

184 · (Raadhuisstraat 30-34) M. combination shops/homes; built in 1897 in the Raadhuisstraat with sandstone façade after design from architect Berlage; top has an asymmetric spout-gable; just recently classified as a monument.
(186-188-190-192) four houses were demolished to make room for the Raadhuisstraat; the first major change in the city since the girdle was finished; the Herengracht façades were well preserved until 1895, so there has been no talk of widening the street, unlike the situation on the Vijzelstraat (see pp. 129 and 131).

184　(30-34)　　　(192·190·188·186)

Raadhuisstraat

213 newly built in 1896 by the Van Gendt brothers, who also designed the galery of shops and housing along the Raadhuisstraat on the opposite side of the canal (see Herengracht 194); stone above entrance.
215 newly built ± 1910; asymmetrical; frontal stoop.
217 there was a neck-gable here until 1937; now used as a bicycle stall; future restoration?
219 M. bell-gable; 1683 date on stone; fronton since removed from the top.
221 M. 18thC bell-gable; top slightly changed in the 19thC; corridor on right gives entrance to Gemeente Giro office on the Singel.

213   215   217   219   221

194   200·198·196   202

202 M. 19thC façade with cornice, 2 consoles and hipped roof; little alteration, window railings on the 1st floor; the awnings are in contradiction of Monument rules.

200 built just after 1900 in same style as nos. 196 and 198; entrance less successful.

196·198·200 M. 6 window wide façade with 17thC elements e.g. relieving arches above the windows; upper windows changed later; top gables replaced by cornice in the 19thC.

194 the side-end of a shopping galery with housing above designed in 1896 by the Van Gendt brothers; many sculptured animals on the Raadhuisstraat façade.

223-225 M. 6 window wide house which looks older than it actually is; in
1928 no. 225 was torn down and no. 223 widened in period style; the *attiek*
from ± 1850 with balustrade and ornamentation has been retained.
227 M. 17thC pilaster façade; top altered and fronton removed in the 19thC.
231 M. 17thC building with a 18thC stone, street front; 19thC cornice and
dormer in half-circle form.
233 M. 18thC elevated cornice with 2 consoles; transverse roof; 18thC
doorway lintel and door framing; little alteration.
235 M. 18thC building with 19thC alterations, e.g. unusual wooden top;
18thC door framing has been retained.

223-225   227   231   233   235

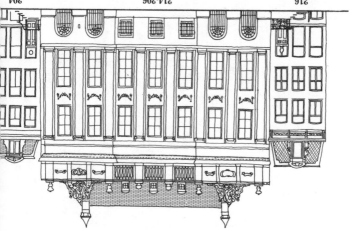

204   214-206   216

Herengracht 204-216

204 radically rebuilt ± 1890; cornice and dormer added; the stoop, however,
was not altered.
206-214 five older houses were demolished for this 1918 building housing
the Pierson Bank. Built in neo 17thC classical style with its pilasters and
festoons, it looks much older than it actually is. The *attiek* and vases are
also from 1918.
216 rebuilt in ± 1890 (see no. 204); the stoop is original, but not the stoop
railing.

237 M. building from 1881 neo-Renaissance characteristics (emphasis on horizontal lines); recently classified as a monument.

239 M. building from 1889; meant as extension of 237.

241 M. 18thC building; heightened by one floor and topped with 19thC straight cornice.

243 17thC house; rebuilt ± 1850 when one floor was added; gable altered into cornice façade; walls stuccoed.

245a building from 1900; wooden street front altered later; statuette on 1st floor corner.

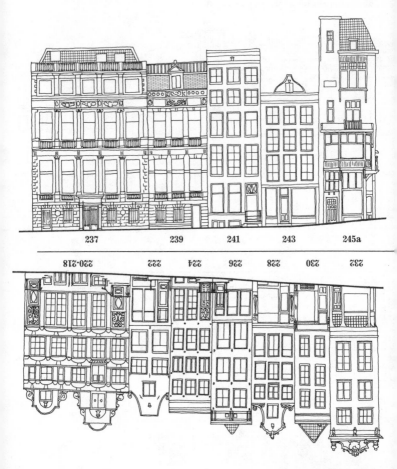

237   239   241   243   245a

232   230   228   226   224   222   220-218

218-220 M. ± 1620 step-gable twin, father and son; fine fanlights and cushion doors; window cross-frame gone; few alterations; original construction.

222 M. rebuilt ± 1800; front from same period; top of façade altered into what now resembles bell-gable; the 2 voluten are probably older; pull bell.

224 M. rebuilt ± 1825; altered into cornice façade with ornamented anchors.

226 façade altered ± 1870; cornice façade with 3 pairs of consoles.

228 M. fine bell-gable ± 1760; street front changed end 19thC and now shows Jugendstil elements.

230 M. early 19thC cornice façade; street front altered later; finely ornamented.

232 M. cornice façade from ± 1740 with 2 ornamental vases and consoles; street front altered end 19thC.

Herengracht 218-232

245 M. built 17thC.; thoroughly rebuilt in 1843 (see yearstone); straight cornice dates from year of alteration.

247 M. cornice façade largely 19thC; fine fanlights; window railings.

249 M. 17thC neck-gable with pilasters and frontal stoop; fronton disappeared during reconstruction; wooden street front altered; right door still 17thC width; owned by 'Stadsherstel'.

251 M. late 18thC bell-gable; many alterations; wooden street front rebuilt in brick just before 1900; frontal stoop.

253 M. built 17thC; rebuilt ± 1800; straight cornice; wooden street front altered in 19thC.

Gasthuismolensteeg

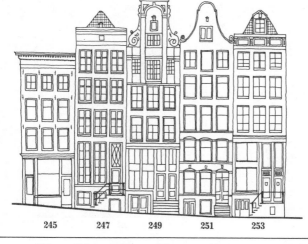

245   247   249   251   253

234   236   238   240   242   246-244

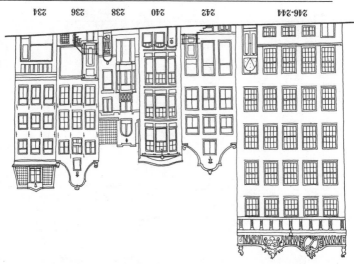

Hartenstraat

style using the 18thC attic of no. 246; windows all of equal size.

244-246 M. two houses torn down in 1929; present house built in an older **242** M. bell-gable from ± 1770; façade slightly changed in 19thC.

240 sandstone façade with 3 bay windows, ± 1915.

238 asymmetrical building with transverse roof ± 1900; door Jugendstil? installed much later.

236 M. bell-gable with fine door framing ± 1770; large lower window

234 corner house with straight cornice ± 1800; street front altered later.

Herengracht 234-246

255a built in 1894; 255 was added in 1923 in same style; complex is
connected with 4 houses at Singel nos. 288-290-292-294.
257 M. fine sandstone neck-gable with pilasters ± 1660; door style Louis
XV ± 1770; well preserved.
259 mainly 19thC; stucco, window framing and straight cornice with
consoles; street front altered around 1900; Jugendstil elements e.g.
tilepictures.

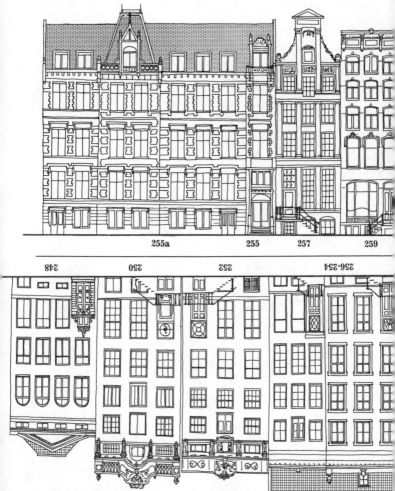

255a	255	257	259

248	250	252	256-254

a sandstone façade with window framing.

254 has a brick façade and straight cornice from before 1780; no. 256 has

254-256 M. 2 façades under one straight cornice and transverse roof; no.

consoles and gable stone 'Meelbaal' (flour bag); well preserved.

252 M. façade with ornamented *attiek* ± 1730; cornice with windows, 4

2 parts; few alterations.

250 M. cornice façade with *attiek* and crest ± 1740; fine Louis XV door in

1886.

and fronton on top ± 1800; windows on second floor arched; entrance from

248 M. 4 window wide façade with straight cornice enclosing windows

261 M. 18thC bell-gable; much of façade dates from 19thC, e.g. windows.
263 M. 17thC neck-gable; 2 corner vases; few alterations.
265 façade dates from 1882 (see top); street front possibly older.
267 high 19thC building; tiled tableau over each door.
269 M. fine step-gable from 1656; original construction.
271 M. 17thC house with 19thC straight cornice.
273 M. 17thC building; 19thC straight cornice.

261   263   265   267   269   271   273

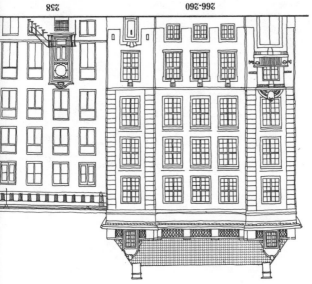

258   266-260

258 rebuilt in 18thC into cornice façade 4 windows wide; sandstone door framing; many times altered; 1st floor even has double windows.
260-266 4 houses torn down in 1917; adapted architecture from 1919 by Van Gendt brothers; year inscription in top right.

275 M. late 17thC neck-gable; segment shaped fronton; few alterations;
pothouse on the side.
277 rebuilt in the 1950's when all windows under the cornice became of
equal size; stoop gone.
279 M. 17thC (e.g. wooden street front); many alterations; altered into
cornice façade just before 1800; frontal stoop.
281 M. rare 17thC elevated neck-gable; claw and wing pieces; 18thC street
front altered (compare no. 281).*
283 M. no. 281's twin brother; original street front; slight alterations (e.g.
sash work).*

275   Romeinsarmsteeg   277   279   281   283

268   270   272

19thC as well as lower part of façade.
272 M. second floor still early 17thC part around hoist beam rebuilt in
and 5 vases ± 1770; sculptured window frames.
270 M. 18thC double house; sandstone façade with straight cornice, *attiek*
pilasters from same period.
268 M. 4 window wide cornice façade from ± 1810; door framing with Ionic

285 M. neck-gable; sandstone ornamentation on top is old; the rest was poorly rebuilt in the 1930's when basement and stoop were removed; door at street-level (compare 287).

287 M. fine $\pm$ 1750 bell-gable (most bell-gables are from this period); few alterations.

289 $\pm$ 1880; 3 floors of equal height; unlike most old houses, no saddled roof.

291 newly built in the 1920's; spout-gable style; ornamental masonry.

285   287   289   291

274   276   278   280   282

Herengracht 274-282

274 M. cornice façade with *attiek*, ballustrade, corner vases and gable stone 'd'Witte Leli' (the white lily) $\pm$1740; entrance with arched doorway lintel; frontal stoop $\pm$ 1800.

276 M. 18thC cornice façade 19thC simplification of cornice.

278 alterations in façade on first and second floor after 1900; Jugendstil elements over door.

280 M. sandstone façade; cornice with *attiek* and coat of arms $\pm$ 1720.

282 M. 18thC; altered in 19thC; straight cornice and hipped roof.

293-305 seven houses were torn down around 1920 and replaced by this large-scale new building; Singel 332-340 were also torn down in the same period; building stretches from Herengracht to Singel; rebuilt and enlarged again in 1953 with even less success.

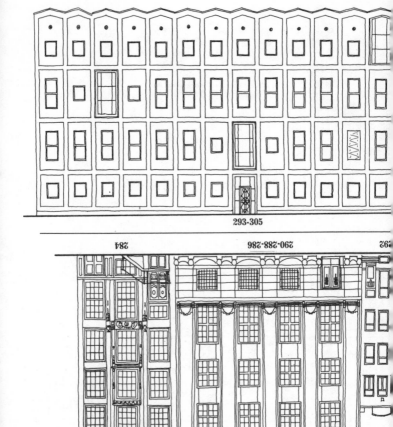

293-305

284 M. Van Brienenhuis; well preserved sandstone cornice façade with ornamented *attiek* ± 1720; owned and occupied by Hendrick de Keyser'; fine interior.

286-288-290 three houses were replaced by this 1921 construction.

292 rebuilt in 1920's; windows nearly equal in size.

307 (now 303) unusual 20thC building with Amsterdamse School characteristics, e.g. much ornamentation in brick, stoop, dormers and 3 dimensional façade.
(Oude Spiegelstraat 12) 17thC side façade with enlarged dormer; pothouse; saddle roof clearly visible.
(Oude Spiegelstraat 11) 17thC side façade; street front ± 1890; upper part stuccoed.
309-311 two houses from before 1600; torn down and rebuilt in 1935 into one house with shop front and double bell-gable; roof clearly visible between the two tops.
313 M. just over 3 meters wide; façade from ± 1810; straight cornice.

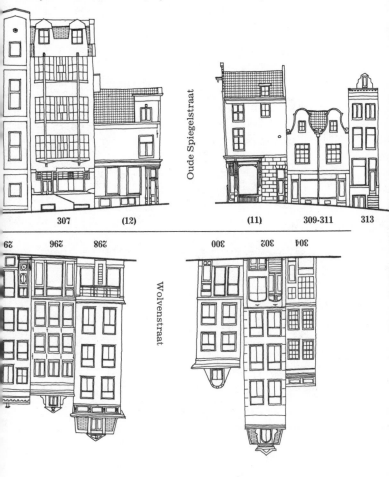

307   (12)   Oude Spiegelstraat   (11)   309-311   313

29   296   298   Wolvenstraat   300   302   304

304 cornice façade from ± 1870; older street front reconstructed in 1965.
302 built in ± 1890; street front of stone.
300 M. corner house; building height and wooden street front from 17thC; front altered into cornice façade; side wall stuccoed; pothouse around the side; piling problems.
298 either newly built or thoroughly rebuilt ± 1890; straight cornice in front and around the side.
296 M. façade mainly 19thC; straight cornice and dormer.
294 M. 18thC; gable replaced by simple cornice in 19thC.

Herengracht 294-304

315 M. same width as no. 313; façade altered in 19thC; stucco, straight cornice and window framing.

317 M. early 18thC façade with elevated cornice of sandstone; highly ornamented; one vase on top and one at either corner; few alterations.

319 newly built in 1889; year inscribed on turret built over a former alley; 'neo-17thC' style.

321 newly built $\pm$ 1940; adapted architecture; spout-gable style.

323 rebuilt $\pm$ 1940; top of older bell-gable was used in reconstruction.

325 M. early 19thC cornice façade; 3 cushion-doors, the extreme right one of which gives access to an alley that used to connect Herengracht and Singel.

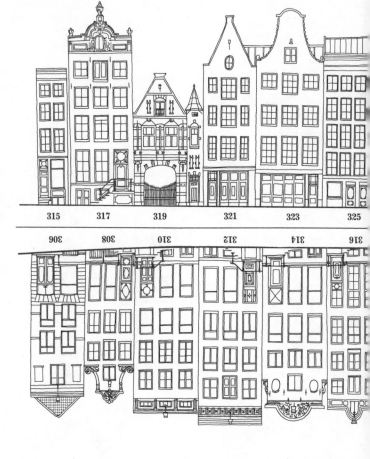

315   317   319   321   323   325

306   308   310   312   314   316

316 M. building with elevated cornice; fine period door $\pm$ 1760; wrought iron railing; few alterations.

314 M. curious building; cross-breed cornice façade and neck-gable from $\pm$ 1720; broad neck-gable with small claw pieces; cornice with ornamented arch; few alterations.

312 M. cornice façade from 1785; ornamented cornice; windows altered later.

310 M. 18thC; *attiek* disappeared around 1810 when cornice was simplified.

308 M. bell-gable $\pm$ 1740; few alterations.

306 M. thoroughly rebuilt around 1880; cornice façade; street front with rustica stucco; fanlight with house number.

327 M. 17thC; transverse roof; 2 stoops and 2 doors giving access to different living quarters as originally intended; straight cornice 19thC.
329 M. 17thC neck-gable; fronton gone; the gable stone 'de Vogelstruys' (the ostrich) is a remnant from a house on Singel.
331 M. bell-gable from ± 1750 with vase; period window framing; few alterations.
333 built in 1890; bands and blocks ornament façade; this style was rampant in de Pijp (an area in South Amsterdam); older stoop preserved.
335 M. 18thC cornice façade; originally 1 door, now 2; cornice sobered in 19thC; windows and street front altered and stuccoed.
337 ± 1890; complete areas of Amsterdam are built in this style; straight cornice; old stoop retained.

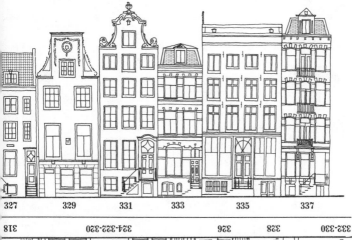

327   329   331   333   335   337

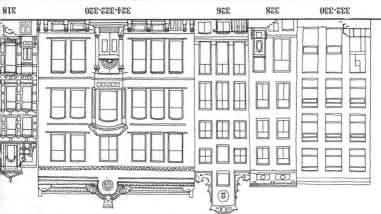

318   324-322-320   326   328   332-330

Herengracht 318-332

318 façade rebuilt around 1890; top looks like neck-gable; stoop unaltered.
320-322-324 3 houses torn down in 1920; new building with façade of sandstone, possibly neo-18thC style; frontal stoop.
326 early 18thC neck-gable; stoop removed and former door converted into window; entrance moved to basement.
328 M. 18thC; straight cornice; consoles date from before 1800.
330-332 3 houses torn down to make way for unimpressive building from University of Amsterdam in 1961; the new building stretches behind the monumental façades of nos. 334 and 336.

339 M. 18thC façade with elevated wooden cornice; renovated in 1963.
341 M. 18thC façade of sandstone; painted; *attiek* and stoop gone; renovated in 1963.
343 newly built in 1936; top consists of bell-gable from elsewhere.
345-347 M. 2 houses behind one large cornice façade from early 19thC; pointed iron roof just visible; 2 iron rods used as hoist beam.
349 M. ± 1760; bell-gable with period door framing; few alterations; 2nd entrance under stoop.
353 M. 17thC (e.g. building height and window front); cornice façade from 19thC.
355 M. 18thC; originally had a bell-gable; cornice façade from 19thC; stoop gone; renovated in 1970.

339   341   343   345-347   349   353   355

342   340   338   336   334

334 M. only the façade of 17thC the step-gable house remains; wooden street front converted to brick in 18thC; ornamented *pui* beam.
336 M. from this ± 1745 building only the fine façade left; unusual sandstone bell-shaped cornice.
338 M. beautiful façade with sandstone cornice, consoles and coat of arms ± 1730; period window framing.
340 M. 19thC façade with elevated straight cornice; until 1874 plot was occupied by 2 houses.
342 M. fine sandstone façade with straight cornice, *attiek*, corner vases and coat of arms ± 1720; shape of windows is unique; few alterations.

357 newly built in ± 1910; asymmetric, with bay windows on 2 floors.
359 M. 18thC neck-gable; few alterations.
361 M. small step-gable ± 1650; one of 'Stadsherstel' showpieces; renovated in 1962; gable stone 'Huis Sonnenberg' (House Sun Mountain); original construction.*
363 M. 17thC (e.g. building height and wooden street front); façade changed into cornice façade in 19thC; renovated in 1964.*
365 M. 17thC house with 18thC bell-gable; renovated in 1971.*
369 M. neck-gable from ± 1735; few alterations; around the side; entrance to upper floors from the side.*

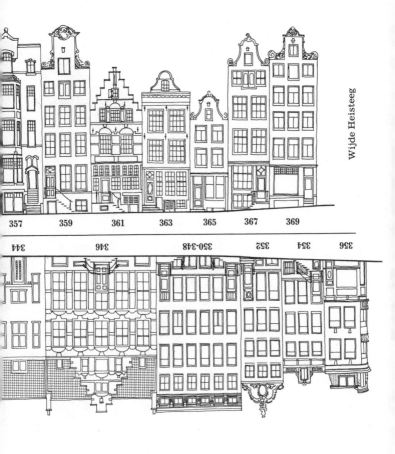

357   359   361   363   365   367   369

Wijde Heisteeg

344   346   350-348   352   354   356

Herengracht 344-356

344 built in ± 1920 where a step-gabled house once stood (see no. 346).
346 M. double house with step-gable ± 1615; transverse roof; well preserved; original construction.
348-350 M. cornice façade twin; painted sandstone façades with wooden cornice ± 1730; *attiek* disappeared later; cornice simplified.
352 M. sandstone façade with straight cornice and fine bell-gable styled top with bust ± 1735.
354 M. 18thC; house used to have neck-gable; top broke off around 1840 and was replaced by straight cornice, ballustrade and dormer.
356 until 1889 plot was taken by 17thC house; replaced by shop; straight cornice; not as high as no. 358.

358 built ± 1900; just a bit too tall.

360 M. 17thC·house; topped with ornate, elevated cornice ± 1745; wooden street front altered after 1900.

362 added to no. 364 in 1918; in adapted style; curious roof.

364-366 and **368-370** M. beautiful sandstone neck-gable foursome 'father, mother and twins'; disigned by Philip Vingboons 1662; frontons above windows; original construction; no. 364's stoop since removed; no. 366 has gable stone: a piece of curved wood, commissioned by one Jacob Cromhout (last name translates: 'curved-wood').

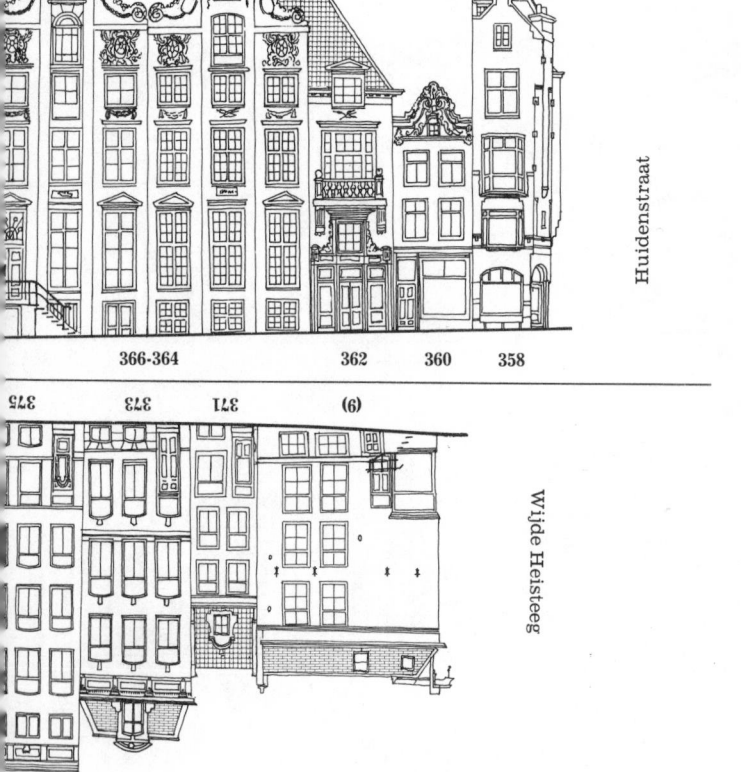

366-364 362 360 358

Huidenstraat

375 373 371 (6)

Wijde Heisteeg

(Wijde Heisteeg 9) M. thoroughly rebuilt in the 19thC; stuccoed side façade with pothouse.

371 M. 18thC; high transverse roof; dormer; straight cornice; frontal stoop.

373 newly built in ± 1880; straight cornice with consoles.

375-385 until 1878 an almshouse was situated here.

375 newly built ± 1880; straight cornice looks older.

377 newly built ± 1880; very common style in the period; straight cornice with consoles.
389 built for Hugo Grothof in 1913; see tiled picture on façade.
391-393 M. 18thC; 19thC elements: straight cornice and hipped roof; street front from no. 391 stuccoed.
395 newly built ± 1880; front- and side façade in step-gable style; tower corner; white cat and pilaster on step-gable.

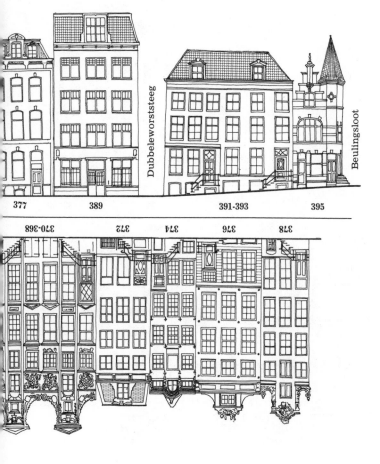

377   389   391-393   395

370-368   372   374   376   378

368-370 M. see text nos. 364-366.
372 M. 18thC; simplified cornice from 19thC; saddled roof altered later; fine cushion-door ± 1800.
374 M. elevated cornice façade; ± 1725; consoles and figurines support cornice; door framing from later period ± 1790; renovated in 1955.
376 M. sandstone cornice façade with bell-shaped elevation, corner vases, statuettes and ashlar street front from ± 1730; few alterations.
378 M. neck-gable from 1740; few alterations; claw pieces with corner vases; an identical façade used to stand at no. 380.

397 M. 17thC; building height a bit increased later; 19thC cornice; street front thoroughly rebuilt.

399 M. early 18thC building with fine door framing; top altered in 19thC; dormer.

401 - 403-(Beulingstraat 10) M. 18thC corner house; cornice with consoles and windows across front- and side façade; 2 stoops; pothouse; few alterations; renovated in 1965.

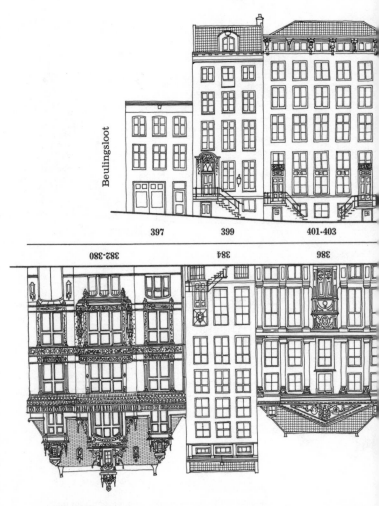

Beulingsloot

397   399   401-403

382-380   384   386

380-382 M. 3 houses used to stand on this plot; present un-Amsterdam double house constructed in 1889 by architect A. Salm; sandstone façade; lavishly ornamented.

384 M. late 18thC; cornice façade; transverse roof, and fine door; now a student house.

386 M. double house; façade ornamented with pilasters; designed by Philip Vingboons in 1663; tympan above straight cornice; hipped roof; door moved to basement; double stoop gone; original construction.

(Beulingstraat 27) M. one of Herengracht's oldest houses; before the 17thC expansion the canal stopped here; row line receded somewhat; front with yearstone 1649; side façade has pothouse and beam ends; renovated in 1964; bell-gable reconstructed (see front façade).

405 M. 17thC; many alterations; straight cornice and dormer from 19thC.

407 M. 18thC with 19thC cornice; well preserved.

409-411 M. 17thC twin neck-gables; renovated in 1954; a similar pair of twins can be seen on the other side (nos. 398-396); 2 frontal stoops.

413 M. 17thC; many alterations; around 1800 top was 'modernized' to straight cornice with 4 consoles; stoop gone.

Beulingstraat

(27)   **405**   **407**   **409-411**   **413**

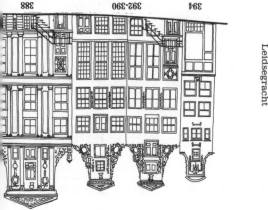

Leidsegracht

Herengracht 388-394

388 M. broad sandstone neck-gable with pilasters from 1655 (see yearstone); beautiful corner vases; few alterations; original construction.

390-392 M. sandstone neck-gable twin from $\pm$ 1665; fine claw pieces representing man and woman; few alterations; original construction.

390 gone; former door converted into window; entrance stoop from no. 390 gone.

394 M. small corner house; bell-gable from 1672 with high wooden street front; street front altered $\pm$ 1900; entrance to upper floors around the side; height of front entrance $\pm$ 1.60 meters; pothouse around the side; gable stone with 'de vier Heemskinderen'; owned by 'Hendrick de Keyser'.

415 this step-gable was built in 1898; on first floor imitation cross-frame windows with neo-Gothic fanlights.
417 M. 17thC bell-gable; remarkable period entrance ± 1670; few alterations.
419 M. built in 1769; frontal stoop; simple, straight cornice and transverse roof from 19thC.
421 M. 17thC; unusual spout-gable on private house (spout-gables were used primarily for warehouses); wooden windows and frames slightly changed later.
423 M. 18thC; formerly topped by bell-gable; 'modernized' to cornice façade in ± 1810; second entrance under stoop.
425 M. detached house, 17thC; slight relief in façade; rebuilt 18thC; top possibly altered; door framing with Ionic pilasters from ± 1800.

415   417   419   421   423   425

398-396   400   402   404   406   408

408 M. 1665; sandstone neck-gable; original construction.
406 M. 1665.
19thC.
404 M. 1665; frontons over windows (see no. 402); straight cornice from
very fine stoop from ± 1760.
402 M. sandstone neck-gable from 1665; frontons over windows and top;
400 M. 1665; neck-gable replaced by straight cornice ± 1780; stoop gone.
and 408 are left with original neck-gable.
400-402-404-406-408 M. in 1665 5 identical houses built here; only nos. 402
from 1665; beautiful window fronts and pothouses.
396-398 M. possibly the most frequently photographed twin of Amsterdam;

427-429 M. fine twin neck-gables, early 18thC; division of windows altered in 18thC except 3rd floor; few alterations; renovated in 1966.*
431 M. back of 17thC church on Singel; wrought iron fence ± 1840.

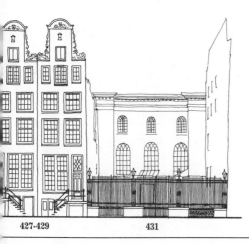

427-429   431

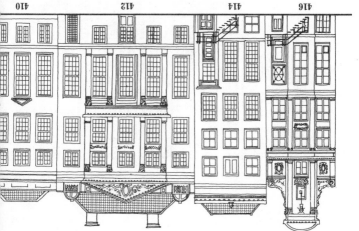

Herengracht 410-416

410 M. style adapted to that of no. 412 in 1938; hipped roof.
412 M. fine double house with sandstone façade from 1664 designed by Philip Vingboons; fronton, pilasters, *attiek* dates from later period; never had a stoop; original construction.
414 M. early 19thC cornice façade; hipped roof; building possibly older.
416 M. beautiful neck-gable with pilasters and oeils-de-boeuf (bull's eyes) from 1667, see year inscription on façade; motto above hoist beam; original construction.

433 M. double house, 5 windows wide from 1720; double stoop; straight cornice and *attiek*; 'blocked' door framing; well preserved.
435 has been adapted in style to no. 433.
437 newly built in 1913 on plot where 2 houses used to stand; cornice façade.
439 newly built in 1904; much glass. (Corner houses like this were often altered or rebuilt.)

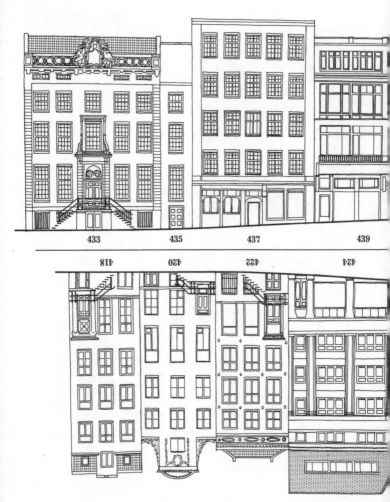

433   435   437   439

424   422   420   418

Herengracht 418-424

418 M. lower part of façade still 18thC; upper part spoiled during 1920's when fine bell-gable disappeared; window framing with Ionic pilasters from ± 1810.
420 M. neck-gable from 1671; unusually short neck; original construction.
422 M. 17thC house; cornice façade result of 19thC 'modernization'; hipped roof.
424 - (Leidsestraat 2) corner houses were often rebuilt and/or elevated; this one was newly built in 1924; street front has Amsterdamse School characteristics.

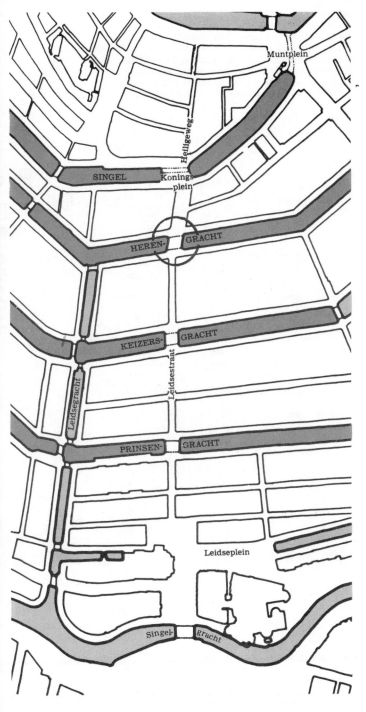

441 corner house 1892; year inscribed on the side façade.
433 M. cornice façade with 2 consoles ± 1810.
445 M. unusual bell-gable ± 1750; lower part altered later.
447 M. 18thC bell-gable with volutes; lower part thoroughly altered.
449 M. 18thC façade with straight cornice, consoles and windows in the cornice; unusual stone sub-structure from 1923.
451 M. stuccoed cornice façade 19thC; stoop is older.
453 19thC façade with straight cornice; *attiek* and dormer.

Koningsplein

441   443   445   447   449   451   453

Leidsestraat

426-428-430 M. over-scaled building from 1901 where once stood 3 houses (see tiles); Jugendstil elements; recently classified as a monument.
432 M. 19thC stuccoed, cornice façade; door disappeared when altered.
434 M. early 18thC sandstone façade unusual circular arch on top; offices behind façade; stoop gone.
436 M. 17thC; thoroughly rebuilt in 1895; *attiek* with e.g. crest and bird.

430-428-426   432   434   436

Herengracht 426-436

455 M. cornice façade; central section comes out slightly; rebuilt $\pm$ 1800; painted sandstone.
457 M. cornice façade; many alterations; arched windows; upper floor again altered in 19thC.
459-461-463 newly built in 1971 on plot formerly occupied by 3 houses; modern stoop; unusually shaped dormers.

455   457   459-461-463

438   440   442

Herengracht 438-442

438 M. late 17thC; straight cornice with *attiek*; 2 vases and coat of arms; many alterations.
440 M. 17thC house; many alterations; double stoop retained; fine door framing probably 18thC.
442 colored green; 5 window wide; outward bending relief in façade; built in 1905; coat of arms of Friesland, Amsterdam and Groningen; entrance at street-level (see no. 440).

465 the original construction was replaced by this new building in 1965.
467-469 newly built 1955, 5 windows wide; double stoop; roof terrace
perhaps less than successfull; replaces two houses torn down in 1954.
471 M. double house with straight cornice; roof probably early 19thC;
awnings.

465   467-469   471

444   446   448

Herengracht 444-448

444 M. 17thC house; façade thoroughly altered in 19thC; windows in *attiek*
and window framing below; door of unusual shape.
446 M. 17thC house with windows of various width, which is unusual;
straight cornice with *attiek* and pinnacles; entrance in sandstone with 4
pilasters; double stoop with wrought iron Empire railing ± 1800; second
entrance under stoop.
448 M. sandstone façade 3 windows wide; cornice of later date ± 1800; door
at street-level (compare nos. 450 and 446).

473 M. late 17thC façade; 19thC straight cornice with rosettes; until ± 1730 joined to no. 475 and part of no. 477.

475 M. one of Herengrachts finest houses both on the inside and outside; façade with straight cornice and *attiek* in sandstone ± 1730; statuettes and globe on **attiek**; 2 ornamented chimneys.

477 M. mainly 18thC house under hipped roof; ornamented straight cornice with windows; double stoop and railing from ± 1800; awnings; 2nd entrance under stoop.

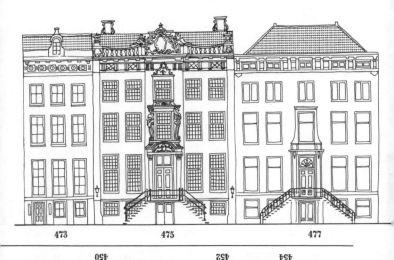

473   475   477

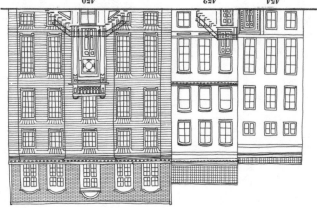

450 M. 1663; house built after design by Philip Vingboons; sandstone façade; in 1922 one floor was added which made alteration of roof necessary.

452 M. 17thC house with sandstone façade and straight cornice; transverse roof from later period; stoop bench retained.

454 M. late 17thC; altered top; cornice and transverse roof from 1820; stoop gone; entrance moved to basement (compare no. 452).

Herengracht 450-454

479 M. straight cornice with large consoles early 18thC; double house with double stoop and ornamented entrance.

481 M. double house; façade shows 17thC ornamentes; festoons and coats of arms; straight cornice with consoles; stoop gone (compare no. 479).

479   481

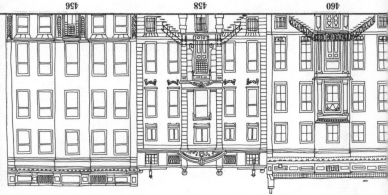

456   458   460

Herengracht 456-460

456 M. early 19thC double house with straight cornice and *attiek*; 20thC windows; sculptured street front; ornaments on either side of door.

458 M. built in 1875; mixture of many styles; *attiek* with 2 vases; corner lisenas; festoons; double stoop.

460 M. double house with 17thC, 18thC, and 19thC elements; straight cornice with *attiek*; double stoop with rare Empire railing $\pm$ 1800; 1st floor central window arched.

483-485 M. mainly early 19thC; all under one hipped roof with straight cornice.

487 M. façade with ornamented, sandstone, bell-shaped conice ± 1740; vase on top; stoop disappeared during later alterations (compare no. 489).

489 M. 17thC house with cornice from later period; door framing and fine door from ± 1750; awnings.

483-485   487   489

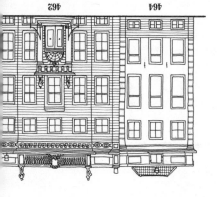

462   464

Nieuwe Spiegelstraat

464 M. cornice façade with *attiek* and hipped roof; corner lisenas which are usually 18thC.

462 M. sandstone façade from ± 1670 from a design by A. Dortsman; straight cornice with oval windows; 2 statuettes on *attiek*; frontal stoop; fine ornamented entrance; thoroughly altered in 1759.

Herengracht 462-464

491 M. 18thC fine sandstone cornice façade with *attiek*, vases and coat of arms; awnings out of place.

493 M. 17thC double house with fronton and 2 fine chimneys; sandstone façade 'modernized' ± 1760; double stoop.

495 M. early 18thC double house; 3 windows wide (compare no. 493 of same width out with 5 windows); sandstone façade with straight cornice and *attiek* topped with vases and coat of arms; unusual balcony over door.

491　　　　　　493　　　　　　495

466　　　　　　468

attiek with 4 vases on top.

468 M. sandstone lower part 17thC, the rest stuccoed; façade mainly 19thC; straight cornice.

466 M. big building, 6 windows wide; built in 1894 using 17thC and 18thC remnants from a house that occupied this plot before; large fronton on

Herengracht 466-468

497 M. 17thC double house; 6 windows wide; fronton from 17thC; façade thoroughly altered in 19thC; 19thC window framing.

499 M. 17thC double house with double stoop; thoroughly altered ± 1750; imitation cross-frame windows.

497   499

470   472   474

474 M. sandstone façade with 18thC characteristics but still primarily a 19thC façade (window framing).

472 M. 17thC house; straight cornice; *attiek* covers only central part; 4 festoons, stoop, door framing and 6 bottle-shaped balusters from ± 1740.

470 M. house 5 windows wide; stoop gone; façade primarily 19thC; straight cornice.

501 M. stuccoed cornice façade; early 19thC sash work; sculptured ornaments next to entrance.

503 M. sandstone cornice façade with hipped roof, primarily 19thC; doors and windows accentuated.

505 M. 17thC bell-gable with one festoon around hoist beam; stoop disappeared over the years; entrance moved to basement.

507 M. 17thC double house with double stoop; Corinthian pilasters and festoons ornamenting the façade; not much alteration.

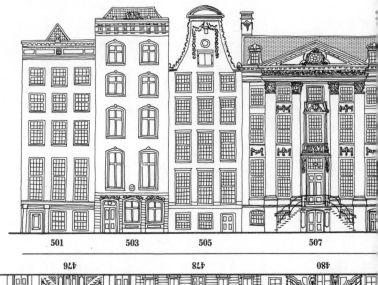

501   503   505   507

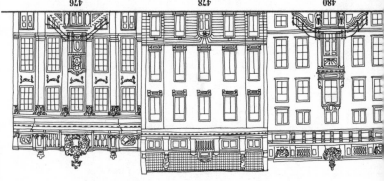

476   478   480

Herengracht 476-480

476 M. one of Herengracht's finest double houses; pilasters and much of façade still 17thC; finely sculptured *attiek* with eagle and vases date from ± 1740; door framing from same period; stoop restored during 1938 renovation, owned by 'Hendrick de Keyser.'*

478 M. late 17thC double house; 5 windows wide; straight cornice and *attiek* with vases and statuettes; lower part altered 19thC; stoop gone (compare nos. 476 and 480).

480 M. 17thC double house; cornice with *attiek* and vase; ornamented double stoop with 18thC harp piece; doorway lintel, ornate fanlight and railing ± 1800; door framing with Ionic pilaster from same period; pull bell next to entrance below stoop.

511-513 over-scaled building from 1928 by architect Rutgers; due to widening of Vijzelstraat (formerly of same width as present Leidsestraat), there is a breach in numbering; no. 515 was torn down in 1917 to make way for Vijzelstraat (see above).

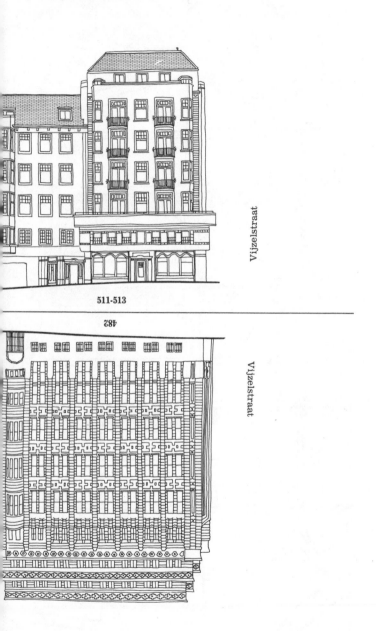

511-513

Vijzelstraat

Herengracht 482-496

482 M. built in 1917 by K.P.C. de Bazel; recently registered as a monument. 8 houses, nos. 482-496, were torn down to make way for this building and the widening of the Vijzelstraat.

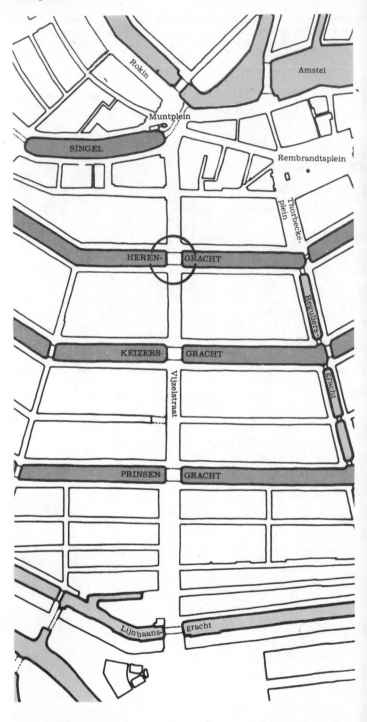

519-525 recent building with sandstone façade remiscent of Paris somehow; 4 older houses torn down in 1923.

519-521-523-525

498

corner lisenas, frontal stoop.

ornamentation ± 1770; door framing from same period; fine fanlight,

498 M. 17thC house; ornamented cornice and *attiek*; Louis XV

Herengracht 498

527 M. double house with hipped roof and 2 chimneys; 18thC façade with Ionic pilasters, all sandstone; tympan with bird; frontal stoop.
529 M. 17thC bell-gable with curious ornamental anchors from 19thC; few alterations; original construction.

527   529

500   502   504

Herengracht 500-504

500 M. 17thC house, altered in 18thC; arched windows; 18thC railing in front; renovated in 1975.
502 M. 17thC house, altered end of 18thC according to designs by Abraham van der Hart (1791); entrance with marble balcony on 2 pillars unusual; official residence of Amsterdam's mayor since 1927.
504 M. 17thC neck-gable with segment-shaped fronton; claw pieces in form of sculptured animals; stoop gone (compare no. 506).

531-533-535-537 since 1968 this building with asymmetric façade has been occupied by municipal registration office; before then 4 houses torn down ± 1910.

531-533-535-537

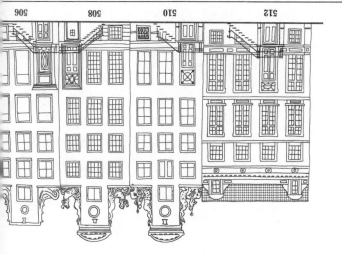

Herengracht 506-512

506 M. late 17thC neck-gable with lion's paws in the claw pieces; top fronton now gone; basement front; door and window framing early 19thC.

508 M. late 17thC neck-gable with fronton; Triton blows his horn in the claw pieces on either side.

510 M. late 17thC neck-gable with exquisite claw pieces that show sculptured sea-gods and dolphins; door and ornate fanlight early 19thC.

512 M. 17thC house; 4 windows wide; many alterations in 19thC; door and window framing from 19thC.

539 M. exquisite sandstone double house; ornamented *attiek* with
statuettes; bust; early 18thC balcony supported by statuettes; modern
lighting next to monumental door.*
541 newly built in 1965 in historical style; double stoop.

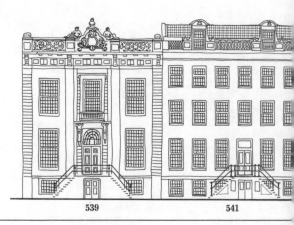

539　　　　　　　　　　541

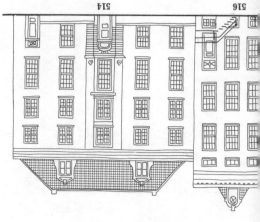

514　　　　　　　　　　516

ornate door with upper and lower halves.
516 M. late 17thC building with altered top; straight cornice from ± 1800;
Louis XVI busts of moors over entrance; ± 1785.
514 M. basically 17thC house; 5 windows wide; many alterations; early

543 M. late 17thC double house with sandstone façade; cornice and *attiek* from 1743; alliance shield on *attiek*; 2 extensible hoist beams.

545-547-549 3 houses here were torn down in 1910 to be replaced by this building designed by architect Staal Jr. in Berlage style; rebuilt in seventies when only the façade was retained.

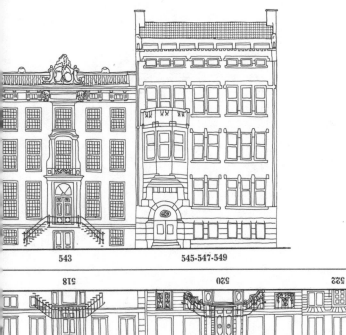

543   **545-547-549**

Herengracht 518-522

518 M. built on 2 plots (like no. 520); straight cornice with consoles from ± 1725; door and framing early 19thC; double stoop; when *attiek* was taken off, roof was altered.

520 M. ± 1725; house built on 2 plots; straight cornice and *attiek* with coat of arms and 4 vases; ornate window framing; fine stoop with harp piece.

522 M. cornice façade with small window in cornice; stoop removed in ± 1800; entrance moved to basement.

551 M. 18thC cornice façade; cornice broken by relief in middle; handsomely sculptured street front ± 1750.

553 M. 18thC façade with early 19thC cornice; size of windows diminishes according to height as in most old Amsterdam houses.

555 M. 17thC façade; formerly bell-gable; very much simplified into what still resembles bell-gable but without any ornamentation.

559 formerly 2 houses; joined under one roof ± 1940.

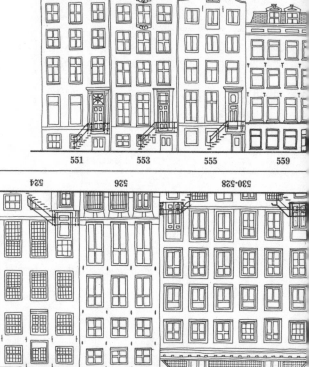

551   553   555   559

524   526   530-528

524 M. ± 1700 neck-gable; fronton op top; ornate period fanlight; late 18thC sash work; original construction.

526 M. late 17thC neck-gable; claw pieces with dolphins; stoop gone; house nicely located in bend of canal.

528-530 M. two 17thC buildings joined by straight cornice and hipped roof ± 1800; door and window framing from 19thC.

561 · (Thorbeckeplein 30) was rebuilt so thoroughly in ± 1840 that all older remnants are gone; joined later under one roof; pothouse on Thorbeckeplein side.

Thorbeckeplein

561-(30)

532   (2)

Reguliersgracht

532 · (Reguliersgracht 2) M. 2 late 17thC buildings joined under one hipped roof; on the left, a side façade; shallow house (common with houses near corners); entrance with side window ± 1800.

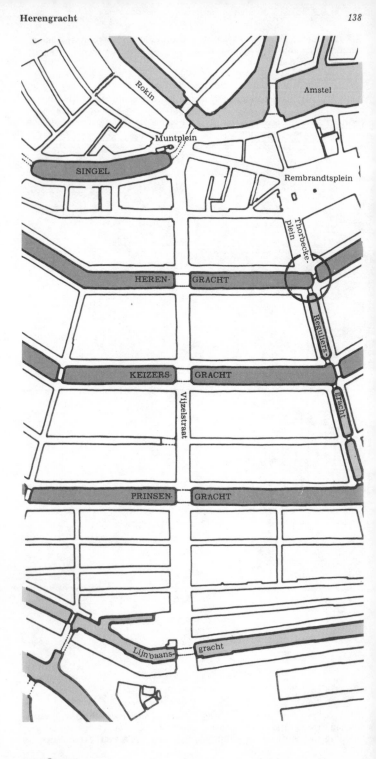

563 · (Thorbeckeplein 19) M. under one big transverse roof; building height characteristic for 17thC; no. 563 was later heightened with an additional floor.

565 M. late 17thC neck-gable; claw pieces with vases; stoop gone (compare no. 567).

567 M. fine 18thC façade with elevated cornice in sandstone; 18thC sash work was restored during 1965 renovation along with stoop; size of windows diminishes according to floor height as with most older houses.

(19)-563   **565**   **567**

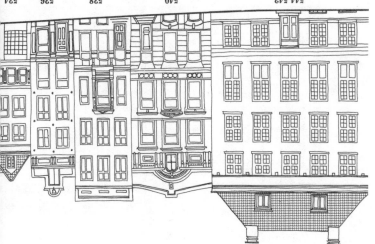

534-542 ... (labels shown inverted: 534, 536, 538, 540, 544-542)

534 M. late 17thC corner house; façade from ± 1870.

536 M. house from 1672 with 19thC façade; straight cornice with dormer.

538 M. 19thC cornice façade; street front and bay window. (Bay windows are few and far between on the canals.)

540 M. typical 19thC façade with finely worked cornice; window framing; frontal stoop.

542-544 adapted architecture from 1930's; completely rebuilt in 1969; building looks much older; original construction demolished down in 1930.

Herengracht 534-544

569 M. formerly topped by bell-gable; changed into cornice façade end 18thC; slightly arched windows; 2nd entrance under stoop.

571 M. late 17thC double house; strong resemblance with no. 573; large triangular fronton; altered in 19thC; stoop gone.

573 M. late 17thC double house having had much rebuilding over the years; 5 windows wide; straight cornice with fronton, 19thC; slight relief sandstone ornamentation on façade under fronton.

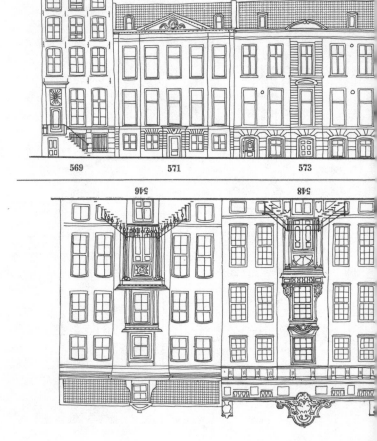

569   571   573

546   548

546 M. house built on 2 plots with 19thC façade; entrance and sash work ± 1800; arched windows; double stoop.

548 M. double house from 18thC; handsomely ornamented *attiek*; 2 vases; central windows with ornamental framing; door framing with Ionic pilasters; double stoop.

575 M. almost identical to no. 577 (see also no. 581).

577 M. door with sidelights, incorporating tree motif, 19thC; (see also no. 581).

579 M. festoons from ± 1670; stoop with Louis XIV balusters ± 1740.

581 M. joined with nos. 579, 577, 575 under one cornice and one transverse roof; between no. 581 and 579 is statuette of St. Michael and dragon; late 17thC complex; original construction.

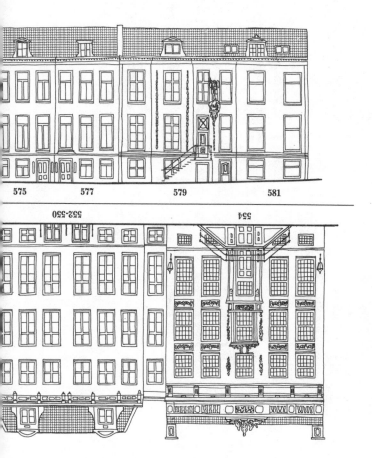

575   577   579   581

Herengracht 550-554

550-552 example of building in historical style; commissioned by the Mees Hope Bank; much old material used; cornice façade under one hipped roof.

554 M. double house; one of the 'Palatals'; 17thC sandstone façade with festoons under windows; balcony; straight cornice and 2 statuettes from later period, ± 1720; 2 chimneys; double stoop.

583 narrow house from ± 1870; small cornice façade; shuttered opening in elevated cornice gives access to loft.

585 high narrow house (basement, 5 floors and *attiek*) from ± 1890; when the building height was increased.

587 corner house from 1883; year inscribed in bay window; flat roof.

583   585   587

Utrechtsestraat

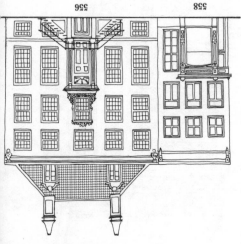

556   558

Utrechtsestraat

556 M. 5 window wide double house with hipped roof and 2 chimneys; late 17thC; 18thC façade; finely worked entrance; ± 1750; double stoop restored during 1930 renovations.

558 M. corner house; 17thC characteristics, e.g. building height; cornice late 18thC; shop front 19thC.

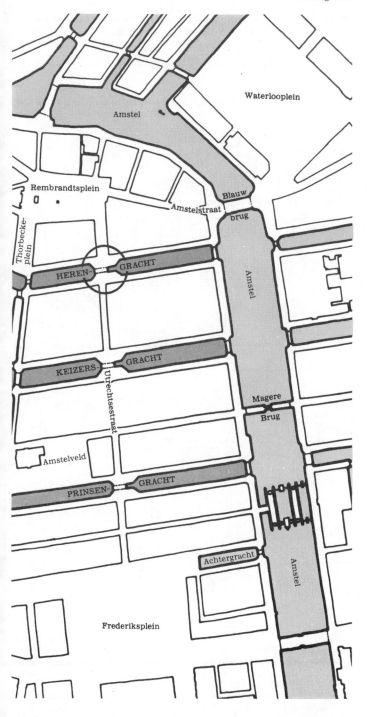

589-595 4 old houses were torn down ± 1930 to make way for this over-scaled new building designed by H.P. Berlage and Ouëndag brothers; after 1969 reconstruction available space was doubled (see nos. 597-599-601).

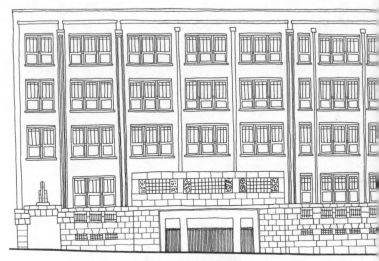

589-591-593-595

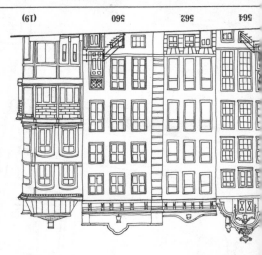

Utrechtsestraat

564   562   560   (19)

(Utrechtsestraat 19) corner house built in 1902; street front changed in 1925.
560 M. 18thC house; cornice from later period and similar to that of no. 562 apart from the panel above.
562 M. 18thC house with cornice from later period; stoop gone (compare no. 560).
564 M. handsome sandstone façade ± 1730; unusual top in which 2 female statuettes and a vase can be seen; sash work late 18thC; some mauve glass panels retained.

597-599-601 in 1969 a fine neo-Gothic building designed by Cuypers in 1889 was torn down for the present construction which, by intermediate relief in the façade suggests being 3 houses; dormers even less successful.

597-599-601

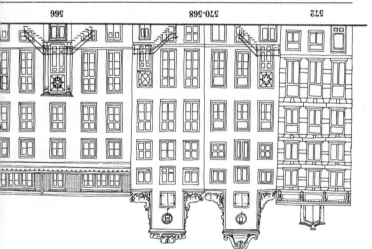

566   570-568   572

Herengracht 566-572

566 M. 17thC house; 5 windows wide; cornice and roof from ± 1910; handsome door framing; double stoop; 2nd entrance under stoop formerly meant for domestic servants.

568-570 M. early 18thC neck-gable twin; claw pieces with sculptured animals; high stoops; no. 568 retained stoop bench.

572 M. 19thC stuccoed cornice façade; entrance at street-level (compare no. 570).

603 built in historical style by AMRO Bank; a genuine old house had to be taken down to give way to present building.

605 M. 'palatial' double house; hipped roof and fine door framing ± 1740; sash work still 18thC; double stoop; building accomodates Willet-Holthuysen Museum; recently garden was laid out in French style of Marot; open to the public.

607 M. late 17thC bell-gable with unusual triangular windows in top; yearstone inscribed 1670; original construction.

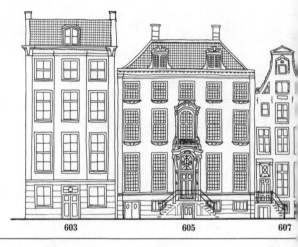

603   605   607

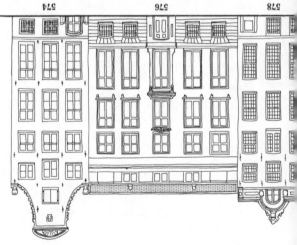

574   576   578

574 M. tall bell-gable from 1686 with segment-shaped fronton and 2 corner vases; stoop disappeared during 19thC alteration; original construction.

576 M. was already double house in ± 1670; thoroughly rebuilt 19thC; low natural stone façade with straight cornice; double stoop gone.

578 M. elevated cornice façade; Louis XV ornamentation over loft-doors (1759); stoop gone; late 18thC sash work.

609-611 M. 2 houses with common sandstone façade and *attiek* ± 1750; no.
609 is 4 windows wide; period stoop and railing; door framing in
sandstone; stoop bench retained.
613 older bell-gable was torn down in 1922; new building dates from 1920's;
windows equally sized on all floors.
615-617 two 17thC houses behind 1767 façade; tympan; fine, stone street
front.

609-611   613   615-617

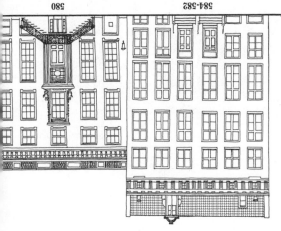

580   584-582

582-584 M. cornice façade twin joined by one transverse roof ± 1800; frontal

580 M. 5 window wide double house ± 1780; thoroughly rebuilt; cornice
with attiek; door framing with cherub on either side; elevated in 1922
when one floor was added; fine double stoop with railing; renovated in
1938.

Herengracht 580-584

619 M. double house from 1666; designed by A. Dortsman; 19thC straight cornice and door framing with motto; double stoop; original construction.
621 formerly plot was taken by house designed by Dortsman; thoroughly rebuilt in 1889; façade completely new; stoop retained.
623 M. one of few remaining houses by Dortsman, who $\pm$ 1670 built several houses here in this style; sandstone façade unfortunately painted over; narrow windows on first floor retained; original construction.

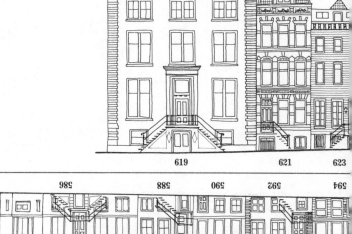

619   621   623

586   588   590   592   594

Herengracht 586-594

586 M. late 18thC building originally 4 windows wide; coach house (right) with its unusual windows was annexed 19thC; double stoop.
588 M. house built just after this part of canal was dug $\pm$ 1680; altered into cornice façade with transverse roof from around 1800.
590 M. 17thC house; rebuilt around 1800; cornice with consoles; hipped roof; lower part was again altered later; stoop gone (compare nos. 588 and 592).
592 M. exquisite house; rebuilt in $\pm$ 1740; ornate sandstone; bell-shaped top; 2nd entrance under stoop originally meant for domestic servants; stoop bench retained.
594 M. thoroughly rebuilt around 1790; cornice with consoles; stoop gone; entrance moved to basement.

625-627 house built in 1902 after design by G. van Arkel; formerly this plot was occupied by 3 houses built by Dortsman (see no. 623).

Amstel

625-627

596   600-598

Herengracht 596-600

596 M. thoroughly rebuilt in 1800; elevated with sandstone *attiek*; unusual arched door dating from period of rebuilding.

598-600 M. late 17thC neck-gable triplets; tops were reconstructed in 1962 with claw piece, frontons and pinnacles; beautiful location at corner of Amstel by the 18thC bridge at the end of the canal.

Magere Brug (skinny bridge)
This old wooden bridge built in 1671 owes its name to its narrow
width. Thanks to many rebuildings, this bridge has managed to
maintain its old character.

Keizersgracht

1 newly built in 1898; tower on top of roof; always been a combination shop and home; original wooden street front much altered.

3 M. ±1865 cornice façade; over 4 meters wide (±12 feet); door at street-level (compare no. 5).

5 M. ±1720 neck-gable with unusual claw pieces; ornamentation around hoist beam; saddle roof replaced by mansarde roof.

7 premodinantly 19thC façade because of straight cornice, dormer and equally sized windows; stoop altered ±1910.

9 M. ±1750 bell-gable; most bell-gables built this period.

Brouwersgracht

stoop older.

8 late 19thC façade with straight cornice, dormer and flat-topped roof;

railings on 1st and 2nd floor; frontal stoops.

4-6 M. twin cornice façades from ±1860; saddle roofs barely visible; window because of its turning approach.

2 M. early 18thC neck-gable; fronton gone; little else changed; stoop unique

19thC; saddle roof replaced by mansarde roof; top of façade altered.

(Brouwersgracht 63) M. 18thC side façade with pothouse; rebuilt end of

11-13 two houses once stood here preceding this newer construction in historical style from 1939; large transverse roof; straight cornice with windows; entrance on street-level.

15 M. ±1735 façade with cornice, transverse roof; handsome *attiek* disappeared over the years; present cornice from beginning 19thC.

17 M. 18thC building; once a neck-gable; somewhat altered; especially top, sobered into bell-like gable in the 19thC.

19 M. ±1740 bell-gable with unusual form (top is wider than normal, compare no. 9); coat of arms on fronton; ornamentation around hoist beam.

21 1904 cornice façade; very few cornices of this kind were built in the 20thC; most cornice façades from the 19thC.

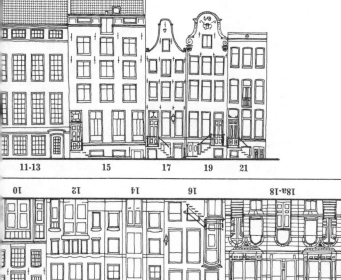

11-13   15   17   19   21

10   12   14   16   18a-18

Keizersgracht 10-18a

10 M. 18thC warehouse; top sobered in 19thC into spout-like gable.

12 M. ±1730 neck-gable with handsome claw pieces and corner vases; lower part of façade altered 1917 when stoop was removed.

14 M. 18thC warehouse; middle part with doors in slight relief; straight cornice; top altered 19thC; lower structure dates from 1917.

16 M. remarkably well preserved neck-gable from 1743 (see claw pieces).

18-18a once a wide step-gable, now typical 19thC complex built 1886.

23 M. remarkably preserved early 18thC neck-gable; 17thC building height; fronton with Roman bust; door has pull bell.

25 newly built in 1896 with ornate straight cornice, dormer and flat-topped roof.

27 M. predominantly 19thC façade; straight cornice; two sculptured heads on door.

29 M. neck-gable with the year of construction, 1689, on fronton; oval windows with sculptured frames (bull's-eyes); ornamental vases.

31 M. façade with straight cornice built beginning 19thC; floor added 20thC.

33 M. 18thC building with altered top; straight cornice with windows from beginning 19thC.

                23   25   27   29   31   33

                20   22   24   26

20 M. ±1740 cornice façade with *attiek*; some elements have disappeared over the years; handsome ornate crest retained.

22 M. until 1929 a church; present building designed by Van Straaten in 1837 (see roman numerals on door frame).

24 M. 17thC warehouse; much altered; hipped roof late 18thC; straight cornice fitted later.

26 M. ±1730 neck-gable; hardly altered; handsome fanlight.

35 M. ±1795 façade with straight cornice; two consoles and hipped roof; little else changed; even sash work original.

37 M. neck-gable with claw pieces, checkered motif; shield above hoist beam dating ±1730; handsome cut-glass fanlight.

39 M. ±1725 neck-gable; lower structure rebuilt early 20thC when stoop was removed and entrance re-positioned.

41 predominantly 19thC façade; floor added 1902; brick cornice; hoist beam missing.

43 M. ±1800 façade with straight cornice, two consoles and hipped roof; sculptured ashlar street front from later period.

45 M. ±1740 neck-gable with ornamented vases and handsome crest on top; sculptured stoop with Ionic balusters; gable stone from ±1860.

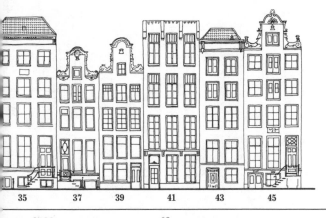

35   37   39   41   43   45

34-28   36

with step-gables that once formed a group of five with nos. 40, 42 and 44.

36 late 19thC 5 window wide cornice façade; replaces two warehouses neck-gables, since demolished.

28-34 newly built in historical style, 1910, with straight cornice, Ionic pilasters, and cross-frame windows on 2nd and 3rd floors; replaces twin

Keizersgracht 28-36

47-63 now 65: adapted architecture drawn according to architects plans; completion scheduled for late 1978; there was once a courtyard here which was replaced by a building in 1913 which in turn was torn down in 1977.
67 M. late 18thC 4 window wide sandstone cornice façade; stoop disappeared over the years as well as entrance; merged with no. 69.
69 M. ±1760 façade with straight sandstone cornice and four consoles; hipped roof fitted somewhat later; unusual window framing from original construction.

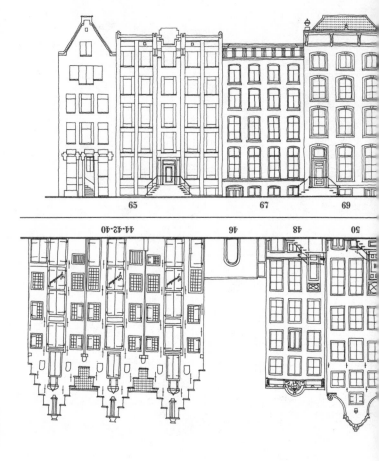

65   67   69

44-42-40   46   48   50

40-42-44 M. 'De Groenland Pakhuizen' (the Greenland warehouses); step-gables from 1621. Originally five identical façades, the group was 'reduced' to triplets when nos. 36 and 38 were torn down in the 19thC. Note covered hoist beams.
46 until 1936 a step-gable; a hole for over 40 years since.
48 M. ± 1760 façade with elevated straight cornice and two consoles; few alterations.
50 M. beautiful bell-gable from ±1750; ornate fanlight and door from ±1800; brick façade; few alterations.

71 M. house built ±1730, once 3 windows wide; handsome *attiek* now gone; new *attiek* fitted 19thC; merged with house on right side ±1860.
73 M. ±1770 façade with elevated cornice pierced by hoist beam straight cornice above 1st floor fitted later.
75 M. early 19thC façade; not much alteration.
77 M. façade with cornice and consoles with Louis XV ornamentation; *attiek* in shape of balustrade and crest in middle dating ±1755.

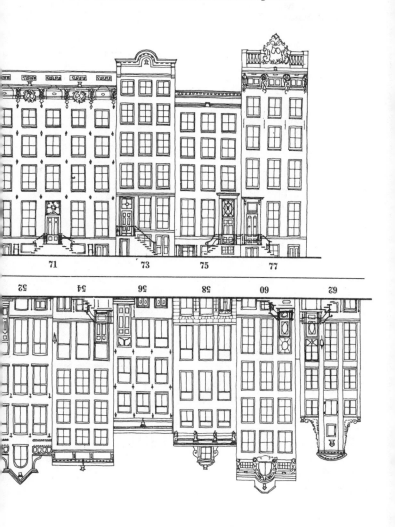

71   73   75   77

52   54   56   58   60   62

Keizersgracht 52-62

52 late 19thC façade with unusual brick dormer.
54 18thC building; floor added 19thC; straight cornice.
56 M. predominantly 19thC façade because of stucco and straight cornice.
58 M. building radically rebuilt 1870 into cornice façade.
60 M. ±1760 cornice façade with elevated, straight cornice; handsome consoles.
62 M. ±1660 neck-gable with fronton and two corner vases; property of 'Stadsherstel'; restored in 1971 together with no. 64.*

79 M. ±1760 façade; top somewhat sobered with another straight cornice in 19thC; wide entrance.

81 M. ±1755 brick façade with straight stone, cornice and ornamented *attiek*; handsome crest and two decorative vases; ornate fanlight with lantern.

83 M. predominantly late 19thC façade with small straight cornice; stoop much older; door and ornate fanlight early 19thC.

85-87 M. once two houses stood here, now 6 window wide cornice façade from ±1870; double stoop.

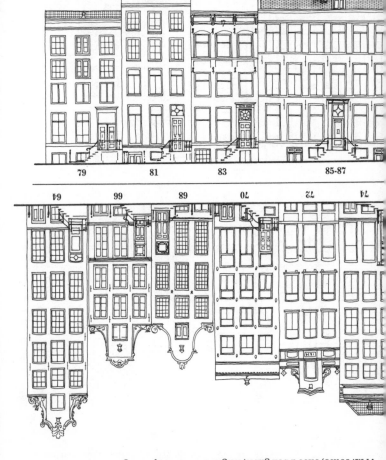

79   81   83   85-87

64   66   89   70   72   74

64 M. 1738 tall neck-gable with handsome ornaments in the top.*

66 M. house with 17thC features; rebuilt into neck-gable 18thC.

68 M. ±1755 bell-gable with asymmetrical Louis XV ornamentation on top;

70 M. ±1870 cornice façade; ornamented anchors; stoop much older.

72 predominantly 1874 façade; top reminiscent of a neck-gable.

74 M. 18thC; once a bell-gable; height increased by straight cornice ±1795.

89 M. once a bell-gable; rebuilt radically in ±1800; now straight cornice with two consoles; late 18thC sash work.

91 late 19thC cornice façade; once a coach house; building height not altered.

93 newly built in 1893 with straight cornice, dormer and mansarde roof; stoop much older; traditional large door replaced by porch with two doors.

95a M. forms one building with Herenstraat no. 40; side façade of little changed bell-gable from 1686; always been a combination shop/home; wooden shop front altered ±1890; two dormers, one with shutters; pothouse; 'family-tree' above door.

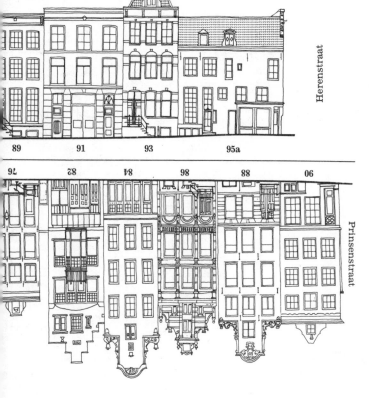

89   91   93   95a   Herenstraat

76   82   84   98   88   90   Prinsenstraat

76 M. 17thC (building height); 18thC façade; 19thC straight cornice and wooden wainscoting on top where there was once a neck-gable.

82 newly built 1907 in 17thC style with step-gable.

84 M. 'reconstruction' from 1934 by making use of sandstone ornaments from demolished building on Zeedijk; stoop not rebuilt.

86 late 19thC façade with many ornaments including, on ground floor, 4 sculptured lion heads and semi-circular fanlights; stoop older.

88 M. ±1720 neck-gable; street front altered early 20thC.

90 M. 17thC wooden street front in altered form; radically rebuilt just before 1800; straight cornice with unique ornaments; pothouse at front.

(Herenstraat 41) M. always been shop/home; upper floors hang out a bit over the street and are supported by the beam ends seen along this side façade; restored by 'Stadsherstel' together with next 7 houses along the Herenstraat.

97 M. 19thC cornice façade; restored by 'Stadsherstel' (see shield left of door).

99 M. early 19thC façade; straight cornice with windows and semi-circular dormer; restored by 'Stadsherstel'; 'family-tree' motif in fanlight.

101 M. façade with elevated sandstone cornice; richly ornamented cornice with two busts from ±1715; hardly altered; beautiful lantern and bottle-shaped balusters.

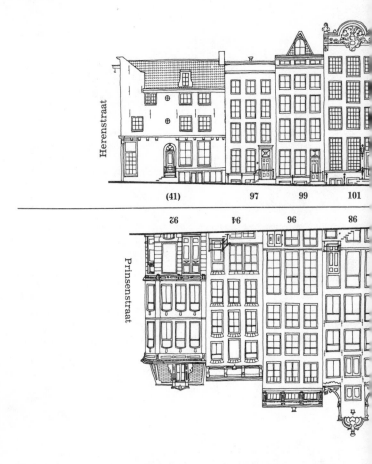

Herenstraat

(41)   **97**   **99**   **101**

92   **94**   **96**   **98**

Prinsenstraat

98 M. ±1730 neck-gable with ornamental vase on top; hardly altered.

96 M. radically altered late 18thC; floor added; handsome straight cornice with windows; stoop disappeared later (compare no. 98).

94 M. predominantly 19thC façade because of stucco and straight cornice.

92 late 19thC corner house with straight cornice and cut-off corner; dormer; still a bakery after centuries.

105 once a 3 window wide façade; neck-gable on left torn down in 1940 and no. 105 extended and reconstructed by making use of old façade fragments; now 5 window wide; designed by D.A. Warners; door frame from ±1760.

107 M. 1933 reconstruction of façade with sculptured whale on straight cornice; hipped roof dating ±1760; lower part altered (balcony fitted); stoop not rebuilt; two hoist beams.

109 ±1875 cornice façade with semi-circular windows on 2nd floor; small frontal stoop.

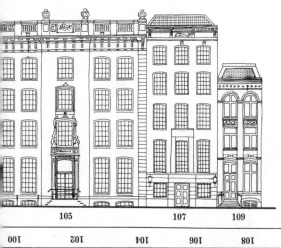

105   107   109

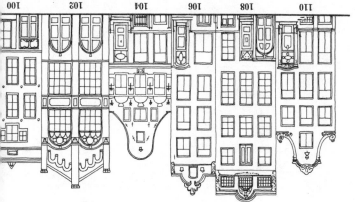

100   102   104   106   108   110

100 M. 19thC cornice façade; double entrance at street-level (compare no. 98); handsome fanlight.

102 M. once a clandestine church; façade from 1876; semi-circular windows on 2nd floor; three pilasters on top.

104 M. early 17thC house; relieving arches above windows on 1st floor; gable stone from same period; top sobered 19thC.

106 M. building from ±1760; elevated cornice with two consoles and two hoist beams; frontal stoop; door in two parts.

108 M. building with elevated cornice and two consoles; hoist beam ±1740.

110 M. 1759 bell-gable with door and door frame from same period; top ornamented in Louis XV style (asymmetrically); little else changed.

112 M. building with straight cornice: bell-shaped crest on top, two corner vases, all in Louis XV style from ±1745; street front altered 1929, then reconstructed during recent restoration.
114 M. late 18thC building with straight cornice, consoles and hipped roof.
116 M. 1745 bell-gable with ornaments at top; doorway lintel.
118-120 M. well known city planner-architect Berlage once lived here (see shield); 19thC façades underneath one hipped roof; one straight cornice with windows and consoles.
122 M. ±1720 neck-gable; family alliance shield above hoist beam.

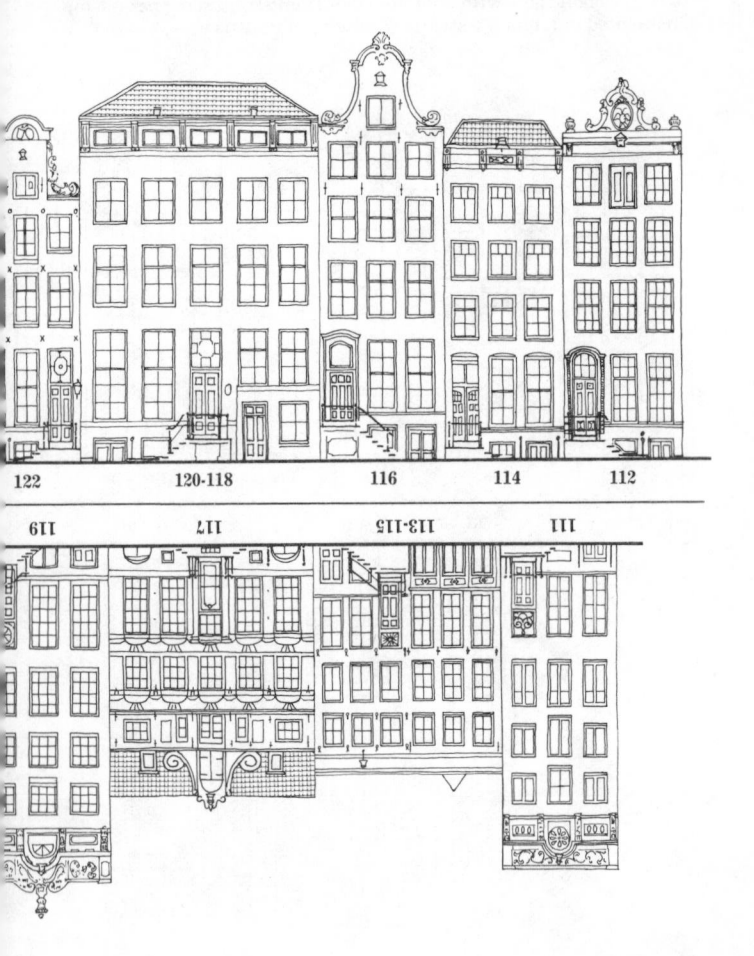

122   120-118   116   114   112

119   117   113-115   111

111 M. ±1740 façade with elevated sandstone cornice and ornamented *attiek*; handsome, cut-glass fanlight.
113-115 M. drastically rebuilt in 1895; old stoop preserved; fanlight in sun design.
117 M. double house built ±1620, original construction; once had step-gable, now peculiar dormer framed in a bell-shaped form; handsome Louis XV door from ±1760.
119 M. ±1735 façade with elevated cornice and ornate, 'closed' *attiek*.

121 M. 6 window wide complex built 1793 with straight cornice, circular windows, transverse roof, double stoop; door from construction period with Louis XVI ornamentation; sash work; semi-circular fanlight; beautiful interior; hardly altered; until just before 1800 a small coach house stood next door.

123 M. palace built 1622 (see date stone); the house with six heads on the façade; step-gable with pinnacles; cross-frames windows reconstructed during 1909 restoration; gate in original style; municipal property.

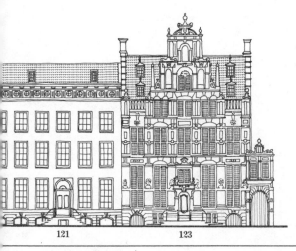

121   123

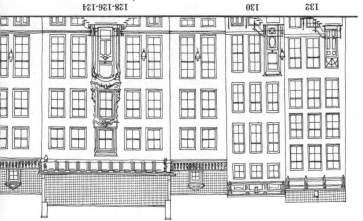

128-126-124   130   132

Keizersgracht 124-132

124-126-128 M. central, 5 window wide building dates from ±1755; nos. 128 and 124 has been merged in same style early 20thC; this sort of double house was seldom built here (in contrast with the bend on the Herengracht between Leidsestraat and Vijzelstraat).

130 M. late 18thC cornice façade with ornaments on top; door framing from same period.

132 M. ±1780 building with straight cornice and transverse roof; interior as well as exterior hardly altered.

125 M. this early 18thC neck-gable was not too well rebuilt in the 19thC: same size windows on all floors; peculiar roof.

127 M. ±1720 double house almost 14 meters wide with straight cornice and consoles; *attiek* and chimneys missing; door frame with Ionic pilasters possibly from same period.

129 newly built 1880 (see commemorative stone and date at top); might be called neo-Gothic style (see pointed arches on 2nd floor and pillars).

131 M. early 19thC cornice façade; stoop older; most houses are 2 or 3 windows wide, this house is 4 windows wide.

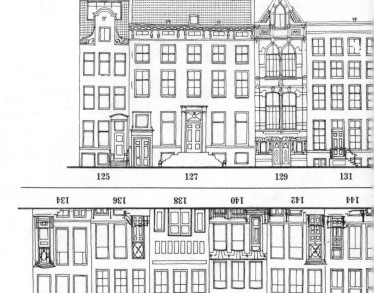

125   127   129   131

134 136 138 140 142 144

Keizersgracht 134-144

134 M. building with elevated sandstone cornice; crest above *attiek* shutter from ±1755; door framing from same period.

136 M. ±1760 bell-gable: entrance early 19thC; pull bell.

138 M. ±1730 neck-gable; lower part unfortunately altered 1919 when stoop was removed.

140 predominantly late 19thC façade; frontal stoop; house does not lean out like its neighbors.

142 M. 18thC building with straight cornice; *attiek* windows from later.

144 M. beautiful façade from ±1760 with elevated cornice executed in Louis XV style (asymmetrically); 20thC door.

133 M. ±1620 wide step-gable with claw pieces, thus original construction; remarkably preserved and well restored.
135 M. façade with straight cornice; *attiek* in shaped of a balustrade and handsome ornate crest ±1760; hardly altered.
137-139 M. 1738 twin cornice façades with elevated cornice and *attiek* in unusual bell-shaped form.
141 M. wide step-gable from 1623; brick façade painted (compare no. 133); top poorly restored in 1878; pull bell.
143 M. late 17thC façade; once a neck-gable before ±1800 replacement by cornice; the rest unaltered.

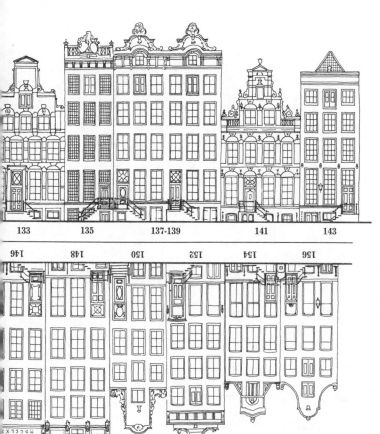

133   135   137-139   141   143

146   148   150   152   154   156

156 M. ±1770 bell-gable; house number above doorway lintel; stoop bench.
154 M. 18thC building with top altered 19thC; hoist beam.
152 M. ±1760 building with straight cornice and bell-shaped *attiek*; door frame from same period; ornamental vases missing.
150 M. ±1725 neck-gable; ornaments above hoist beam; early 19thC cushion-door; frontal stoop; house number in same style.
148 M. façade with ornamented straight cornice and open balustrade; consoles and sculptured acorns from ±1790 below straight cornice; entrance from construction period.
146 M. building from 1780 (see top) with straight cornice and Louis XVI ornamentation; hipped roof (most houses have a saddle roof).

Keizersgracht 146-156

145 M. earlier a neck-gable; altered ±1800 with elevated straight cornice and two consoles; gable stone reads 'Breslaw'; ground floor windows have ornamented corners.

147 M. façade drastically altered ±1800; elevated and finished with straight cornice, two consoles and hipped roof; stoop bench.

149 M. 4 window wide cornice façade; the central statue 'D'Koning van Zweden' (the king of Sweden) was earlier above gate at the side; sun-blind fitted above door.

151-153 newly built in 1880 with straight cornice, dormers and flat-topped roofs; no. 153 has one large window frame around the middle windows.

145	**147**	**149**	**151-153**

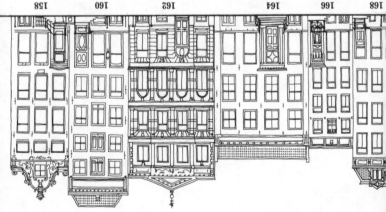

158	**160**	**162**	**164**	**166**	**168**

158 M. 1721 elevated cornice façade; handsome top; door frame early 19thC.

160 M. late 18thC building with straight cornice and two consoles; hipped roof; unusual wooden window framing early 19thC.

162 late 19thC 4 window wide façade; straight cornice with tympan weather vane on roof top.

164 M. late 18thC 4 window wide cornice façade with transverse roof; door frame with Ionic pilasters from same period; frontal stoop with railing.

166 M. 18thC façade with straight cornice; four consoles and hoist beam from later period; door frame late 19thC; door altered still later.

168 M. façade dating from 1899; straight cornice; dormer and flat-topped roof; stoop older.

155 newly built in 1897; same size windows on all floors; straight cornice, dormer and flat-topped roof. (Entire neighborhoods are built in this style). **157** M. 17thC house (as indicated by its height and the remaining horizontal beam over street front); rebuilt considerably; stuccoed in the 19thC when given an ogee-gable (with inward and outward bending profile; there are about 20 ogee-gables in Amsterdam).

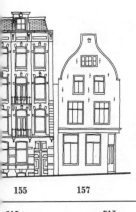

Leliegracht

155   157

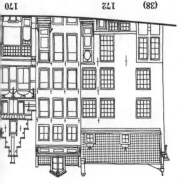

Leliegracht

170   172   (38)

Keizersgracht 170-172

170 M. early 17thC step-gable; original relieving arches above windows still present on 1st floor; top reconstructed in 1947 (see gable stone below top pilaster); shop front fitted in 1899 when stoop disappeared; original construction.
172 M. predominantly 19thC façade with straight cornice, two consoles, dormer and transverse roof; frontal stoop.
(Leliegracht 38) M. ±1750 side façade with pothouse; wooden street front runs around and partly across the side façade; front reconstructed by 'Stadsherstel' who owns many corner buildings. (As soon as such a building has been restored, it often acts structurally as a 'book-end' support for its neighbors).

159 - (Leliegracht 29) newly built 1935; saddle roof well visible from side; same size windows on all floors.

161 M. ±1735 façade with straight cornice, dormer and transverse roof.

163 newly built 1904 with straight cornice; entrance via frontal stoop rather than street-level; house does not lean.

165 newly built 1904 in historical style (even a stoop was built); roof terrace; two hoist beams.

167 M. ±1760 4 window wide façade with straight cornice and two consoles; small double stoop; upper floor has window railings; two hoist beams; little changed.

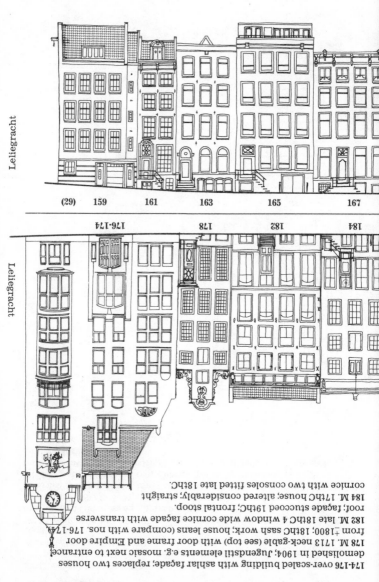

Leliegracht

(29)   159   161   163   165   167

Leliegracht

174-176 over-scaled building with ashlar façade; replaces two houses demolished in 1904; Jugendstil elements e.g. mosaic next to entrance!

178 M. 1713 neck-gable (see top) with door frame and Empire door from ±1800; 18thC sash work; house leans (compare with nos. 176-174).

182 M. late 18thC 4 window wide cornice façade with transverse roof; façade stuccoed 19thC; frontal stoop.

184 M. 17thC house; altered considerably; straight cornice with two consoles fitted late 18thC.

176-174   178   182   184

169 M. ±1725 façade; straight cornice with *attiek* replaced by sobered straight cornice 19thC.

171 M. ±1735 unusual 6 window wide façade; straight cornice with windows, two hoist beams and transverse roof; *attiek* since disappeared (probably due to weather conditions); double stoop.

173 M. 4 window wide sandstone façade with straight cornice and two consoles; two hoist beams and two chimneys from ±1770; door frame; beautiful interior; hardly altered.

175 M. façade with elevated sandstone cornice; elevation around the hoist beam ornamented, *attiek* in form of a balustrade and two ornamental vases dating ±1715.

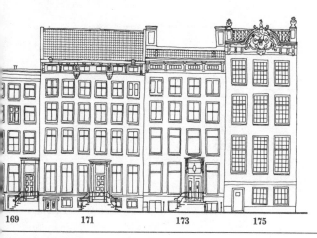

169   171   173   175

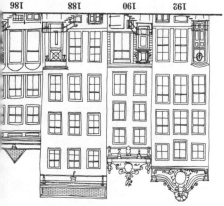

186   188   190   192

186 M. 17thC house (see relieving arches above windows); drastically altered 1880 into cornice façade; old saddle roof barely visible; building height un-altered.

188 M. ±1740 cornice façade; transverse roof fitted later when ornamentation on straight cornice probably disappeared; door framing with Ionic pilasters from 19thC.

190 M. ±1720 sandstone cornice façade; cornice finely ornamented with corner vases, escutcheon, sculptured helmet and two heads; ashlar street front and door frame from same period; hardly altered.

192 M. ±1745 cornice façade; handsome cornice in the shape of a bell; ornamentation around the *attiek* shutter.

177 M. 8 window wide façade with pilasters; complex designed by Jacob
van Campen, architect of Royal Palace on Dam Square; house named after
owner (Coymans houses); original construction from 1624; floor added
in period style 19thC; house on right built-on, also in period style; old door
gone.

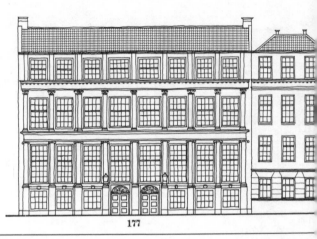

177

194   196   198

194 M. ±1760 façade with cornice in shape of a bell; ornamentation around
attiek shutter; front door early 19thC; hardly altered.*

196 M. façade with unusual sandstone cornice in shape of a bell; two corner
vases from ±1730; door from same period; pull-bell.*

198 the 17thC step-gable twins that once stood here were replaced in 1919
by the present office building with Amsterdam School features (outward
bending relief).

179 M. late 19thC façade with equally sized windows (compare with no. 181); straight cornice; ornamented anchors; older stoop.
181 M. early 19thC cornice façade; window railings on 1st floor.
183 M. step-gable built 1626; altered considerably; façade stuccoed in 19thC; stoop and entrance rebuilt 1922; lamp from 1922.
185 - (Raadhuisstraat 54) newly built in 1902 by architect G. van Arkel. In 1896 no less than 12 houses were demolished for the construction of the Raadhuisstraat; before it was a closed façade wall.

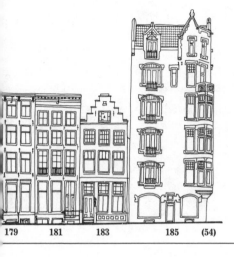

179   **181**   **183**   **185**   **(54)**

197-199 M. newly built 1898 by van Gendt brothers; small tower on corner;
recently classified as monument. These houses form the end of an arcade
of shops that runs back along the Raadhuisstraat to the Herengracht.
201 M. façade with fine tiled tableau above including name of original
owner; Jugendstil ironwork on ground floor window (see text no. 197-199).

(Westermarkt I) M. side façade of 18thC neck-gable; shop front fitted ±1890.
200 M. ±1715 neck-gable; shop front fitted late 19thC when stoop
disappeared.
202 M. ±1740 sandstone façade with elevated cornice and two consoles;
ornamentation around _attiek_ shutter; the grey sandstone has been painted;
door frame and window frames early 19thC.
204 M. early 18thC building, once had neck-gable; top altered into straight
cornice late 18thC.
206 M. late 18thC house with hipped roof; straight cornice with two
consoles; entrance from same period; hardly altered.

203 M. ±1735 unique 7 window wide sandstone façade with straight cornice; two coats of arms and 'closed' *attiek;* door frame from same period; double stoop; small coach house on right; altered considerably.
205 M. ±1750 4 window wide façade with straight cornice and consoles; *attiek* sobered later.

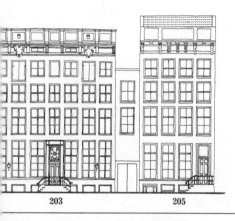

203   205

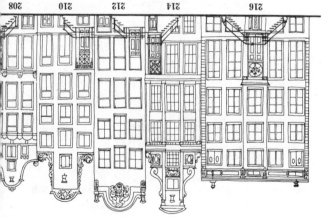

208   210   212   214   216

208 M. 17thC façade (see relieving arches above windows); house earlier had step-gable; top altered into bell-gable ±1750.
210 M. early 18thC neck-gable; decorative door frame from 1790; hardly altered.
212 M. 1709 façade with elevated cornice; ornamentation around hoist beam and two corner vases; well preserved; old door frame now gone.
214 M. one of the comparatively few elevated neck-gables; building date 1656 on cartouche; arched fronton and pilasters on façade.
216 M. ±1740 sandstone façade with sandstone cornice and consoles; double stoop; earlier this 5 window wide house had an *attiek.*

207 M. façade with straight cornice, unusually ornamented window frames (most window frames date from 19thC) and ±1755 door frame; *attiek* gone; straight cornice fitted early 19thC.

209 M. 4 window wide façade with ornate straight cornice and handsome *attiek* in the form of a balustrade; two ornamental vases and statue in middle dating ±1740.

211 M. 17thC house; altered considerably; top sobered into bell-like gable 19thC; lower structure converted to garage 1930.

213 newly built 1910; door at street-level; rebuilt later.

215 M. ±1760 bell-gable with sandstone street front; cabbage shaped gable stone; hardly altered.

207   209   211   213   215

218   220

218 M. rectory; 19thC cornice façade; no stoop (no longer built then).
220 M. neo-Gothic style cruciform basilica designed by Th. Molkenboer; built 1852; three houses demolished for this church.

217-219 M. ±1740 two houses with one façade and one handsome, elevated cornice with closed *attiek* and ornamental vases; four sculptured heads on *attiek;* double stoop; beautiful doors; little changed.

221 M. 4 window wide sandstone façade with straight cornice; *attiek* with coat of arms, two square chimneys and door frame from 1747; double stoop.

223 M. 18thC building; top altered 1869 when balustrade was fitted.

225 M. façade with elevated sandstone cornice and *attiek* in the shape of a balustrade and crest; handsome door frame with relief (construction year 1746); stoop still has bottle baluster in shape of 'S'.

217-219   221   223   225

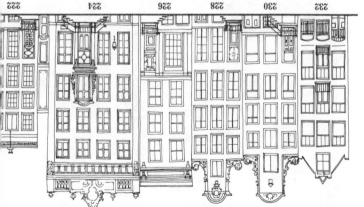

222   224   226   228   230   232

Keizersgracht 222-232

222 M. predominantly early 19thC façade; iron pole on hoist beam just above straight cornice; entrance with handsome doorway lintel.

224 M. 'Saxenburg' ±1765; sandstone façade with straight cornice and *attiek;* ornamented with corner vases and escutcheon; ornamented entrance.

226 M. ±1790 façade with straight cornice and consoles; rare ashlar street front; door varnished instead of painted usual canal-green.

228 M. ±1720 neck-gable with ornamented medallion above hoist beam.

230 M. ±1710 neck-gable; this handsome merchant's home has hardly been altered, only sash work on the windows and the door changed.

232 newly built ±1905; stoop gone; entrance at street-level; house does not lean (compare with no. 230).

227 M. ±1750 bell-gable with handsome top; windows become smaller towards top as in most old Amsterdam houses; stoop bench.

229 M. early 19thC cornice façade; iron extension on hoist beam for easy transport of goods; house number and name of occupants fitted in style.

231 M. façade from 1801; straight cornice with windows; transverse roof and ornamented anchors; sash work on ground floor altered; handsome door from building period.

231a - (Hartenstraat 36) M. 19thC side façade with straight cornice and dormer; shop front with semi-circular fanlights dating 1890; frontal stoop.

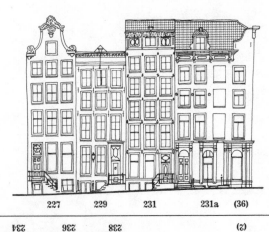

227   229   231   231a   (36)

Hartenstraat

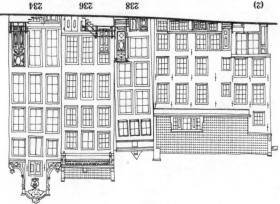

234   236   238   (2)

Reestraat

Keizersgracht 234-240

234 M. fine neck-gable from ±1740 with corner vases; early 19thC entrance with semi-circular doorway lintel; hardly altered.

236 M. drastically altered into cornice façade late 18thC; transverse roof; most houses have saddle roofs (compare with no. 240); nos. 234 and 236 are part of a hotel situated on the Prinsengracht (no. 323).

238 M. 18thC building; altered considerably; once had a neck-gable; rebuilt into straight cornice early 19thC; frontal stoop.

240 (Reestraat 2) M. side façade of 18thC bell-gable with pothouse; wooden street front runs around the corner; ±1755; hardly altered.*

233 17thC building height unchanged throughout 330 years; shop/home with straight cornice and flat roof dating late 19thC.

235 M. house built ±1735; shop front from same period, altered later; façade altered early 19thC.

237 M. 18thC façade with early 19thC straight cornice and dormer with fronton; 'Aristoteles' has restoration intentions.

239 M. façade with straight cornice and handsome ornamentation in form of bell with sculptured sun; two ornamental vases from ±1740; hardly altered.

241 M. ±1790 sandstone façade with straight cornice, two consoles and hipped roof; large early 19thC, door with ornate fanlight.

233   235   237   239   241

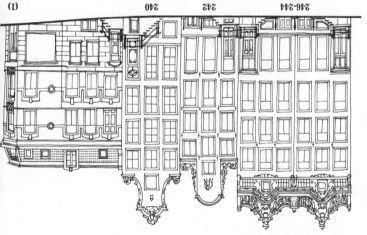

(I)   240   242   244-246

Keizersgracht 240-246

(Reestraat 1) late 19thC shop/home; flat roof; stoop older.

240 M. ±1750 bell-gable; handsome ornamentation at top; ornamented stoop; cushion-door in two parts; hardly altered.

242 M. ±1715 neck-gable; hoist beam sticks out through cartouche; hardly altered.

244-246 M. beautiful twins with elevated cornices and *attieken* (2) built 1730; both cornices enclose small windows and ornamented *attiek*; *attiek* in shape of balustrade has one ornamental vase above the shutters; hoist beam; well preserved.*

243-245 M. earlier two houses; merged 18thC; now 5 window wide cornice façade; 18thC door frame; double stoop.

247 M. ±1760 bell-gable with bust on finely ornamented top; middle window on 2nd floor once had loft-doors.

249 M. late 18thC cornice façade; top floor still has original sash work; beautiful ornate fanlight.

251 M. façade 'modernized' with straight cornice early 19thC; once a neck-gable; transverse roof also fitted early 19thC (most houses have saddle roofs).

253 M. early 19thC façade; at that time stoops no longer built; ornamented windows from same period (see souterrain and ground floor).

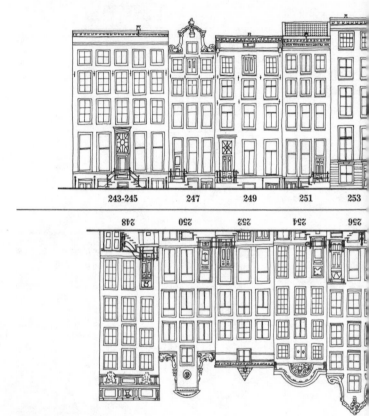

243-245   247   249   251   253

248   250   252   254   256

256 M. ±1750 bell-gable with much ornamentation at top; stoop bench.

254 M. handsome sandstone façade with elevated cornice ±1740; ornamentation around hoist beam; house number fitted in same style; pull bell; remarkably little changed.

252 M. early 18thC façade; top altered into straight cornice ±1800; old roof not altered (compare with no. 250).

250 M. ±1700 neck-gable with fronton on top; once a twin with no. 252; hardly altered.

244 and 246 have open *attieken)*; two coats of arms below cornice; sandstone façade now painted.

248 M. ±1710 sandstone façade with straight cornice and closed *attiek* (nos.

Keizersgracht 248-256

255 M. ±1740 façade; beautiful top replaced with straight cornice and transverse roof early 19thC; door with two rosettes.

257 M. ±1760 façade with straight cornice; transverse roof; door frames and arched windows.

259 M. predominantly 19thC cornice façade; arched windows; dormer.

261 M. ±1740 façade with straight cornice, four consoles and *attiek; attiek* sobered early 19thC; door frame with consoles.

255   257   259   261

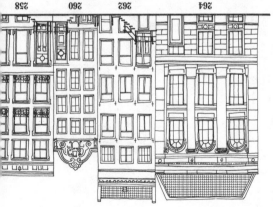

258   260   262   264

Keizersgracht 258-264

258 M. 18thC building; rebuilt drastically 1870; window frames and straight cornice fitted then; 19thC window railings.

260 M. ±1750 building with decorative, elevated, wooden cornice; two consoles and crest; hardly altered.

262 M. 18thC sandstone façade with straight cornice and transverse roof from just before 1800; once a neck-gable; traditional large door replaced by porch and two doors (compare with no. 260).

264 M. two older houses demolished in 1876 for this building; pilaster façade with straight cornice and hipped roof; entrance at street-level; large pull bell; house does not lean (compare nos. 268 and 262).

263 M. building with elevated cornice; hoist beam tucked away in elevated cornice over coat of arms; two ornamental vases dating ±1735.

265 M. ±1735 façade with straight cornice, four consoles and sobered, 'closed' *attiek;* in most houses entrance is either on right or left but here the sandstone door frame and window frame are in the middle.

267 M. 18thC building now with straight cornice, two rosettes and two consoles; sun awnings fitted.

269 M. ±1800 façade with straight cornice, four consoles and transverse roof; exceptionally handsome interior.

263   265   267   269

278   276   274   272   270   268

278 M. early 18thC façade with ornate cornice once had an *attiek* which hid roof; roof now just visible above cornice.

276 M. ±1715 façade with elevated cornice and two consoles; ornamentation around hoist beam; house number fitted twice.

274 M. ±1740 sandstone façade with elevated cornice; handsome ornaments and *attiek* with dormer ±1800; door from same period.

272 M. 18thC building, earlier a neck-gable; altered into straight cornice and *attiek* with dormer ±1800; door from same period.

270 M. 18thC façade (lower part); top altered into kind of 19thC neck-gable.

268 M. 18thC house; originally a neck-gable; top removed after 1800 and 'straightened', with a cornice.

271-273-275 demolished in 1955 for the present bank building which
architect A.J.Westerman tried to blend in with the surroundings; limited
building height; double stoop.
277 newly built in 1967 (see stone below stoop); stoop built in historical
style; windows are less successful than nos. 271-273 and 275 because of
missing sash work.
(Nos. 271-303 once comprised 16 seperate houses which have since
disappeared).

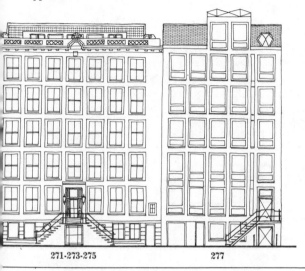

271-273-275   277

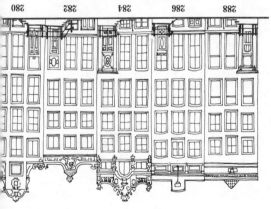

280   282   284   286   288

280 M. ±1720 neck-gable; hoist beam sticks out through a cartouche; house
number above doorway lintel.
282 M. ±1730 façade with unusual elevation in the cornice; vase above the
ornaments around the hoist beam; handsome fanlight.
284 M. ±1765 building; fine cornice with straight elevation and *attiek*; two statues
at top; early 19thC entrance.
286 M. ±1770 façade with straight cornice and consoles; *attiek* disappeared
over the years; arched windows.
288 M. 18thC building; top sobered into cornice façade early 19thC; old
roof unchanged.

279-283 predominantly 1900 façade; windows of peculiar form reminiscent of 17thC cross-frame windows; stone ornamentation, arches, and pilasters give relief to façade.

285 built in historical style; commissioned by Nederlandse Credit Verzekering Mij; door frame with gable stone, double stoop and sash work; opened June 16, 1975; the NCM also intends to build on the site next door.

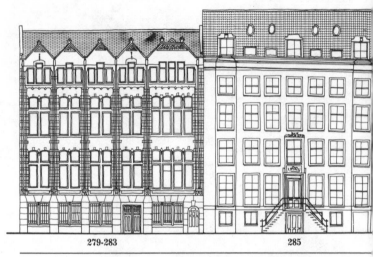

279-283   285

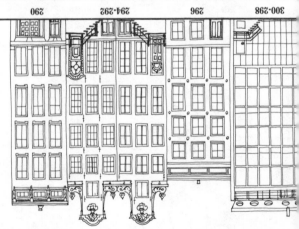

300-298   296   294-292   290

Keizersgracht 290-300

290 M. predominantly 19thC façade; stoop disappeared with rebuilding (compare nos. 292 and 294); entrance moved to souterrain; cornice with consoles dating early 19thC.

292-294 ±1730 twin neck-gables with beautiful claw pieces and corner vases; no. 292 still has original door and ashlar door frame.

296 M. predominantly 19thC façade; ornamental anchors; stoop gone; entrance at street-level.

298-300 newly built 1955; a monstrosity which does not harmonize with its surroundings; too much glass, too little brick.

nos. 293 and 295 were demolished in 1964; no. 297 in 1953; nos. 299 and 301 in 1951; no. 303 in 1950; as the data show, the houses were torn down one after another resulting in 'urban removal'. To prevent this, it is important that, as soon as one house is demolished, another is built to take its place and soon; if this does not occur, there is a big chance that the surrounding houses will also deteriorate.

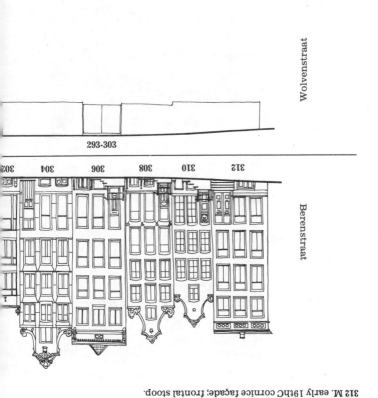

293-303

Keizersgracht 302-312

302 narrow house, just over 3 meters wide (∓9 feet); renovated completely 1909; corner vases are the oldest elements.

304 M. ∓1775 neck-gable with Louis XV ornamentation in claw pieces; merged with no. 302 in 1909; stuccoed 19thC; ornamented door slightly 'sunken', resulting in two fanlights.

306 M. early 19thC straight cornice with two consoles, sculptured acorns and small windows; hoist beam missing.

308 M. bell-gable with large, Louis XV top ornaments ∓1770 and crest above hoist beam; ornamented anchors above ground floor.

310 M. ∓1770 bell-gable; arched windows; pull-bell and stoop bench.

312 M. early 19thC cornice façade; frontal stoop.

305-309 M. newly built in 1912 designed by P.H. van Niftrik; house number above door set in a kind of gable stone; lower structure ornamented; three houses once stood here.

311 M. 1738 façade; top sobered with straight cornice and 'closed' *attiek* early 19thC; 18thC sash work repaired during restoration.

305-309   311

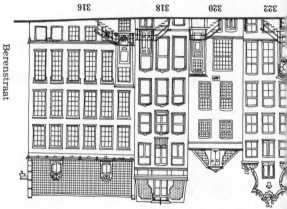

316   318   320   322

316 William Koch, building, built in 1935; well known example of 'modern' architecture in historical style designed by A.A. Kok, an architect who was much involved in restoration.

318 M. building from 1765 with unusual window frames; top altered early 20thC with dormer and flat roof.

320 M. 1788 façade with straight cornice; 17thC gable stone 'in the town Bordee'; door frame with Louis XVI ornamentation from same period.

322 M. ±1750 finely ornamented bell-gable with original door frame; door in two parts; hardly altered.*

313 newly built 1914; designed by P.A. Warners.

315 predominantly 1884 façade; cornice with windows; same size windows on all floors (compare with no. 317); entrance at street-level.

317 M. ±1713 handsome brick façade with straight cornice and 'closed' *attiek* with ornamentation including two vases and two sculptured waternymphs; well preserved.

319 M. 1639 elevated sandstone neck-gable designed by Philip Vingboons; pilasters, frontons on top and above two windows.*

313   315   317   319

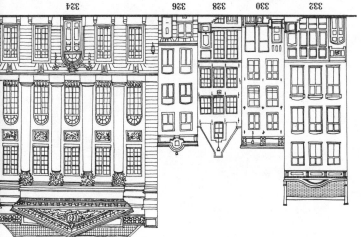

324   326   328   330   332

324 M. built 1788; unusual, palatial building for a city more well known for its houses; straight cornice and fronton; façade with four Corinthian pilasters; named 'Felix Merites'.

326 M. 19thC façade with elevated cornice; entrance at street-level.

328 spout-gable built in historical style, 1914.

330 M. ±1860 cornice façade; hoist beam fitted to the side.

332 cornice façade from 1913 with ashlar street front; one of the doors leads to the Claes Reynierzoon alms courtyard built 1618 (renovated 1913).

Keizersgracht 324-332

321 M. house built ±1650; once a step-gable before drastic rebuilding in ±1740; floor added and transverse roof fitted 18thC; stucco removed during restoration in 1958.

323 M. ±1730 façade with ornate, elevated cornice and two corner vases.

325 M. until 1914 bell-gable dating ±1750; now straight cornice.

327 M. ±1795 sandstone façade with straight cornice, two consoles and hipped roof.

329 M. façade with elevated cornice; ornamentation in front of _attiek_ loft-door dating ±1740; lower structure altered drastically ±1900; beautiful Jugendstil elements include iron work on balcony and in front of porch.

331 M. house built ±1740; once a twin with no. 329; present straight cornice from ±1800; little else changed.

321   323   325   327   329   331

370   372   374   376   378

370 M. 18thC building; rebuilt 19thC when straight cornice with two consoles and dormer were fitted; stoop gone.

372 M. early 19thC cornice façade with transverse roof; entrance at street-level.

374 M. early 19thC cornice façade; stoop older; handsome Empire door from ±1800; once a neck-gable.

376 built ±1860; straight cornice, dormer and flat-topped roof; arched windows; entrance at street-level (compare with no. 374).

378 M. ±1800 building with straight cornice and two consoles; saddle roof barely visible; façade altered 1890; entrance moved to souterrain.

333 M. house built ±1710; altered late 18thC with straight cornice and hipped roof (*attiek* disappeared then).

335 M. early 18thC house; once a bell-gable; sobered into straight cornice 19thC; old roof visible.

337 M. early 18thC house; once a neck-gable; sobered into straight cornice 19thC.

339 M. late 17thC house; once a neck-gable; altered somewhat; straight cornice fitted ±1800; renovated 1977.

341 M. ±1740 façade with ornamented elevated cornice; hardly altered.

343 M. predominantly ±1800 façade; four handsome consoles.

| 333 | 335 | 337 | 339 | 341 | 343 |

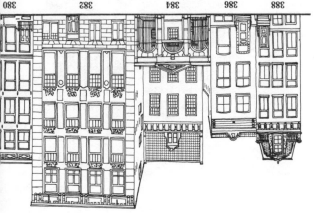

| 380 | 382 | 384 | 386 | 388 |

388 M. 19thC façade with early 19thC straight cornice; balustrade, dormer and flat roof late 19thC; frontal stoop.

386 M. 19thC façade with straight cornice; arched windows.

384 M. sandstone gate with three portals and a fronton; once entrance to a theatre that burned down in 1772; present façade from 1773; the yellow bricks on the small court indicate private ownership.

382 in 1902 and 1919 rebuilt in such a way that little was left of the 18thC house; ornamentation above windows; flat roof; ashlar street front; entrance at street-level.

380 ±1860 cornice façade; rebuilt 1923; remarkable stoop railing.

345-345a M. early 18thC building; floor added, straight cornice and closed *attiek* fitted ±1800; door frame from ±1800.

347 M. 19thC cornice façade with ashlar street front (in 19thC stoops were no longer built); entrance at souterrain level.

349 M. 18thC building; once a bell-gable, now straight cornice.

351 M. late 19thC cornice façade; ornamented anchors; stoop older.

353 M. ±1720 sandstone façade; unique cross between a cornice façade (see straight cornice) and neck-gable (see claw pieces).

355 M. ±1705 neck-gable with fronton; bay windows from 1899.

357 M. shop/home dating 1711; circular windows with ornamental frames; this neck-gable has always had a shop front, present one from 1907.

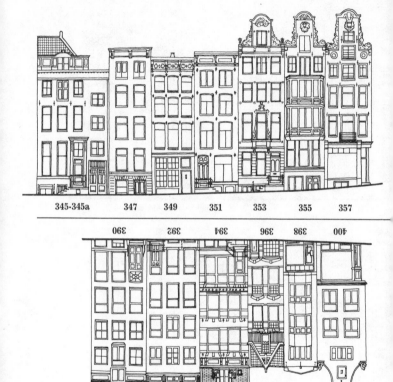

| 345-345a | 347 | 349 | 351 | 353 | 355 | 357 |

| 390 | 392 | 394 | 396 | 398 | 400 |

390 M. ±1800 rebuilt into cornice façade with transverse roof; frontal stoop; beautiful door.

392 M. 18thC house drastically rebuilt ±1800 when straight cornice fitted.

394 ±1895 façade; ornamented with natural stone (compare the brick front of no. 392); straight cornice, dormer and flat roof; stoop older.

396 house with wooden pointed gable (unusual for Amsterdam); from 1897; saddle roof barely visible; small stoop.

398 façade with outward bending relief with two bay windows and one balcony from 1924; door from same period.

400 M. ±1770 shop/home with bell-gable (most bell-gables built at this time); shop front early 20thC.

359-361-363 four houses stood here until November 1966 when they were demolished; the number of gaps on the canals is small and this one will be filled soon.

Huidenstraat

Runstraat

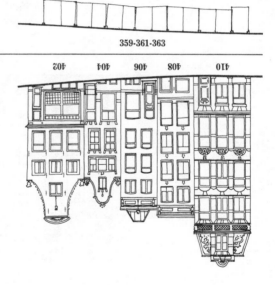

359-361-363

402 404 406 408 410

Keizersgracht 402-410

402 M. 1682 bell-gable with two corner vases and fronton with shell motif ornamentation; shop front early 20thC.

404 M. ±1770 bell-gable; white stone work above windows fitted 19thC.

406 M. façade drastically altered ±1880 with straight cornice and two consoles; arched windows.

408 façade drastically altered ±1875 with straight cornice (could be older) and two consoles; stoop gone; entrance moved to souterrain level.

410 ±1890 façade with brick dormer; straight cornice; flat-topped roof; ashlar street front; door at street-level.

365-367 M. ±1725 building; a curiosity is the portal of the Oude Zijds Herenlogement fitted here in 1874; once the portal, dating 1647, stood on the Oude Zijds Voorburgwal and was the entrance to an elegant hotel; part on left built-on in 19thC style.

365-367

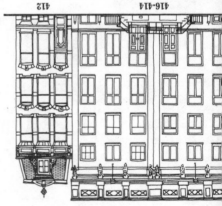

412   416-414

Keizersgracht 412-416

412 1881 façade; straight cornice and ornamented dormer; flat roof; stoop gone; entire districts were built with this kind of house.

414-416 M. twin cornice from ±1730; straight cornice with eight consoles and open *attiek*; two stoops almost make a double stoop; door of no. 414 varnished instead of usual canal-green paint; hardly altered.

369 five beautiful houses stood here until 1938; demolished in that year for this over-scaled building designed by architect J. van der Steur; building completed 1940.

369

Keizersgracht 418-430

418-424 example of 'modern' architecture built in historical style 1930 (see fanlight); architect A. Ingwersen tried to design a building that would fit the surroundings; straight cornice with brick dormer; double stoop.
426 M. ±1740 façade with elevated cornice and four consoles with sculptured heads; hardly altered; beautiful door.
428-430 M. late 19thC façade with straight cornice, four consoles and transverse roof; adapted advertisement in the shape of a wrought iron sign board.

379-381 twin neck-gables stood here until 1940; now fencework.
383 M. ±1700 neck-gable; little less than 4 meters wide (±13 feet).
385 M. late 17thC neck-gable with fronton and sculptured, shell motif.
387 M. 1668 handsome, elevated sandstone neck-gable (two large and two
small claw pieces) with fronton on the top and above some windows;
remarkably preserved; property of 'Hendrick de Keyser'; original motif.
389 M. late 18thC sandstone façade with straight cornice and two consoles.
391 M. brick façade (compare with nos. 387 and 389); straight cornice with
small windows ±1810; stoop older; handsome Empire entrance.

| 379-381 | 383 | 385 | 387 | 389 | 391 |

| 432 | 436-434 | 438 |

for this.
and too much glass; two houses were demolished
438 newly built 1897 with unusual façade for Amsterdam: too little brick
cornice fitted 19thC.
434-436 M. twin cornice façades; until 1897, triplets built ±1720; straight
top altered.
432 M. coach houses were rare on the canals; here an example from ±1720;

393-395 M. 1665 twin elevated neck-gables; frontons on top; original construction, though altered considerably.
395 rebuilt 19thC; house does not lean; handsome Louis XV door.
397 M. $\pm$1790 façade; 'cut-off' straight cornice; hipped roof.
399 M. 17thC neck-gable; rebuilt totally in 18thC while retaining 17thC top.
401 M. $\pm$1665 elevated sandstone neck-gable with pilasters; gable stone.
403 M. 1669 warehouse with spout-gable; lower structure altered 1949.

393-395   397   399   401   403

442   444   446   448   450

442 M. sandstone façade with straight cornice and 'closed' *attiek*, two ornamental vases and two hoist beams; two windows have decorative frames dating $\pm$1740.
444-446 M. $\pm$1720 sandstone façade with straight cornice and *attiek*; no. 444 adopted in style 1758; double stoop removed 1881.
448 M. 18thC façade; straight cornice and 'closed' *attiek* from late 18thC; straight cornice above ground floor, hardly altered.
450 M. $\pm$1685 neck-gable; fronton on top; door frame early 18thC; handsome pull-bell; hardly altered, possibly original construction.

405 M. warehouse; altered considerably; top with straight cornice from
±1800; lower structure 'beautification' from 1911 by J. Warners.
407 M. 1665 pilaster façade (see date stone); top altered into bell-like gable
early 19thC; small cornice on top.
409 M. ±1670 sandstone façade with straight cornice; front altered ±1790.
411 M. rare bell-like top from 1770; ornamental crest above hoist beam;
sandstone façade; hardly altered.
413 M. house built 1671 (see *pui* beam, roof and stoop); predominantly
19thC façade.
415 M. 1671 stuccoed neck-gable with fronton and festoon around hoist
beam; hardly altered; possibly original construction.

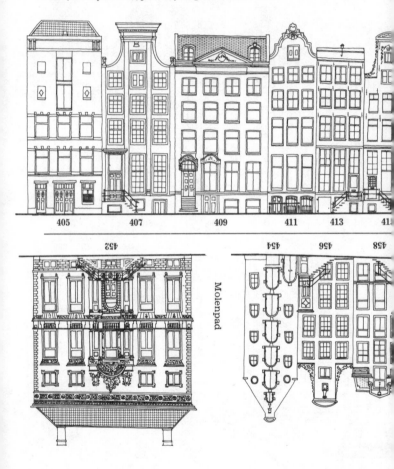

405   407   409   411   413   415

Molenpad

452 M. even in the 17thC this building was as wide as it is now, almost 18
meters; not much was left when it was rebuilt in 1860; façade richly
ornamented (see straight cornice); double stoop.
454 M. warehouses are unusual on the stately Keizersgracht; here a
specimen from ±1685 that came through three centuries almost unscathed;
most warehouses were built with a spout-gable like this one.
456 M. ±1680 neck-gable with fronton above hoist beam; once part of a
triplet with nos. 458 and 460; servants' entrance below stoop.
458 M. see no. 456; neck-gable altered into cornice façade ±1880.

417 newly built 1897 making use of old stoop; same size windows on 1st and 2nd floor; white blocks worked into façade; house does not lean as do nos. 419 and 415.
419 M. late 17thC corner house; altered considerably; 18thC façade with 19thC top in shape of a bell; fronton; stoop on corner of house; pothouse around to the side.

Leidsegracht

417   **419**

460   **462**

Leidsegracht

Keizersgracht 460-462

460 M. (see no. 456); neck-gable altered into cornice façade late 19thC; straight cornice with four consoles fitted then; old saddle roof replaced by this unusual flat-topped roof; house number fitted in same style; 2nd entrance below stoop.
462 M. once looked like no. 456; although it was earlier a bell-gable; pothouse from that period; old roof removed ±1880; dormer and flat roof fitted then; the 'Amsterdamse maatschappij tot Stadsherstel' has its office here.

(Leidsegracht 27) M. side façade of a sobered neck-gable from 1684; saddle roof well visible; pothouse with windows and window railings; hardly altered; original construction.

421 newly built 1911 with bay windows and balcony; old stoop preserved (with unusual, turning approach).

423 M. 19thC façade; house somewhat wider than 3 meters (± 10 feet).

425 M. 'neo-spout-gable' from 19thC; reminiscent of 17thC warehouse that stood here earlier; altered again 1916 together with no. 423.

427-429 M. recently completely rebuilt; twin cornice façades with hipped roof; houses dating from 17thC; façades are predominantly 19thC; handsome, wooden street front.

Leidsegracht

(27) 421 423-425 427-429

Leidsegracht

474 472 470 468 466 464

Keizersgracht 464-474

464 M. 1936 reconstruction of a shop/home, making use of materials from a demolished house from elsewhere; bell-gable with wooden street front.

466 M. early 19thC cornice façade; dormer with semi-circular top; entrance almost at street-level; three stoop posts.

468 M. 17thC house; wooden street front altered later; rebuilt considerably. **470** M. house built 1671; altered considerably; rebuilt ±1800; straight cornice with windows fitted then; house number above handsome doorway lintel; 2nd entrance below stoop.

472 M. ±1790 façade with straight cornice, two consoles and hipped roof; handsome fanlight; hardly altered.

474 the only genuine 'old' part is the straight cornice with four consoles ±1800.

431 somewhat elevated pointed gable from 1896; old stoop preserved.
433 M. predominantly 19thC cornice façade with transverse roof; stoop older.
435 M. wide façade from 1686; straight cornice and two hoist beams ±1790.
437 M. neck-gable from 1684; rebuilt 19thC; stoop missing.
439 newly built ±1895 with dormer and unusual roof.
441 M. 1684 neck-gable with festoons; stoop removed in 1925.

431   433   435   437   439   441

476   478   480   482   484   488-488

476 M. early 19thC façade with straight cornice and transverse roof; three stoop posts.
478 M. early 19thC façade with straight cornice; shop front from 1920.
480 19thC façade; top altered into step-like gable 1892; bay window fitted later; house does not lean (compare with no. 482).
482 M. predominantly 18thC façade with elevated cornice and two ornamental vases; elevation includes *attiek* loft-doors; stoop removed in 19thC.
484 M. late 17thC house; once a bell-gable; floor added and 'finished' with straight cornice; ornamented anchors on rebuilt part.
486-488 M. twin neck-gables from 1686 (see date stone) with corner vases, frontons and oval windows; no. 488 still has the festoon around the hoist beam; portal between houses with gable stone, 'Messina'.

443 M. late 17thC house with *pui* beam, stoop; altered considerably; straight cornice.

445 M. late 17thC house; once a neck-gable; altered considerably.

447 M. once a neck-gable (1672); predominantly 19thC façade with straight cornice; lower structure altered with bay window 1904.

449 M. handsome bell-gable from ±1760; top ornamented in Louis XV style (asymmetrical, see crest); shop front designed 1933 by G.Th Rietveld.

451 M. ±1740 building with straight cornice and four consoles; *attiek* since removed.

453 M. 1669 elevated neck-gable with fronton and festoon around hoist beam.

| 443 | 445 | 447 | 449 | 451 | 453 |

| 490 | 492 | 494-496 | 498 | 500 | 502 |

490 M. narrow house built 17thC 3.3 meters (10½ feet); oval windows from same period; altered considerably; neck-gable altered into cornice façade 19thC.

492 house had 17thC neck-gable until 1909; altered considerably; stoop gone; ornamented ashlar street front; window railings.

494-496 until 1909 two houses stood here; sandstone façade with straight cornice; entrance at street-level; window railings on 1st floor.

498 drastically altered 1901; a much too large window fitted on 2nd floor; cornice façade; ornamented anchors; old stoop preserved.

500 newly built 1892; dormer and flat roof.

502 newly built ±1910 with top like step-gable; shop front fitted 1917; entrance at street-level (compare with no. 504).

455 four houses were demolished in 1891 for this unusual building; small tower above cut-away corner; many statues; round 'pent-house'; makes use of much glass (designed by G.Th. Rietveld 1933).

Leidsestraat

455

506-504   508

Leidsestraat

Keizersgracht 504-508

504-506 M. twin neck-gables built 1671; earlier identical neck-gables stood on both sides of these twins; festoon around hoist beam and fronton on top; no. 504 altered least; old stoop preserved with 2nd entrance below; no. 506 has shop front dating 1896; sash work repaired recently; original construction.

508 M. corner house built 1881 (see underside of bay window); with small tower on cut corner; richly ornamented; street front altered later; bay window supported by sculptured lion-heads; recently classified as a monument.

(Leidsestraat 33) newly built 1910 with stoop; bay window at corner.
463 M. ±1795 brick façade with straight cornice and two consoles;
ornamentation above windows on ground floor dating from same period.
465 M. 1675 neck-gable with fronton, festoon and altered wooden street
front; hardly altered; restored in same year as no. 463 (1958).
467-469 M. little left of the original construction after so many rebuildings.

(33)   463   465   467-469

Leidsestraat

(35) 508a 512-510 514 516

Leidsestraat

shop front from 1913.
516 M. ±1795 façade with straight cornice and two consoles; hipped roof;
window; sash work from same period; house once had neck-gable.
514 M. predominantly 19thC façade with straight cornice and small
scaled shop front from 1904.
510-512 M. upper part of façade dating ±1800; cornice on right with consoles
supposed to be older; both houses have hipped roof; stuccoed 19thC; over-
3rd floors; shop front with Jugendstil elements including tiled tableaus
and ironwork on corner.
508a - (Leidsestraat 35) 19thC side façade; same size windows on 2nd and

471 M. 19thC cornice façade with gable stone; 1905 shop front.
473-479 four buildings demolished 1896 for this design by architect Poggenbeek; completed ±1900; over-scaling in width, fortunately not in height.
481 M. once a coach house with only one floor, built ±1670; wooden street front somewhat altered; façade renovated 20thC.
483 M. ±1680 warehouse with spout-gable; street front altered later.

| 471 | 473-479 | 481 | 483 |

consoles.
530 M. 18thC building; sobered 19thC with straight cornice and four
528 M. ±1770 bell-gable; once a neck-gable; top sobered.
526 bell-like gable from 1875; fronton above hoist beam.
ornate fanlight with lantern from same period.
524 M. 18thC building with cornice and four consoles; *attiek* sobered ±1800;
frame with Louis XVI ornamentation from ±1790.
522 M. late 18thC façade with elevated cornice around *attiek* shutters; door
520 M. predominantly 19thC façade with straight cornice; transverse roof.
façade with straight cornice, two hoist beams and hipped roof.
518 17thC house as identified by *put* beam and stoop; altered considerably;

Keizersgracht 518-530

532 M. early 18thC building; considerably altered; *attiek* removed as well as double stoop; middle window on ground floor once a door; one floor added.

534 adapted architecture from 1973; brick façade with ashlar street front; small terrace provides easier access to hoist beam.

536 M. 17thC bell-gable with fronton on top; two oval windows with sculptured frames (bull's-eyes); ornamented stoop and door from ±1750; hardly altered; original construction.

538-540-542 M. three houses with original straight cornice and transverse roof from 1671 which is unusual for a period when most houses had individual roofs; 17thC festoons have disappeared as well as date stone; middle house is 4.5 meters wide (14½ feet); hardly altered; original construction.

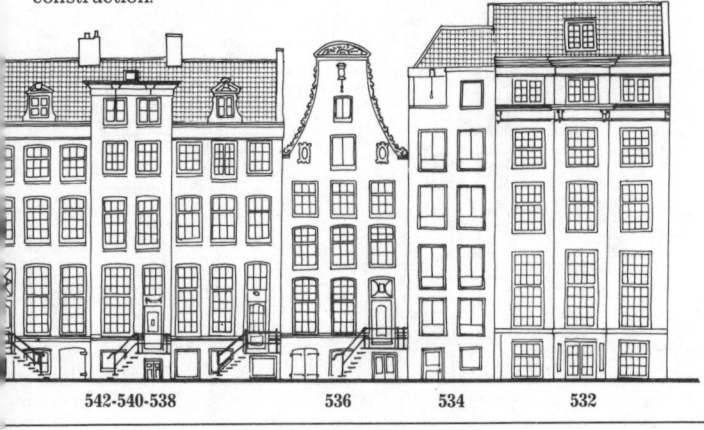

542-540-538   536   534   532

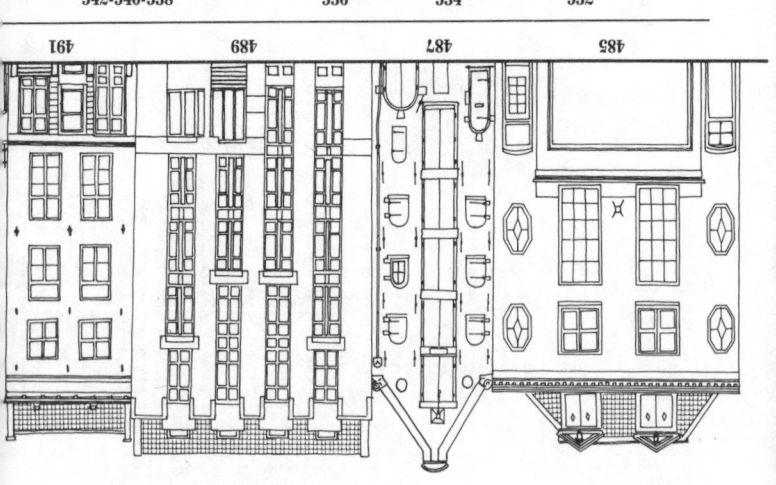

491   489   487   485

491 M. 19thC cornice façade with two hoist beams and transverse roof; once a warehouse.

489 once two warehouses stood here that were identical to no. 487; now a good example of adapted architecture from 1974.

487 M. of seven warehouses that once stood here, only this one remains; most 17thC warehouses had spout-gables; here the loft-doors indicate height of floors; hardly altered; original construction.

485 M. two warehouses once stood here; identical with no. 487; rebuilt into coach house 1838; straight cornice and two dormers with 'shutters'.

493 M. unusual double warehouse; extra large because it merged with house next door 1872; now warehouse with straight cornice; name of warehouse, 'Indie' on straight cornice above ground floor; ornamented anchors.

495-495a newly built in 1891; repeated alterations followed; dormer nearly changed into top-gable; façade ornamented with pilasters.

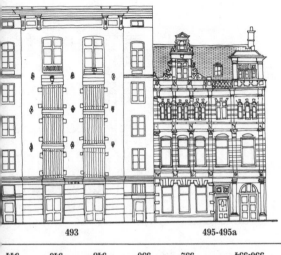

493   495-495a

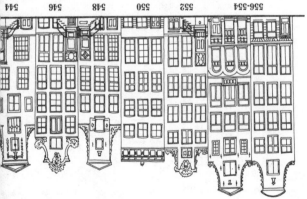

544 M. ± 1675 neck-gable with triangular fronton and festoon around hoist beam; sash work on 2nd floor still 17thC; below that, façade altered 18thC; little else changed since.

546 M. possibly the most beautiful bell-gable in Amsterdam, dating from ±1760; exuberantly ornamented on top; 3rd floor still has loft-doors.*

548 M. 18thC façade with 17thC top (claw pieces, triangular fronton); 18thC sash work fitted during restoration.

530 M. early 18thC façade with straight cornice and ashlar cellar front.

532 M. neck-gable, rebuilt 1908 by making use of (too) small, early 18thC top.

534-556 M. twin bell-gables from ±1695; altered somewhat since.

497 M. large complex, almost 19 meters wide from early 19thC ($\pm$ 61 feet); earlier combination warehouse, stables and home built $\pm$1670; straight cornice with small windows; two hoist beams; hipped roof.

501-503-505 M. earlier neck-gable triplets built $\pm$1680; no. 501 altered most, though it retained its stoop; stoops at nos. 503 and 505 gone; top altered into cornice façade; old roof barely visible above cornice; street front of no. 503 altered; entrance at street-level (compare no. 505's entrance at souterrain level).

497

501-503-505

560-558   562   564   566

from a design by the Salm brothers.

566 until 1888 a 17thC double house stood here; church built same year

altered saddle roof barely visible above cornice; not altered.

564 M. once twin with no. 562; altered into straight cornice early 19thC; un-
disappeared, leaving a straight cornice on top.

562 M. $\pm$1690 bell-gable with festoon around hoist beam; fronton

replaced just after 1800; stoop at no. 560 is missing.

558-560 M. two houses built $\pm$1690 underneath one roof; straight cornices

515 repeated rebuildings in this century have left nothing of what once
stood here; house looks older than it really is; double stoop and door fitted
in same style.
517 newly built 1909; designed by Van Gendt brothers; point-shaped gable;
ashlar Jugendstil-like ornament at top; iron hoist beam; entrance at street-
level.

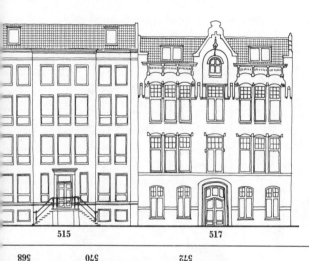

515   517

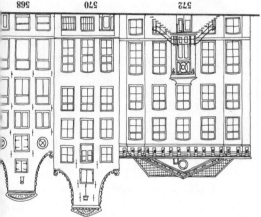

568   570   572

568 M. 1695 bell-gable with fronton and sculptured shell ornamentation;
circular windows shed light into *attiek*; stoop gone; entrance moved to
souterrain.
570 M. 1685 bell-gable with triangular fronton; hardly altered; only stoop
is missing.
572 M. double house from 1770 with straight cornice and fronton; two
17thC houses underneath one roof once stood here; parts of which were
used for the construction of this 5 window wide building; ornamented
door frame from that period; double stoop.

519 M. ±1725 neck-gable with fronton and sculptured shell ornamentation; beautiful, ornate fanlight; stoop bench; hardly altered.

521 M. ±1695 neck-gable with festoon around hoist beam; fronton disappeared over the years (compare with no. 519); street front altered ±1880.

523 drastically altered 1896 into straight cornice, four pairs of consoles, balustrade, dormer and flat roof; balcony also fitted then.

525 newly built 1896 with straight cornice, dormer and flat roof; brick façade ornamented with white stones; two doors.

527 1875 façade; straight cornice with two dormers; restored by 'Stadsherstel'.

529 M. ±1760 cornice façade with transverse roof; chimneys gone.

519   521   523   525   527   529

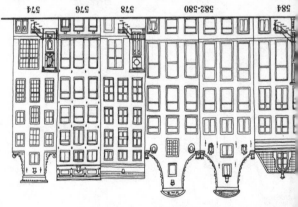

574   576   578   582-580   584

584 M. built 1687; semi-circular dormer and hipped roof from ±1800.

580-582 M. twin bell-gables from 1687 with frontons, corner vases and oval windows with sculptured frames; stoops since removed (compare with no. 584); original construction.

578 M. house built ±1690; earlier part of a triplet with nos. 574 and 576; lower structure hardly altered; top changed into cornice façade ±1800.

576 M. house built ±1690; 17thC elements almost entirely gone; once a triplet with nos. 574 and 578; predominantly 19thC façade because of straight cornice with four consoles.

574 M. ±1690 neck-gable; fronton replaced by small straight cornice ±1800; stoop bench; original construction.

531-533 two neck-gables stood here earlier (see nos. 535 and 537); building from 1926; asymmetrical window arrangement; two dormers and two hoist beams; two entrances; house does not lean (no.535 does).

535-537 M. dollhouse-like, twin neck-gables built ±1690; window grouping altered later (earlier one wide window and two narrow windows next to it); hardly altered; door frame of no. 535 from same period.

539-541-543 earlier three shop/homes stood here; neck-gables; part of wooden street front still remains; upper part of façade torn down 1949; 'Stadsherstel' intends to rebuild the three façades.

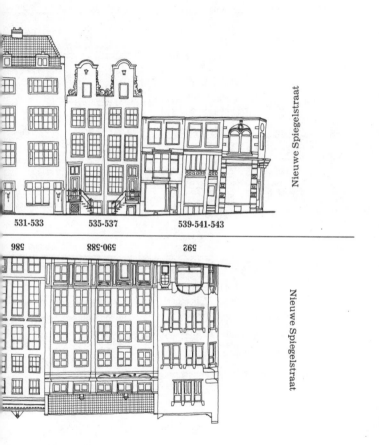

531-533   535-537   539-541-543

Nieuwe Spiegelstraat

586   590-588   592

Nieuwe Spiegelstraat

586 M. house built 1687; earlier belonged to a group of four bell-gables, nos. 584, 582 and 580; predominantly 19thC façade because of stucco and straight cornice (old roof barely visible above cornice); stoop gone.

588-590 M. part on left (3 windows wide) from ±1785; house has rare Louis XVI ornamentation (see straight cornice); *attiek* sobered later; ornamented ashlar street front. The part on the right was built in 1960 in the same style from a design by architect Bart van Kasteel.

592 until 1912 two small bell-gables stood here; in that same year this shop/home was built; mostly brick used; building height adapted to historical surroundings.

Keizersgracht 586-592

555 · (Nieuwe Spiegelstraat 17) six houses were demolished in 1917 for this over-scaled building in historical style from a design by J.B. Postumus Meyes; sash work in windows; fronton with ornamentation; 'monumental' chimneys.

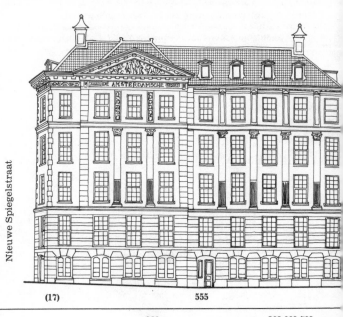

Nieuwe Spiegelstraat

(17)   555

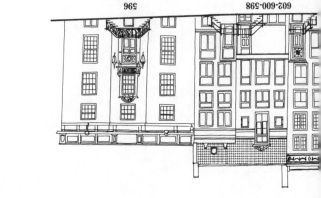

Nieuwe Spiegelstraat

596   602-600-598

Keizersgracht 596-602

596 M. palace-like, double house built ±1740 with cornice and 'closed' *attiek*; middle part in slight relief; handsome entrance with lanterns; double stoop with Empire ironwork from ±1800; hardly altered.

598-600-602 M. three houses built ±1670 underneath one straight cornice and one transverse roof; altered considerably; new, straight cornice with two hoist beams fitted early 19thC at no. 598; unattractive shop front at no. 600 dating 1902; floor added at no. 602 late 18thC and topped by straight cornice with Louis XV ornamentation; old stoops preserved; original construction.

557 M. 18thC building with straight cornice and transverse roof from early 19thC; since restored; sun awnings; over 3.5 meter wide ($\pm$11 feet).

559 M. $\pm$1680 neck-gable with fronton; this house never had a high stoop (compare with no. 561); ironwork repaired at restoration; sun awnings.

561 M. $\pm$1770 bell-gable; most bell-gables built during this time; sash work repaired at restoration.

563 M. $\pm$1680 bell-gable (see difference with 18thC bell-gable next door); fronton on top; hardly altered; sun awnings; 2nd entrance below stoop; original construction.

557   559   561   563

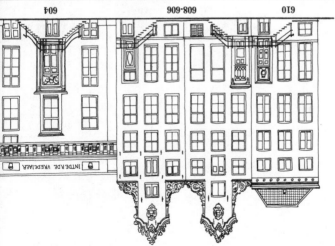

604   606-608   610

604 M. 1670 double house almost 15 meters wide (48 feet) built 1670; straight cornice with small windows and unusual brick *attiek* with proverb, 'Int derde vredejaar' (in the third year of peace).

606-608 M. built $\pm$1730; perhaps the most handsome twin neck-gables in Amsterdam, certainly the tallest; both hoist beams stick out through a cartouche; houses have coach house on the Kerkstraat (backside); the pinnacle of Amsterdam house architecture.*

610 M. until $\pm$1790 part of a triplet with nos. 608 and 606; now cornice façade with hipped roof.*

565-567 M. built ±1672; on right side once stood an identical complex; left, gate that led to old stable; above it, floors for storage of goods; somewhat altered 19thC; no. 567 4 window wide cornice façade from ±1679 (most old houses 2 or 3 windows wide); somewhat altered in 19thC (new straight cornice).

569-571 predominantly 1923 façade; reminiscent of Gothic style (see pointed-arch entrance); upper floor added later.

565-567   569-571

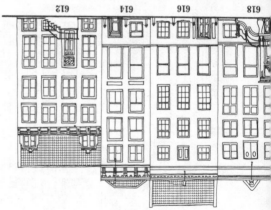

612   614   616   618

618 M. 18thC building; top sobered into straight cornice ±1800; handsome interior; ornamented stoop includes harp piece which hides the steps standing in front; pull bell.

616 M. ±1800 cornice façade with transverse roof, ashlar street front; stoop posts with chains.

614 M. early 19thC façade with straight cornice, hipped roof; window frames and entrance at street-level; stoop gone (compare with no. 618).

612 M. 4 window wide house from ±1675 (most houses 2 or 3 windows wide); 17thC cornice replaced by a somewhat larger specimen early 19thC; original construction.

Keizersgracht 612-618

573-575 ±1770 façade with straight cornice and tympan with garland drastically altered 1910; many original elements lost.

577 M. 1665 double house almost 15 meters wide (48 feet) with hipped roof; altered in 19thC when large fronton disappeared; straight cornice, dormer and door then fitted; handsome door frame.

573-575   577

620   622   624   630-628-626   632

Keizersgracht 620-632

620 M. ±1680 neck-gable with fronton; original construction.

622 M. neck-gable, altered 19thC making use of sandstone claw pieces and fronton from ±1680; old door missing.

624 M. early 19thC façade with straight cornice and two consoles; two hoist beams and hipped roof; house number fitted in same style.

626-628-630 built ±1680; once belonged to a group of five neck-gables together with nos. 624 and 622; these three still have oval windows with sculptured frames (bull's-eyes); no. 630 is best preserved; stoop gone.

632 M. 18thC building; once a neck-gable; altered considerably.

579-581 newly built 1919 designed by van Gendt brothers; asymmetrical window grouping; sort of cross-framed windows on 2nd floor; use of plate glass.

583-585 M. houses built under one transverse roof with straight cornices and door frames from ±1700; doors on left are original and once led to stable; early 19thC window railings on 1st floor; little else changed.

579-581   583-585

646-634

and is just visible above straight cornice.
changed into cornice façades early 19thC; old roof remained unchanged
at street-level; lowest part of façade altered with ashlar; nos. 644 and 646
converted into windows (entrances moved to souterrain); no. 634 entrance
no. 640 preserved its stoop; the remaining six had their entrances
634-646 earlier, seven almost identical neck-gables dating from ±1700; only

Keizersgracht 634-646

587-589 M. eight houses were demolished in 1916 for the widening of the Vijzelstraat and this newly built design by K.P.C. de Bazel built 1917-23; classified as a monument in 1973.

Keizersgracht 648-650

648 earlier a row of eight identical neck-gables with its neighbours on the right, this one altered most; elevated cornice with *attiek* from 19thC; old roof just visible above cornice; street front altered 19thC; stoop gone; three stoop posts.

650 until 1917 five houses stood here; two were demolished in 1917 for the widening of the Vijzelstraat and three for a new roofed row of shops with flats above in 1927-28 which were torn down again in 1962; this most disputed bank building in Holland is a design by Prof. Duintjer. In spite of all the protests against the over-scaled size, it was opened in November, 1973; the building runs back crossing over Kerkstraat until Prinsengracht.

660 1927 corner house with round bay windows at the corner; Amsterdam School features (outward bending relief in façade, ornamentation in brick).

662 M. predominantly 19thC façade with straight cornice, dormer and transverse roof.

664 M. building with elevated cornice and consoles with Louis XV ornamentation; transverse roof and *attiek* shutter in elevated cornice from ±1755; late 18thC sash work (small panes); handsome Louis XV door from original building; house leans (compare with no. 666); little else changed.

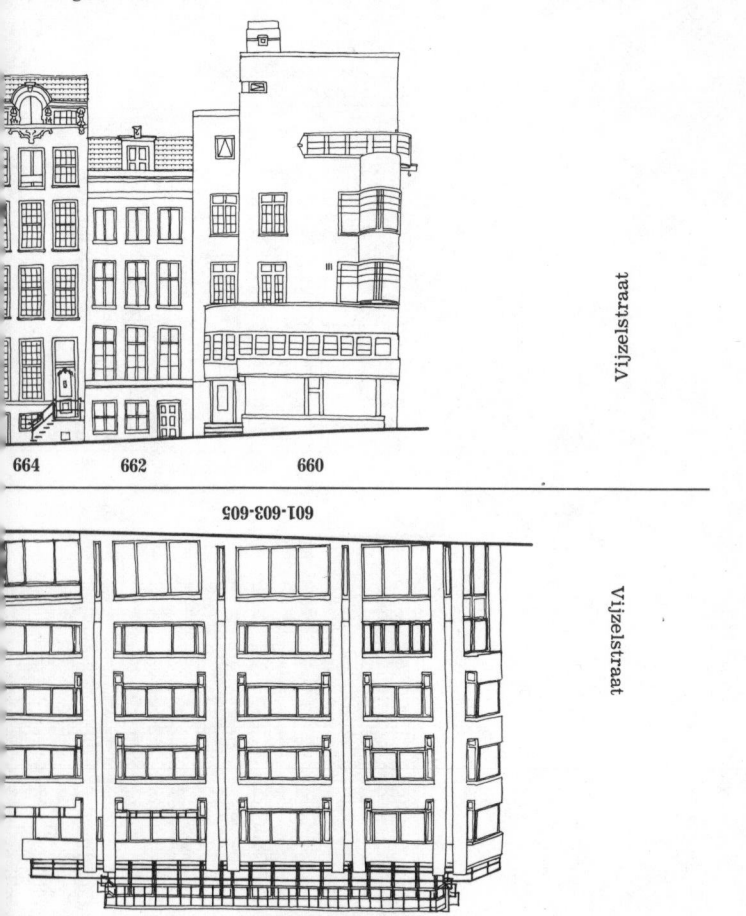

664   662   660

Vijzelstraat

601-603-605

Vijzelstraat

601-603-605 on this spot, where once three houses stood, Hollenkamp built something new in 1903; it was demolished in 1971; the present bank building from 1976 is, concerning its exterior, much better adapted to its surroundings than its predecessor (much better brick used this time). The vertical relief breaks up the façade into elements the size of individual houses.

607 M. nearly 15 meters (48 feet) wide coach house built 1672 and belonging with Herengracht 502; top floors used once for storage; three dormers and three hoist beams; remarkably preserved; original construction.
609 M. before 1861 a coach house; converted that year into a museum by order of the deceased owner, C.J. Fodor; sandstone façade with straight cornice from a design by architect C. Outshoorn.

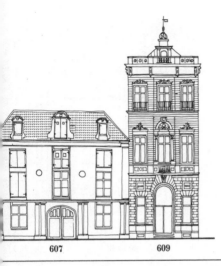

607　　　　　　609

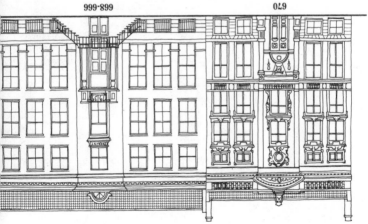

999-899　　　　　　　　　670

Keizersgracht 666-670

666-668 newly built in historical style 1939 (see ironwork on balcony) by architects C.B. Posthumus Meyes and Van der Linden; building looks much older than it really is; brick façade with straight cornice and sandstone door frame; double stoop. This building is open to criticism but it still does harmonize with its historical surroundings. Until 1937 two buildings stood here.
670 M. ±1675 house, nearly 15 meters wide; drastically altered 19thC when balustrades and window frames were fitted and double stoop removed resulting in double door 'sinking' to street-level.

672-674 M. two double houses or palaces built 1671; sandstone façades with straight cornices and 'open' *attiek* with four statues on top; houses designed by well known 17thC architect A. Dortman; one of the first houses with a balcony; no. 672 recently became a museum; interior worth seeing; garden with splendid garden house from original building period; also stables on Kerkstraat; double stoop from 18thC; original construction.*

674-672

611·613 M. twin neck-gables built 1716; both stoops preserved with 2nd entrances underneath; hardly altered.
615 M. ±1720 neck-gable; exeptionally fine claw pieces with statues, mounted on sculptured dolphins; hoist beam in ornate frame; door frame and door Empire from ±1800.

617-629 seven houses were demolished here in 1912 and replaced the same year by this over-scaled building; design by P.J.S. Pieters and built in historical style with straight cornice, four pilasters; center part of façade in relief; 'monumental' entrance; frontal stoop with sculptured elephants on both sides.

617-629

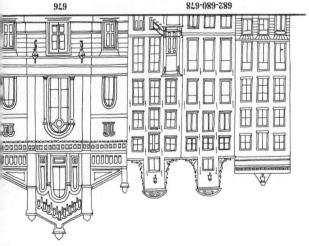

676   678-680-682

Keizersgracht 676-682

676 earlier a late 17thC double house; now a church built 1856 from design by architect A.N. Godefroy; sandstone façade.
678-680-682 M. once, together with nos. 684 and 686, a row of identical neck-gables built in ∓1690; original construction; no. 678 with fronton is best preserved; middle windows on 2nd and 3rd floor once had loft-doors; no. 682 converted into cornice façade 19thC.

631 M. late 19thC cornice façade with hipped roof; ashlar lower structure and ornamented anchors; entrance 'sunk' almost to street-level.

633 M. earlier a coach house with two floors for storage; converted into homes 19thC; predominantly 19thC façade (because of straight cornice and ornamented anchors); roof unchanged.

635 M. nearly 15 meters wide (48 feet) building; once a garage for coaches; rebuilt twice in 20thC; lower structure is good example of over-scaling in width; handsome roof gone.

637 M. late 17thC house; once had portal leading to stable; lower part of façade altered ±1870; house leans (compare with no. 635).

631   633   635   637

684-686   690-688   692

692 see text no. 694 and 696.

688-690 M. house built just before 1700; earlier twin neck-gables; original construction; both houses rebuilt at same time into cornice façades, ±1795, with semi-circular dormers and hipped roofs; since, little else changed.

684-686 M. built in ±1690; once formed a row of identical neck-gables with nos. 678, 680 and 682; out of the five, no. 684 damaged most; façade repeatedly altered; street front changed in 20thC; stoop gone; entrances at street-level; saddle roof converted into ugly transverse roof; no. 686 'modernized', with straight cornice with 10 consoles 19thC.

639 coach house converted into homes 1883; old roof preserved; façade ornamented in historical style.

641 M. ±1860 stuccoed building with straight cornice, two consoles and a slanted, 'closed' *attiek;* (in 19thC stoops no were longer built).

643 M. building from ±1740; now cornice façade; stoop gone.

645 M. ±1700 house that once had a neck-gable; façade drastically altered 19thC when straight cornice and hipped roof were fitted.

647 M. ±1685 neck-gable with fronton and ornamental vases crowning the claw pieces; stoop gone; entrance moved to street-level.

649 M. ±1690 neck-gable with corner vases and oval windows.

639   641   643   645   647   649

694-696 forms single complex with no. 692; built in ±1685; original construction; neck-gable of no. 692 sobered into bell-like gable with triangular fronton 19thC; no. 694 only 3.5 meters wide (±11 feet); façade altered 19thC; straight cornice and dormer; no. 696 best preserved; neck-gable still has original claw pieces; fronton on top.

698 M. house built ±1690; original construction; stoop gone; ashlar street front fitted 19thC; altered considerably.

700 M. earlier a neck-gable (see nos. 702 and 704); now 19thC cornice façade.

702-704 M. ±1700 twin neck-gables with handsome claw pieces and fronton.

651 M. small coach-house narrower than 3.4 meters (±11 feet) built ±1686; the present façade is early 19thC and has a straight cornice.

653 M. early 17thC house, once had a bell-gable; top converted into straight cornice with two consoles 19thC.

655 M. predominantly 19thC façade (because of straight cornice and window grouping); street front altered 1907.

657 newly built in 1903 with spout-like top and two bay windows; fine Jugendstil tilework around windows above door.

659 M. late 17thC house; rebuilt ±1770; consoles from that period (Louis XV ornamentation); door not painted usual canal-green; sun awnings over ground floor.

661 - (Reguliersgracht 38) M. two houses with straight cornice underneath one transverse roof; festoons on front from construction date ±1690.

651   653   655   657   659   661   (38)

706   708   710   714-712

Keizersgracht 706-714

706 M. 5 window wide, double house (15 meters/48 feet); altered considerably 18thC; straight cornice fitted ±1795.

708 M. ±1670 bell-gable with cluster ornaments on sides; fronton with sculptured bird fitted later; once a warehouse (see top); larger part of façade altered 19thC.

710 M. ±1670 warehouse with spout-gable (warehouses were seldom built on this stately canal); lowest part altered.

712-714 M. two houses built ±1670; earlier twin bell-gables, now twin cornice façades; cornices fitted early 19thC.

(Reguliersgracht 39) M. side façade of one of the most photographed bell-gables in Amsterdam; shop/home built ±1690; saddle roof fully visible; altered somewhat, especially in 18thC; pothouse; original construction.
663 M. early 18thC house, a bit over 3 meters wide (±9 feet); with arched cornice; stoop gone; iron railing at street-level.
665 façade drastically altered in 1891 with straight cornice and four consoles; saddle roof just visible above cornice; 19thC door frame; late 17thC stoop preserved.

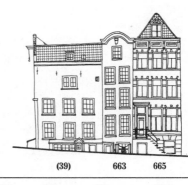

Reguliersgracht

(39)   663   665

716   718   720   722

Reguliersgracht

Keizersgracht 716-722

716 M. dollhouse-like shop/home built 1671; one of the first bell-gables in Amsterdam; wooden street front preserved in altered form; pothouse on side façade; 17thC building height (compare with no. 720).
718 M. predominantly 18thC building with early 19thC straight cornice, semi-circular dormer and hipped roof; stoop bench.
720 M. house built 1672; altered considerably; façade predominantly 18thC with straight cornice and topped with hipped roof dating ±1795.
722 M. 18thC building; floor added and topped with straight cornice with eight consoles 19thC; windows become smaller towards top as in most houses.

667 M. 18thC façade with straight cornice; mansarde roof just before 1900.
669 built 1890 with straight cornice, consoles and ornamented dormer.
671 M. ±1780 façade (17thC building height) the days of richly ornamented
bell-gables have by this time passed; door frame from same period.
673 M. late 17thC house as identified by building height and stoop;
drastically altered 19thC.
675 M. late 17thC house as identified by building height, saddle roof, and
stoop; converted into cornice façade.
677 M. late 17thC house as identified by building height, saddle roof and
stoop; converted into cornice façade.
679 M. late 18thC house; cornice façade with *attiek* in shape of balustrade.
681 M. earlier a bell-gable; 'modernized' into
cornice façade 19thC.

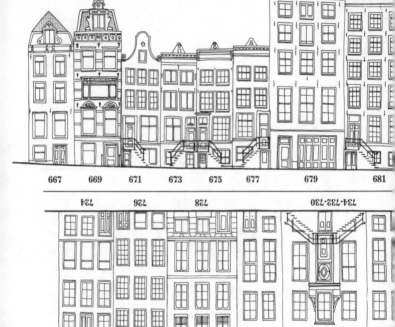

667   669   671   673   675   677   679   681

724 M. predominantly 18thC façade with straight cornice; transverse roof
from ±1790; upper two floors still have loft-doors; stoop missing.
726 M. early 19thC façade with circular windows in straight cornice;
transverse roof; entrance moved to souterrain; early 19thC sash work.
728 M. 17thC house; altered considerably; 19thC cornice façade; street
front early 20thC; round corners in tops of windows.
730-732-734 three houses behind one sandstone façade with straight cornice
from 1671; design by A. Dortsman, one of the best known 17thC architects
who also designed nos. 672 and 674; *attiek* with statues disappeared over
the years; stoops gone at nos. 730 and 734; at no. 732, double stoop and
handsome fanlight.

724   726   728   734-732-730

683 M. this building once had a bell-gable; top altered early 19thC; a new 'old' cornice fitted recently.

685-689 newly built 1971 in historical style with elevated straight cornice; until recently three houses stood here.

691-693 M. two late 17thC cornice façades with unusual brick *attieken*; transverse roof; at no. 691 stoop removed ±1830; remaining street front with two entrances dating from that period; at no. 693 lower structure also altered; stoop disappeared in 1912 and entrance was moved to street-level; original construction.

683   685-689   691-693

736   738   740   742   744   746   748

transverse roof.

748 M. predominantly 19thC façade with straight cornice, dormer and transverse roof.

746 M. 18thC building; sobered with straight cornice early 19thC; flat-topped roof.

744 M. late 19thC cornice façade with straight cornice, four consoles and reconstruction of street front, ±1890.

742 M. 19thC cornice façade with transverse roof; street front altered.

740 M. early 19thC cornice façade; entrance moved to street-level; during reconstruction of street front, ±1890.

738 M. 19thC cornice façade; windows become smaller towards top.

736 M. predominantly 19thC façade because of straight cornice, consoles, stucco and widow frames; two hoist beams.

695 M. ±1690 neck-gable; handsome claw pieces with sculptured figures; hoist beam sticks out through cartouche; stoop gone.

697 M. predominantly 19thC façade with straight cornice and hipped roof that was altared later; twin with no. 699 before reconstruction.

699 M. ±1690 neck-gable with fronton, shell motif, two ornamental vases.

701 late 19thC façade with straight cornice, four consoles, dormer and *attiek*.

703 M. early 19thC cornice façade, restored by 'Stadsherstel' (see plaque).

705 ±1890 façade with straight cornice; stoop older.

695   697   699   701   703   705

754-752-750   756   758   760   762

762 M. twin with no. 764 (see next page).

760 M. predominantly 19thC façade with straight cornice, and transverse roof; stoop gone; narrow house, just over 3 meters wide (±9 feet).

758 newly built 1912 with elevated cornice (for hoist beam); entrance at street-level (compare no. 756); door rounded at top.

756 M. 18thC building with straight cornice and *attiek* in shape of a balustrade with ornamental vases; ornamented stoop with fine door frame from ±1740.

754-752-750 M. once neck-gable triplets; houses built ±1680; original construction; no. 754 converted into cornice façade ±1800.

Keizersgracht 764-764a

764 M. twin no. 762; both late 17thC houses which were altered considerably; new straight cornice fitted 19thC; floor added same time; door frame still 17thC; at no. 762, a bay window with balcony was fitted in 1904; no. 762 has a small pothouse.

764a - (Utrechtsestraat 48) newly built 1927 has always been a shop/home; brick façade (which was most usual for the 1920's); house does not lean as no. 764.

Utrechtsestraat

(48)   764a-764

709

Utrechtsestraat

709 two shop/homes stood here until 1904 when this building was constructed; stuccoed façade with green and yellow bricks; cut-corner with bay windows; unusual tower on corner, possibly Jugendstil; circular window underneath hoist beam.

711 M. 17thC house as identified by building height; façade from 1887; straight cornice; shop front fitted 1912 when pothouse disappeared.
713-715 newly built 1905 making use of old stoop; design by architect C.B.P. Posthumus Meyes; house looks older due to application of step-gable and relieving arches above windows.

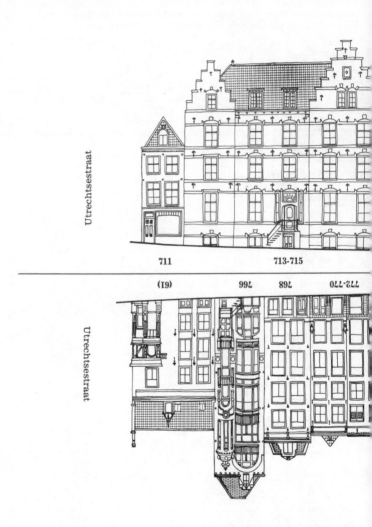

Utrechtsestraat

711   713-715

(61)   766   768   772-770

Utrechtsestraat

(Utrechtsestraat 61) M. has always been a bakery shop and home; side façade sobered 19thC (pothouse removed); part of wooden street front on Keizersgracht from 1887.
766 1894 façade with ornaments; unusual for Amsterdam.
768 M. ±1880 façade; straight cornice with three consoles, dormer and flat-topped roof (saddle roofs were no longer built at that time); ornamented anchors.
770-772 M. predominantly 19thC façades with straight cornices from period when stoops were no longer built (±1880).

717 M. building from 1696; 'modernized' with new straight cornice 19thC; door frame with house number early 19thC.

719 'modern' reconstruction from 1910; altered again later.

721 M. late 17thC house; neck-gable replaced by a top with a (too) large, semi-circular *attiek* window in 1875; street front also altered somewhat in that period; two doors from 19thC.

723-725-727 M. until 19thC neck-gable triplets from 1697; nos. 725 and 727 are best preserved; tops retained their fronton with shell ornaments; old stoops gone; entrance moved to street-level (compare with no. 721); no. 723 floor added and finished with straight cornice early 19thC.

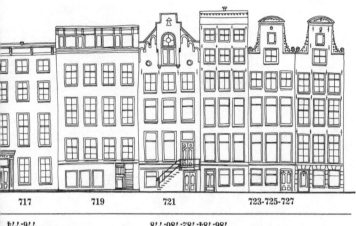

717   719   721   723-725-727

774-776   778-780-782-784-786

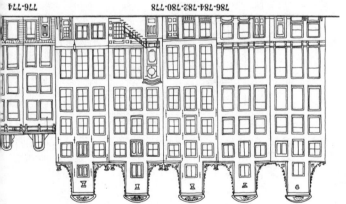

774-776 M. until 19thC twin neck-gables stood here; still twins, but now straight cornice façades with semi-circular dormers; 17thC building height retained by reconstruction.

778-780-784-786 M. group of five neck-gables from 1688; frontons with shell ornaments and sculptured claw pieces; nos. 784 and 786 lost their ornamental vases; only no. 780 preserved its high stoop and door at ground floor level; handsome doorway lintel; original construction.

729-731-733 M. now cornice façade triplets, earlier neck-gable triplets; houses built 1708; all three neck-gables 'cut-off' early 19thC and replaced by straight cornices; old roof just visible above cornices; old stoops gone; no. 733 has wrought iron railing.

735 M. late 19thC façade; straight cornice with mini-window and semi-circular dormer; ornamented anchors; entrance at street-level; house number above doorway lintel.

737-739-741 M. neck-gable triplets built ±1700; at no. 741 fronton gone; no. 741 old stoop preserved (compare nos. 737 and 739); no. 739 has handsome fronton with coat of arms; original construction.

729-731-733   735   737-739-741

790-788   792   794   796   798   00

788-790 M. twin neck-gables built ±1690; oval windows with sculptured frames; no. 788 altered least; stoop gone at no. 790; street front renovated.

792 M. predominantly 19thC façade; stuccoed; hipped roof; window frames; original construction.

794 M. 17thC house; festoon around hoist beam; ornamental vases; mortared-over oval windows with sculptured frames from late 17thC; 1st and 2nd floor window railings.

796 M. 17thC house with 18thC elements but 19thC straight cornice.

798 M. 19thC façade with straight cornice and window frames.

800 M. stuccoed façade dating ±1800; cornice façade; handsome window frames with sculptured heads of girls.

743 M. double house built 1670; original construction; house nearly 15 meters wide (48 feet); altered ±1800; double stoop; two pull-bells.

745 M. earlier a coach- and warehouse; wooden street front from building period ±1770; façade altered 19thC.

747 M. predominantly 19thC façade with straight cornice, two consoles and hoist beam at same height as no. 745.

749 M. neck-gable built 1697; top still late 17thC; window grouping altered later; stoop gone; entrance moved to souterrain.

751 until 1910 a neck-gable identical to nos. 749 and 751; stuccoed.

753 M. neck-gable built 1697; top two floors still have late 17thC window-grouping; stoop gone; original construction.

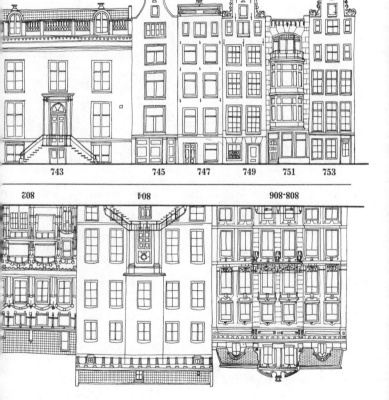

743   745   747   749   751   753

802   804   808-806

Keizersgracht 802-808

802 richly ornamented, late 19thC brick façade (compare flat brick façade of no. 804); designed by Van Gendt brothers 1895; later altered repeatedly.

804 M. double house built 1761 with straight cornice and transverse roof; altered ±1800; sandstone door frame with Ionic pilasters; double stoop with wrought iron railing from ±1800.

806-808 M. ±1720 façade, nearly 15 meters wide (48 feet); altered drastically in 19thC when straight cornice, dormers, balconies and window frames were fitted; double stoop removed in 19thC.

755 M. one of the few preserved 'garages' for coaches and carriages; built ±1700; drastically altered in 1906 when semi-circular doors on 1st and 2nd floor were removed and straight cornice was fitted; stuccoed.

757 M. double house built ±1670; this nearly 15 meters wide (48 feet) house was drastically altered late 18thC when straight cornice with fronton and street front were fitted.

759-761-763 M. neck-gable triplets built 1704; hardly altered; top of middle house rebuilt with restoration; stoops with 2nd entrance below retained; original construction.

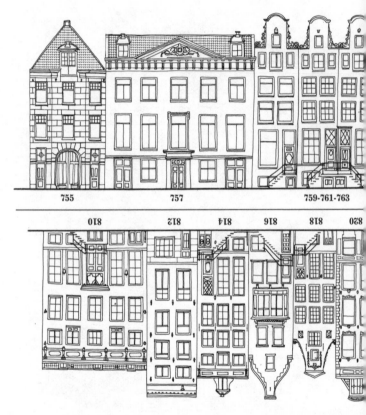

755   757   759·761·763

810   812   814   816   818   820

810 M. ±1750 5 window wide façade with straight cornice and consoles; *attiek* disappeared over the years; house once had double stoop; sandstone door frame from building period.

812 M. 19thC stuccoed façade with window frames and straight cornice; house does not lean (compare with no. 814).

814 M. late 17thC house, once had a neck-gable; top of neck-gable was 'cut-off' in 1891 and replaced with straight cornice; handsome cushion-door; pull bell.

816 older house converted in 1912 into ogee-like gable (with S-curve profile).

818 M. 1672 bell-gable with festoon around hoist beam; oval windows with sculptured frames (bull's-eyes); triangular fronton.

820 M. straight cornice from ±1885; façade with ornamentation on corners; window frames.

765 M. this house, transversely constructed on the canal, was built ±1670; once a coach house that belonged to the corner house; straight cornice fitted in 19thC when entrance to coach house was removed; door with sculptured heads of girls; original construction.

767 M. reconstructed in same way as no. 826 (opposite); 11 meter side façade (±35 feet); same size windows on all floors; door nearly at street-level.

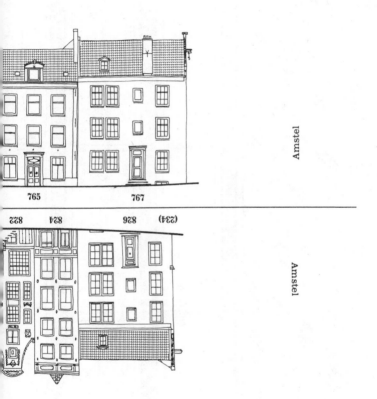

Keizersgracht 822-826

822 M. bell-gable from 1672 (see date stone); fronton on top; oval windows with sculptured frames; flower ornaments along top; door in two parts; stoop bench remarkably preserved; original construction.

824 M. 1869 cornice façade with ashlar street front; ornamented anchors and arched windows.

826 - (Amstel 234) M. not too well reconstructed in 1938; same size windows on all floors; door nearly at street-level.

Prinsengracht

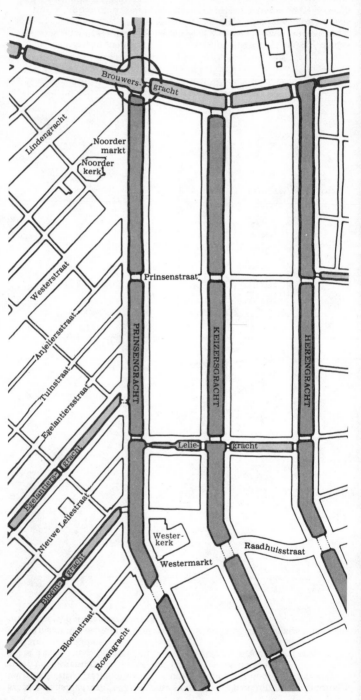

1 · (Brouwersgracht 101) M. side façade; together with Brouwersgracht 97 and 99 this corner was restored to its original state in 1972 by 'Stadsherstel'; building height and pothouse remained 17thC.

1a M. 17thC house somewhat rebuilt; wooden street front remains in altered form; top sobered into spout-like gable in 19thC; earlier a neck-gable; property of 'Stadsherstel'.

3 M. middle 19thC façade; dormer with framing and hoist beam; straight cornice with two ornamented consoles; property of 'Stadsherstel'.

5 M. 18thC building; sobered into bell-like gable in 19thC (no ornaments at top); 'Stadsherstel' would like to restore it.

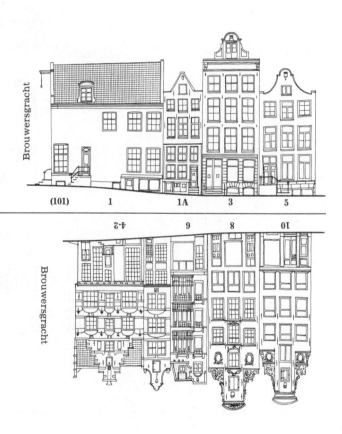

Prinsengracht 2-10

2-4 M. beautiful shop/home dating 1641; wooden street front; *pui* beam, step-gables on front and side façade; step-gables rebuilt during 1955 restoration; no. 4 once had a step-gable which was replaced in 1755 with a bell-gable; property of 'Hendrick de Keyser'.*

6 asymmetrical façade with balconies and shop front dating ±1910.

8 M. ±1660 neck-gable with segment-shaped fronton; festoon and two oval windows with sculptured frames; gable stone; 'Stadsherstel'.

10 M. ±1660 elevated neck-gable with fronton and two oval windows; window grouping altered 19thC; wooden street front from same period.

7 M. ±1750 bell-gable, door frame with postal horn emblem; top sobered in 19thC when ornaments disappeared; pull-bell by door.

9 M. 19thC façade with straight cornice, ornamented dormer and saddle roof; two doors and frontal stoop; gable stone 'nooit weer' (never again) fitted in 1976.

11 M. 18thC building; finished and elevated with straight cornice in 19thC; door frame 18thC; frontal stoop; gable stone fitted 1973.

13-15 M. once two houses; beginning 19thC joined together by means of one straight cornice with consoles; no. 13 has hipped roof and hoist beam.

7   9   11   13-15

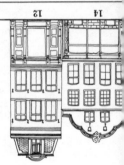

14   12

Prinsengracht 12-16

12 simple cornice façade with ornamented dormer and almost flat roof; same size windows on 1st and 2nd floors (compare no. 14); ±1870 shop front; ornamented anchors.

14-16 M. ±1760 unique cornice with two *attiek* shutters; ornament at top of cornice; two hoist beams, unusual 4 window wide façade (most houses are two to three windows wide); 19thC shop front.

17-19 M. early 18thC houses; earlier a twin neck-gable, now a twin cornice
façade from ±1800; street windows slightly arched; street front of no. 17
stuccoed; at no. 19 the large traditional door was replaced by a porch and
two doors; no. 17 has a stoop-bench.
21 M. façade predominantly 19thC by its straight cornice, dormer with
fronton; ornamented anchors; saddle roof replaced by flat-topped roof.
23 M. ±1790 façade with straight cornice, consoles and Louis XVI
ornamentation; hipped roof; varnished door; frontal stoop.
25 M. neck-gable with unusual ornamentation at top; claw pieces with
checkered motif from ±1740; property of 'Stadsherstel'.
27 M. ±1740 neck-gable with richly ornamented claw pieces.

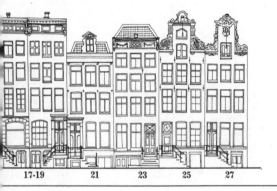

17-19   21   23   25   27

Noordermarkt

29 early 19thC building, stoop older; windows on 1st floor altered; old roof and upper floor altered at end of 19thC; semi-circular fanlight; handsome door; straight cornice.

31-33-35 rebuilt from older houses in 1938; same size windows on all floors (in old houses, windows become smaller towards top); doors at street-level, therefore no stoop; when rebuilding no. 35 the sandstone ornamentation from a neck-gable was used; gable stone with 'fisherman' fitted in peculiar place after rebuilding.

37 M. predominantly middle 19thC façade with straight cornice, dormer and almost flat roof; portraitures of a man's and woman's head in door frame; stoop from later period.

39 M. 18thC building; tall door frame from ±1860; top altered into cornice façade same time; three fine bottle-shaped balusters and stoop bench.

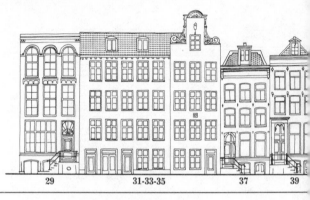

29	**31-33-35**	**37**	**39**

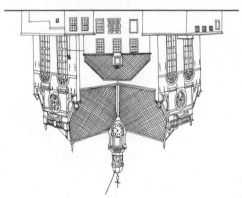

Prinsengracht-Noorderkerk

Noorderkerk built 1622 (see date on so called celebration tower); design by either Hendrick Staets, the architect of the 1612 large city expansion plan or by Hendrick de Keyser, the architect of the Zuiderkerk and Westerkerk. The most notable feature of this church is its floor plan; it was built in the shape of a Greek cross (four equal arms); four façades with pinnacles, balustrades and a circular window.

41 M. early 19thC cornice façade; sash work of windows on 1st floor altered; street front has wooden and five fanlights.

43 ±1890 façade with straght cornice, four consoles, dormer and flat-topped roof.

51 M. 18thC building; floor and straight cornice added 19thC.

53 early 18thC warehouse with spout-gable; roof somewhat altered; little else changed.

55 example of adapted architecture; design by Baanders in 1930.

41　　　　**43**　　　　　**51**　　　　**53**　　　　　　**55**

Noordermarkt

71 M. early 19thC façade with straight cornice and two consoles; façade interrupted by cornice over 1st floor.

73 M. 18thC; somewhat rebuilt; top drastically altered into cornice façade with brick dormer ±1860; large door removed.

75 façade with simple, straight cornice, dormer and flat roof; same size windows on all floors dating from ±1880; frontal stoop.

77 M. ±1735 neck-gable; center window below dormer once had loft-doors; stoop bench; little alteration.

79 M. ±1760 bell-gable with Louis XV ornamentation (see crest).

81 M. 17thC (e.g. wooden street front); bell-gable predominantly 18thC; stoop with turning approach.

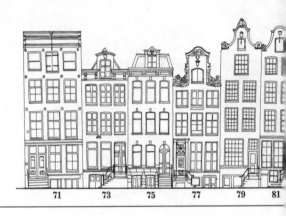

| 71 | 73 | 75 | 77 | 79 | 81 |

Noordermarkt

83 M. 18thC building; top altered into cornice façade 19thC; stucco removed from brick during restoration; fan railing next to souterrain entrance.
89-113 M. 'Starhofje' dating from 1804 (see below clock); middle building shows its backside here; sandstone door frame and double stoop. The buildings house a Roman Catholic Chapel and a trustee-chamber founded by A.J. van Brienen.

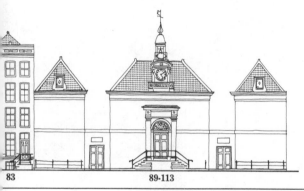

83   89-113

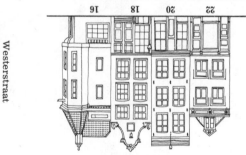

Westerstraat

16   18   20   22

Prinsengracht 16-22

16 side façade of shop/home with brick wing added on corner in 1926; chimney visible from many sides.
18 M. ±1760 bell-gable with wooden street front; most bell-gables built in this period; windows become smaller towards top as in most old houses; frontal stoop; three doors.
20 M. predominantly 19thC façade with straight cornice which was probably raised a bit in the 19thC when new windows were installed; hoist beam with iron extension hook fitted to move goods.
22 ±1870 shop/home with straight cornice, dormer; and shop front; building height from early 17thC.

135 M. bell-gable dating 1772 (see date below top ornament on right); *pui* beam; lantern on front; a 3rd door underneath stoop; Jacob's staff at top.
145 M. 18thC building with wooden street front and two stoops; handsome bottle-shaped balusters; façade above street-level predominantly ±1860; formerly a different top but now a cornice façade.
151 19thC façade with straight cornice; later drastically altered; e.g. door sunken to street-level; unusual sash work.
153 stucco façade predominantly from ±1860 with spout-like top; wooden street front; everything painted white.

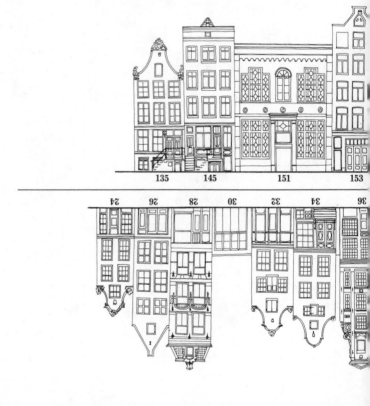

135   145   151   153

24   26   28   30   32   34   36

24 M. 17thC house (see building height); façade with Louis XV ornamentation on top dating from ±1765; bell-gable; wooden street front.
26 newly built 1969 in historical style; similar to spout-gable.
28 built ±1855 with straight cornice and dormer.
30 another gap in the wall of façades. Prinsengracht seems to have the most gaps.
32 M. 17thC house as identified by height and wooden street front; bell-gable dates from ±1760.
34 M. late 18thC bell-gable with simple top (compare with no. 32).
36 M. handsome, elevated neck-gable with pilasters, fronton, festoon, two oval windows and date stone 1650, gable stone, 'De Veersack' (the featherbag).*

155 M. ±1740 warehouse with spout-gable; little changed.
157 M. predominantly early 19thC façade with straight cornice and loft-doors within; two stoops (unusual); two doors.
159-171 Zon's hofje (Sun's courtyard) built 1765; open to the public and the interior is worth seeing.
173 1893 façade (see window 1st floor); small stone blocks.
175 M. step-gable from 1661 (see middle gable stone); restored.
177 late 19thC façade with ornamentation below window sills.
(Prinsengracht 30) late 19thC side façade with same size windows.

155   157   159-171   173   175   177   (30)

Prinsenstraat

Anjelierstraat

40-38   42   44

Prinsengracht 38-44

38-40 here, in 1973, two houses were torn down. Previously houses had to be demolished if the foundation was bad, now the foundation can be restored.
42 newly built 1906 with brick, bay-windows, and balcony with wrought iron railing; simple roof cornice includes dormer with ornamentation; lower structure ornamented with glazed brick.
44 late 19thC façade; roof altered 20thC; wooden shop front; 17thC building height; awning over windows.

(Prinsenstraat 27) side façade with top-gable in shape of tower built ±1910; iron *pui* beam.
179 newly built ±1905 with flat-topped roof; iron *pui* beam easily visible; name of house, 'Pax Vobis' (Peace for All) above windows 1st floor; railing with Jugendstil elements.
181 newly built 1903 (see tiled tableau) with wooden bay windows; asymmetrical façade with Jugendstil elements (see door, mail box and ornamental anchors).
183 early 19thC cornice façade; street front altered ±1900; rebuilt after early 20thC fire.

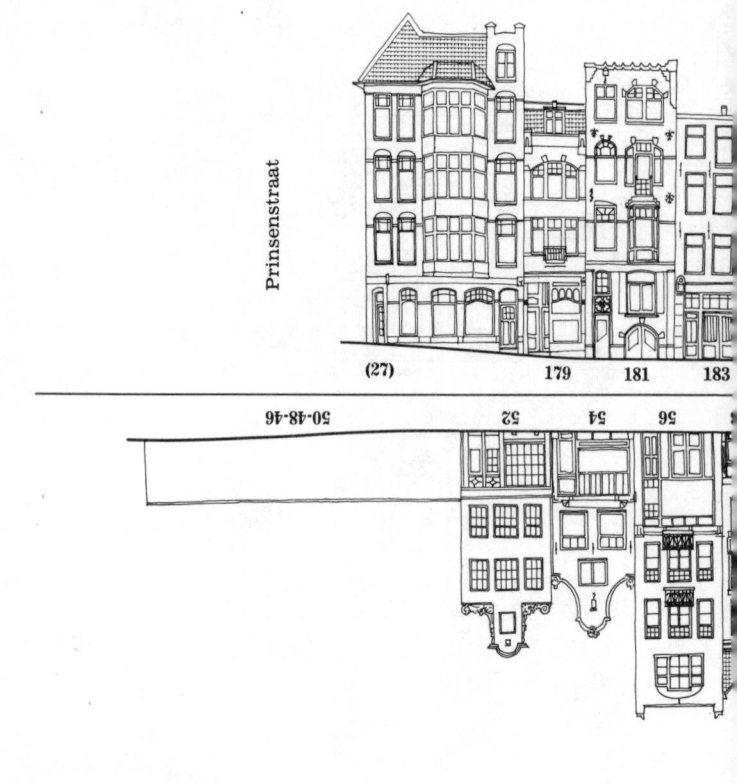

Prinsenstraat

(27)   **179**   **181**   **183**

50-48-46   52   54   56

two bay windows, one was hit by a truck.
and dormer; later altered somewhat; now one wooden, bay window; earlier
58 narrow house, becomes wider towards back; ±1890 façade with cornice
worked into façade.
ironwork; absence of straight cornice; iron hoist beam; small glazed bricks
56 newly built 1913 includes two small balconies with ornamental
not lean! (compare with no. 54).
52 M. reconstructed early 18thC neck-gable; at which time the façade did
46-48-50 in 1958 three houses were torn down here leaving this gap.

185 19thC façade with straight cornice interrupted by a brick dormer; same size windows on all floors.

187 17thC warehouse with spout-gable; rebuilt 19thC; two hoist beams.

189-191-193 M. ±1750 warehouses with spout-gables; little changed; floor heights easily discernable from outside; some of the loft-doors disappeared when the buildings were renovated into homes; entrances no higher than 1.80 meters (5¾ feet).

195 M. warehouse with spout-gables from ±1750; lower structure altered end 18thC; floor added 20thC.

185   187   189-191-193   195

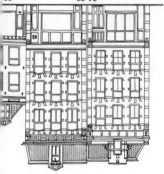

Tuinstraat

with natural stone; ornamented shop fronts.

62-64 newly built in 1895 with straight cornice and flat-topped roof; same size windows all floors; no. 64 has a brick dormer; façade ornamented ornamented anchors.

60 ±1860 cornice façade with saddle roof; dormer and hoist beam;

Prinsengracht 60-64

197 M. 18thC warehouse with spout-gable; ornaments on side of top are missing (compare nos. 189-191 and 193); lower structure altered 19thC.
199 M. oldest part is 18thC ashlar street front; 19thC spout-gable.
201 façade with straight cornice; small dormer with fronton; hoist beam and saddle roof dating ±1860; large door from same period.
203 a-b two warehouses from ±1700; rebuilt in 1884; one old and one new hoist beam; spout-gables.
205 used to be a warehouse as suggested by its people; now three flats built ±1860; door renovated; spout-gable.

197   199   201   203   205

89   70   72   76   78

Tuinstraat

68 the small house that stood here was torn down in 1944.
70 M. neck-gable with wooden street front from 1741 (see fronton); once shop/home; door in middle.
72 M. 1741 neck-gable with beautiful top ornament; middle window on 3rd floor once had loft-doors as did the 4th floor windows; lower structure drastically renovated 20thC.
76 newly built in 1911 with spout-like façade.
78 M. early 17thC house (see building height); changed to bell-gable ±1755; wooden street front altered in 19thC; early 19thC cushion-door.

207 ±1910 warehouse with two crenelles and iron hoist beam; top ornamented with yellow brick.

209 M. warehouse with spout-gable from ±1630; rebuilt considerably; the large window was installed during last renovation; height of building never changed.

211-213-215-217 M. four identical warehouses with spout-gables and volutes dating ±1690; semi-circular shutters on top; nos. 215 and 217 renovated by University of Amsterdam; little altered.*

207   209   211-213-215-217

80   82   84   86   88

Egelantiersstraat

Prinsengracht 80-88

80 ±1860 cornice façade with ornamented, wooden street front; same size windows all floors; property of 'Aristoteles'.

82 façade with straight cornice, dormer, and an almost flat roof from ±1875 (after 1860 saddle roofs were seldom built).

84 M. house with interesting wooden street front (slightly altered) and festoons; gable stone, 1658; top sobered 19thC into spout-like façade; restored in 1977 by 'Aristoteles'.

86 M. ±1650 house with wooden street front; top sobered 19thC into spout-like façade; restored in 1977 by 'Aristoteles'.

88 M. ±1650 house; façade altered ±1870 when a straight cornice with two consoles were fitted; restored in 1977 by 'Aristoteles'.

225-227 in 1938 eight houses were demolished for this wide, over-scaled, newly built in 1939; asymmetrical façade.

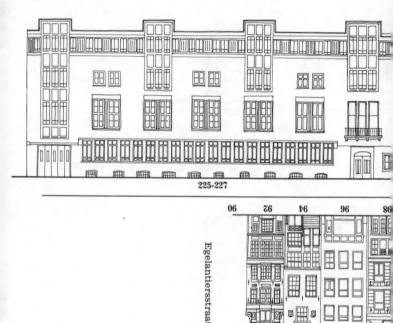

225-227

Egelantiersstraat

90 a 17thC house was torn down here in 1945 leaving a gap.

92 M. elevated neck-gable with pilasters; two oval windows with sculptured frames and segment-shaped fronton; gable stone, date 1661; lower part of wooden street front altered.

94 M. ±1680 neck-gable with triangular fronton, and two oval windows with sculptured sandstone frames; handsome wooden street front with frontal stoop; company's name inscribed in period style.

96 newly built in 1930 with spout-like façade; entrance at street-level (compare no. 94); house does not lean as do nos. 94 and 98.

98 newly built, spout-like gable; predominantly ±1865; stuccoed.

235 M. 19thC façade; tympan with a ship, a dog and two men (they are the assumed founders of the city in ±1200); tympan is from elsewhere, dating from 1649; low construction.

237 built ±1855; top has many consoles; 3 window wide center part in slight relief; windows and doors semi-circular; once a workhouse for the poor; after 1871 became a fire-station.

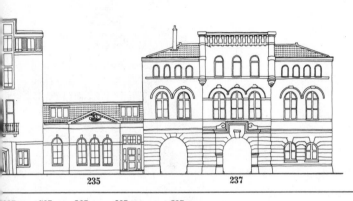

235   237

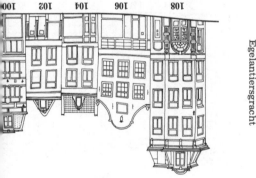

Egelantiersgracht

100 newly built in ±1855 with straight cornice, dormer and almost flat roof; ornamented shop front.

102 M. building height not altered in ±350 years; façade of larger part dating from ±1860 includes straight cornice, dormer, same size windows; ornamented shop front from same period.

104 M. building height not changed since ±1620; façade predominantly 19thC; transverse roof early 19thC; semi-circular dormer.

106 M. early 18thC house; bell-gable; 1920's shop front.

108 M. unusually shaped building; three windows on Prinsengracht and one on the Egelantiersgracht; straight cornice with consoles and mansarde roof dating from ±1865; ornamented street front.

239 late 19thC building with large transverse roof and 2 dormers; entrance
almost at street-level; semi-circular windows on ground floor; brick
ornamentation below roof cornice.

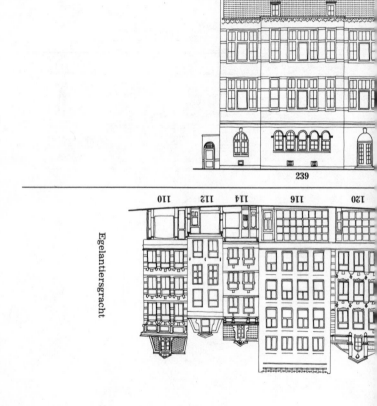

239

Prinsengracht 110-120

110 newly built in 1889 with ashlar façade; dormer and almost flat roof;
same size windows on all floors; shop front renovated.
112 ±1865 façade with straight cornice, dormer and shop front.
114 M. ±1860 façade with straight cornice, four consoles, ornamented
dormer; almost flat roof.
116 façade from 1926; 4 windows wide simple brick and stone
ornamentation at top; shop front.
120 1877 façade with ornamentation below windows; mansarde roof; round
hoist beam; shop front renovated in 1926 (see no. 116).

Egelantiersgracht

241 newly built in 1966; replaces five houses demolished the year before; brick façade; 'interesting' glass dormers; now student dormitory.

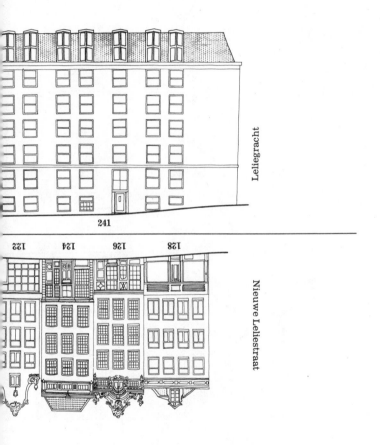

241

Leliegracht

Nieuwe Leliestraat

122   124   126   128

Prinsengracht 122-128

122 M. 1744 bell-gable with two corner vases; renovated 1926; wooden street front from same period.

124 M. late 18thC façade with straight cornice and two consoles; windows in cornice; hipped roof; shop front; restored in 1969 by 'Diogenes'.*

126 M. façade with exceptionally handsome elevated cornice in shape of a bell; two corner vases from ±1755; wooden cornice ornamented with sculptured man's head and an asymmetrical crest in Louis XV style; owned by 'Diogenes'.*

128 ±1855 cornice façade with dormer and hoist beam; 4 windows wide; shop front has Amsterdam School features from ±1920.

(Leliegracht 51) M. 19thC corner house; side façade with straight cornice, semi-circular windows on 1st floor; handsome front cornice with three consoles above 1st floor.

247 M. 17thC warehouse with spout-gables; lower structure rebuilt many times; street front ornamented with consoles.

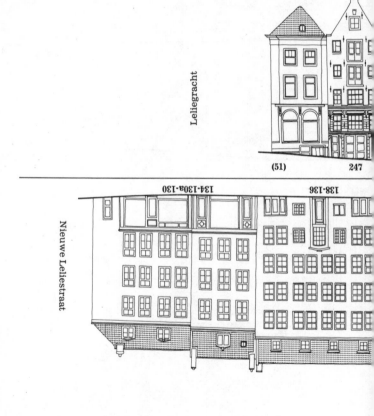

Leliegracht

(51) 247

Nieuwe Leliestraat

134-130A-130 **138-136**

Prinsengracht 130-138

130-130A-134 brick façades in historical style with roof cornice and wooden street front dating 1954; transverse roof with three chimneys; sash work. **136-138** over-scaled architecture from 1940; 8 windows wide; cornice and transverse roof with two chimneys; sash work; stone door frame.

249 ±1870 façade with straight cornice and dormer; the usual large door
has disappeared; stoop older; house does not lean.

251 M. lower structure 18thC; upper part late 19thC, neck-gable from
earlier; straight cornice; low doors; pull-bell.

253 M. wooden street front reminiscent of 17thC house; altered ±1800; top
changed into cornice façade same time; cushion-door.

255 M. this bell-gable was renovated in the 1940's; since then, same size
windows on all floors; stoop gone.

257 late 19thC cornice façade with flat-topped roof; hoist beam above
dormer.

249   251   253   255   257

144-142   146   148   150

Bloemgracht

150 M. corner house with bell-gable from ±1760; top comes from elsewhere.

148 M. ±1760 bell-gable (most were built at this time); wooden street front;
frontal stoop; restored in 1966 by 'Stadsherstel'.

146 M. late 18thC cornice façade; wooden street front; hipped roof; straight
cornice fitted 19thC; restored 1966 by 'Stadsherstel' (see plaque).

142-144 M. two 17thC houses under one transverse roof; one floor added
during restoration in 1966 by 'Stadsherstel'; wooden street fronts.

Prinsengracht 142-150

259 building with cornice-like façade from ±1930; simple cornice; same size windows on all floors; *pui* beam.

261 M. warehouse witp spout-gable dating ±1700; rebuilt considerably; loft-doors on lower floors gone; renovated below the iron *pui* beam.

263 M. most sought after building on the Prinsengracht, the Anne Frank House; has rear annex, like many houses on the canals; façade dating from ±1740; straight cornice fitted 100 years later.

265 M. built 1635; somewhat rebuilt; top altered ±1800; straight cornice with two consoles fitted ±1800; stoop preserved; annexed by Anne Frank House.

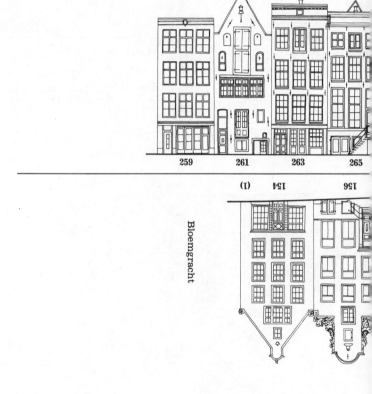

259   261   263   265

(I)   154   156

Bloemgracht

154 · **(Bloemgracht I)** M. 18thC home with unusual spout-gable (most spout-gables are on warehouses); late 18thC wooden street front.

156 M. early 18thC neck-gable; handsome claw pieces; door frame from later period; sash work gone (compare no. 154); now T-windows from ±1870; earlier only one door; little else changed.

(Westermarkt 36-58) sequence of demolitions; no. 267 in 1861, no. 269 in 1956, no. 271 in 1951, no. 273 in 1956, no. 275 in 1961. Present over-scaled building from 1961; the use of brick is an attempt to harmonize with the surroundings as is the decreasing size of the windows towards the top; roof-terrace; student dormitory.

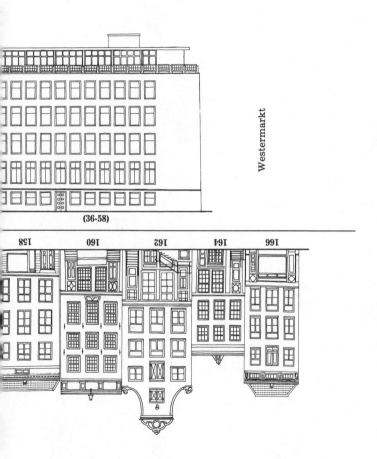

Westermarkt

(36-58)

158   160   162   164   166

Prinsengracht 158-166

158 M. early 19thC cornice façade with hipped roof and street front.

160 M. 18thC house; earlier a bell-gable; top 'modernized' beginning 19thC into cornice façade; wooden street front altered at same time.

162 M. early 18thC bell-gable; top 'beautified' late 18thC; wooden street front altered with brick; two stoops.

164 M. 17thC house; wooden street front; building height altered later; façade predominantly early 19thC with straight cornice; frontal stoop.

166 M. ±1790 façade with straight cornice, two consoles and hipped roof; middle window now has a 'life-shutters' (loft-doors with glass).

277 spout-like construction newly built in the 1930's with circular windows; gate with fronton; relief with skull above gate; (there is a stone-cutters shop behind where grave stones are made).

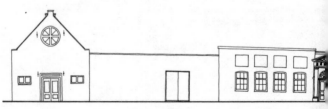

277

Westerkerk M. designed by Hendrick de Keyser; construction begun in 1620; the largest reformed church in Holland, as well as the highest tower in Amsterdam: 85 meters (272 feet); beautiful interior; Rembrandt was buried here.

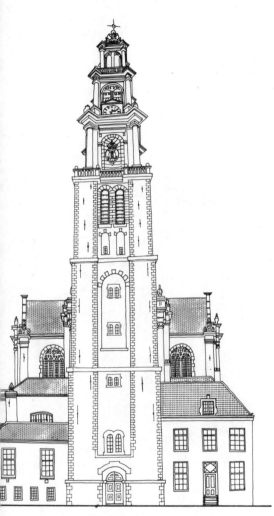

Westerkerk

Prinsengracht 168-172

168 M. 17thC warehouse with wooden street front; the barely altered façade has a spout-gable; two volutes and fronton above hoist beam.
170 newly built in 1910 with wooden bay windows and balcony; asymmetrical façade; brick dormer; almost flat roof.
172 newly built in ±1915 with bay windows, small balcony; symmetrical façade (compare with no. 170); almost flat roof; iron hoist beam; shop front.
(Bloemstraat 1) once walled, now a gap; used mostly as playground.

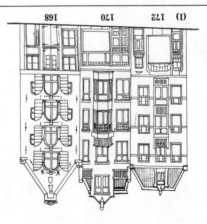

Westermarkt

Bloemstraat

168   170   172   (1)

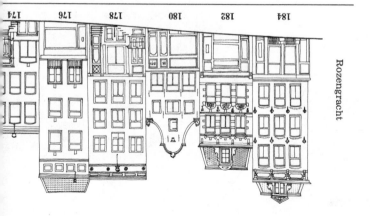

Prinsengracht 174-184

174 ±1860 façade with simple straight cornice; door frame.

176 newly built in 1934; hipped roof; straight cornice; does not lean.

178 M. 18thC façade; building height increased beginning 19thC when straight cornice with ornamentation, four rosettes, was added; earlier a bell-gable; two stoops.

180 M. 17thC house with façade that was altered later; bell-gable from ±1765; shop front from same period altered later.

182 newly built in 1890 with roof cornice, ornamented dormer and flat roof.

184 newly built ±1890 with straight cornice; ornamented dormer has hoist beam.

283 M. ±1740 handsome bell-gable with crest above hoist beam; façade drastically altered in 19thC; sash work gone.
285 M. ±1855 cornice façade with door frame, portal and two doors.
287 M. early 18thC warehouse with spout-like gable; spoiled considerably; converted to living function; earlier, probably a garage for carriages.
289 M. ±1720 neck-gable with beautiful top; lower structure altered 20thC; stoop gone; house leans (compare with no. 291).
291 newly built in ±1905; rounded bay windows; glazed brick used in asymmetrical façade; door on street-level; Jugendstil.

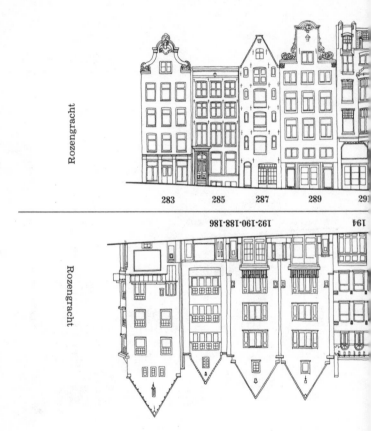

Rozengracht

283   285   287   289   291

Rozengracht

192·190·188·186   194

unusual place; over-hanging cornice.
194 newly built in 1908; semi-circular fanlight on 3rd floor; chimney in and hoist beam; no. 188 has brick bay windows.
block but four separate houses, each with its own roof, door, pointed-gable
186·188·190·192 early example of adapted architecture from 1932; not a solid

293 shop front from ±1905 (see no. 291); during this time a late 19thC façade
was built with glazed bricks; wooden bay window.
295 1903 façade (see commemorative stone) with flat roof and three
balconies; Jugendstil ornamentation (see street front).
297 ±1800 façade with flat roof and same size windows.
299 M. ±1740 façade with ornamented, elevated cornices, ornamental vases.
301 M. ±1720 neck-gable; hardly changed; Empire entrance with cushion-
door dating ±1800; sash work from same period.
303 M. ±1750 bell-gable (most bell-gables built in this period); sash work
late 18thC; little changed.

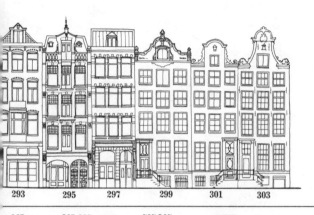

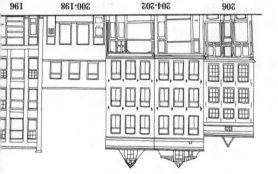

Rozenstraat

street front.
206 M. predominantly 19thC façade; floor added 20thC; 19thC wooden
ornamented anchors; shop fronts.
202-204 twin cornice façade from ±1860; dormer with hoist beam;
198-200 top of building gone.
196 newly built in 1908 with brick ornamentation at top; two crenelles.

Prinsengracht 196-206

305 M. rare façade with bell-shaped cornice built ±1725; sometimes called a sunken bell-gable.

307 M. ±1720 neck-gable, tall, fronton with shell motif; late 18thC sash work; 19thC door frame; very little altered.

309 M. backside vicarage of church on Keizersgracht; cornice façade with transverse roof dating ±1850; below the stoop is a 2nd entrance.

311 M. predominantly early 19thC façade; straight cornice; stuccoed.

313 newly built ±1905 with glazed bricks; Jugendstil elements (see top); iron hoist beam; balcony.

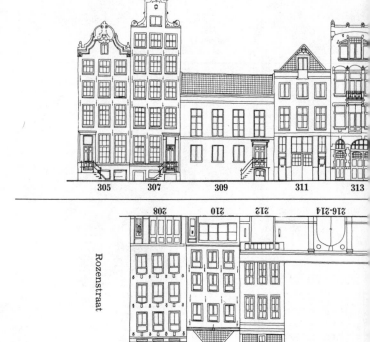

208 newly built with straight cornice; dormer and almost flat roof; in ±1870 many districts were filled with this type of architecture; street front altered later ±1915.

210 newly built in ±1860 with simple roof cornice which holds the hoist beam (fitted later); in this period the last saddle roofs were built; shop front from 1920's.

212 newly built 1932 in historical style with straight cornice and transverse roof.

214-216 the two houses that stood here were torn down in 1937.

315 rebuilt warehouse with spout-gable; now hotel (see no. 323).

317 M. 17thC warehouse with spout-gable; fronton at top; wooden street front from later period; now hotel (see no. 323).

319 M. ±1740 neck-gable; oval windows with sculptured frames below claw pieces; stoop bench; now hotel (see no. 323).

321 M. 19thC warehouse with straight cornice and almost flat roof; now hotel (see no. 323).

323-325 hotel (Pulitzer) consisting of nine buildings on Prinsengracht and four buildings on Keizersgracht; unique operation from 1970 resulting in 175 hotel rooms; designed by Bart van Kasteel.

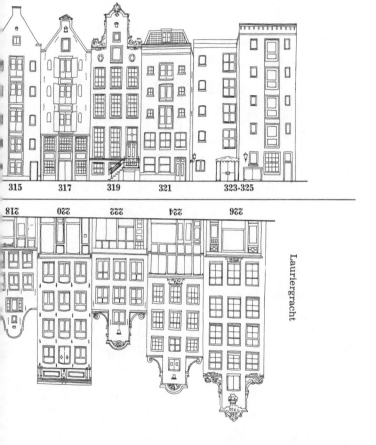

315   317   319   321   323-325

Lauriergracht

Prinsengracht 218-226

218 M. early 18thC house (earlier neck-gable); sobered 19thC into bell-gable like façade (no ornaments); wooden street front.

220 ±1875 façade with straight cornice, two pairs of consoles, and sculpture of small man.

222 neck-gable from ±1725; shop front constructed 20thC.

224 M. 1723 neck-gable (see gable stone); fronton with sculptured bird; wooden street front altered repeatedly.

226 M. 1733 neck-gable (see ornamented fronton) above wooden street front altered repeatedly; gable stone; little else changed.

327 M. early 18thC warehouse; top rebuilt; handsome gable stone 'D'Nieuw Goudsbloem' (the new marigold); (see no. 23).

329 M. 18thC bell-gable; late 18thC stoop; sash work (see no. 323).

331 built 1970 in historical style (see no. 323).

333-335-357 M. reconstruction by 'Stadsherstel' 1968 of 17thC wooden street fronts, building height; upper part of façades 19thC (straight cornices); wooden street fronts altered later.

339 M. reconstructed bell-gable ±1760; wooden street front and pothouse probably 17thC by 'Stadsherstel' in 1968 (see plaque).

327   329   331   333-335-337   339

228   230   232

Laurierstraat

with put cornice.

232 newly built 1915 with brick ornamentation on top; wooden shop front brick, iron hoist beam.

230 newly built ±1905; asymmetrical façade with windows, balcony, yellow

228 newly built ±1915 with roof cornice and dormer; wooden street front.

Prinsengracht 228-232

341 · (Reestraat 27) shop/home built 1883; relieving arches with ornamentation above windows, straight cornice, dormer and almost flat roof.

343 M. early 19thC building; straight cornice, two ornamented consoles with transverse roof, beautiful ornate fanlight, *pui* beam, frontal stoop; belongs to 'Aristoteles'.

347 M. 17thC house; building height, wooden street front altered later; 18thC façade sobered into 19thC bell-like gable.

349 M. rare warehouse with bell-gable dating ±1650; fronton at top; little altered; original construction.*

351 M. ±1740 bell-gable with family arms above hoist beam (compare the top ornaments with those of no. 349).

Reestraat

341   343   347   349   351

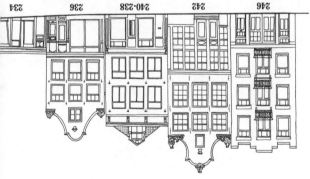

234   236   240-238   242   246

246 newly built in ±1910 with stone ornamentation on top.

242 M. 17thC house (by its wooden street front and building height); façade about 100 years older ±1765; bell-gable with beautiful Louis XV ornaments (see asymmetrical crest); wooden street front altered later.

17thC building height remains unchanged.

238-240 ±1860 cornice façade, dormer with hoist beam and shop front; 17thC building height.

236 M. ±1765 bell-gable (most bell-gables were built in this period); wooden street front altered repeatedly; this one dates from ±1880.

234 shop front; family tree motif still intact in fanlight.

353 M. warehouses with bell-gables are unusual; here is an example from ±1730; old roof altered; little else changed.

355 M. 18thC house; rebuilt 19thC into bell-like gable.

357-357a M. twin bell-gables from ±1730; house on left side still has original top with two medallions; lower structures altered.

359 M. ±1730 bell-gable with sandstone, ornamented fronton; next to *attick* shutter two medallions; window shape is unique.

361 M. 19thC cornice façade with unusual window grouping in lower part.

369 this narrow house with entrance gate to the 'Nieuwe 'Suykerhofje' (New Sugar-courtyard with nos. 365-371); courtyard now gone; now annexed to another building.

353   355   357-357a   359   361   3

248   250   252   254

Lauriergracht

248 M. 18thC façade; 1743 inscribed on *pui* beam; sobered into cornice top; late 18thC wooden street front.

250 M. 18thC façade (earlier genuine bell-gable) with 19thC bell-gable like façade 19thC; ornamented dormer; 19thC shop front.

252 M. neck-gable from ±1730 (top somewhat 'sunken'); hoist beam sticks out through a cartouche; altered street front; pothouse.

254 remains of 19thC house; three-flat building until 1966, now a one -floor roof terrace.

373 ±1860 façade with wooden street front, straight cornice, dormer and mansarde roof; ornamented white block above windows.
375 newly built in 1896 (see top) with flat roof; lower structure changed.
377 newly built in 1910 (see gable stone above windows 1st floor); remarkable top with fronton and two pinnacles; wooden street front.
379 rebuilt late 1920's; straight cornice missing; brick closure at top; iron hoist beam.
381 newly built in 1903 with wooden bay windows and wooden top; frontal stoop.
383 newly built in 1890 with flat roof; dormer changed into what is almost a tower; ashlar street front with semi-circular windows.

73   375   377   379   381   383

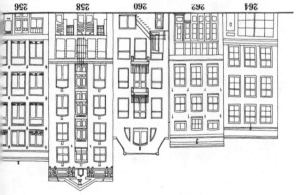

256   258   260   262   264

256 ±1865 cornice façade with ornamented anchors and window railings; iron hoist beam.
258 most warehouses were built in the 17thC; this warehouse from ±1870 with straight cornice and fronton; lower structure 1920's; ornamented doors.
260 newly built in 1950's with stoop and trapeziodal-shaped top; balconies; iron hoist beam; high stoop.
262 M. ±1840 cornice façade; lower structure altered 20thC.
264 ±1860 cornice façade with same size windows (compare with no. 262).

Prinsengracht 256-264

397 façade from 1897 with elevated, straight cornice; hoist beam on elevation; all windows arched; ornamented anchors; stoop older.
399 M. little remains from 19thC cornice façade.
401 when will this be restored?
403 M. early 18thC street front, athough altered later, is oldest part of house; now cornice façade from ±1850; porch and two doors.
405 ±1860 cornice façade; street front altered later; entrance at street-level (compare with no. 403).

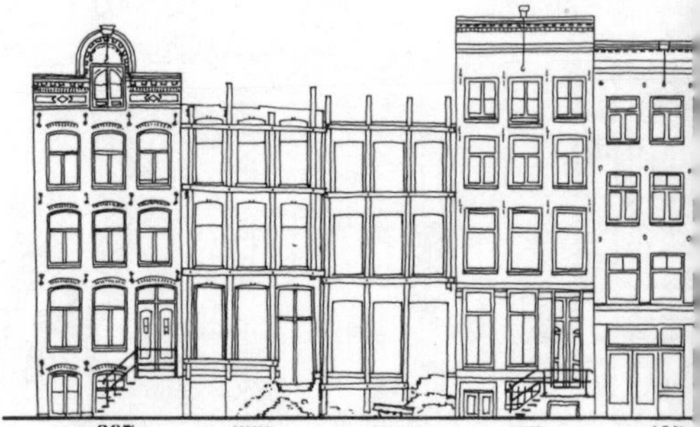

397 399 401 403 405

Prinsengracht 268-274

268 newly built in 1941 with straight cornice and two dormers; (corner lisenas); earlier two houses stood here.
270 pointed gable newly built in 1931 with brick-bay windows.
272 M. 18thC bell-gable rebuilt in 1938; same size windows on all floors; stoop gone.
274 late 18thC bell-gable rebuilt in 1937 without making use of old brick; same size windows on all floors; stoop gone.

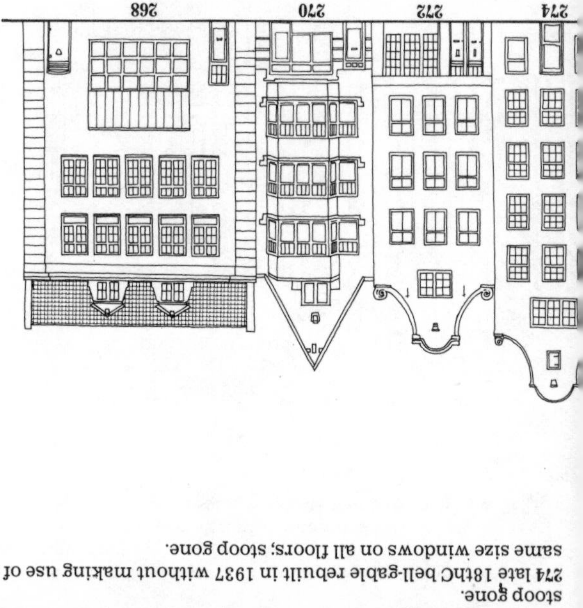

268 270 272 274

407-409 adapted architecture from 1977 housing 18 separate apartments.
411 ±1865 house with straight cornice, two dormers, mansarde roof and
large window frames; window railing.
413 M. 18thC house; earlier a neck-gable, now with straight cornice from
19thC; building height unchanged; *pui* beam; earlier one door.
415 M. 18thC building; elevated and fitted with straight cornice in 19thC;
railing on stoop renovated.
417-419 this pilaster façade was built in 1918 (see top) on a site where once
stood two houses; it looks older.

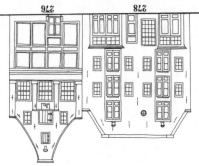

407-409   411   413   415   417-419

Elandsstraat

276 M. 17thC house identified by building height, wooden street front,
gable stone, pilasters; top altered into bell-like gable 19thC; wooden street
front altered; original construction.
278 M. 17thC double warehouse; rebuilt somewhat; tops sobered into
trapezoidal-shaped gable; garage doors (for carriages) next to large window;
both installed 19thC.

421 unusual example of adapted architecture from 1975 with concrete elements and brick, the latter recently painted.
437 newly built in 1950; an almost glass façade with iron window frames; no brick or wood used.
439 newly built in 1901 (see top); bay window with Jugendstil elements (see tiled tableau); transverse roof.
443-445-447 early example of adapted architecture from 1953; sash work; two hoist beams; straight cornice.

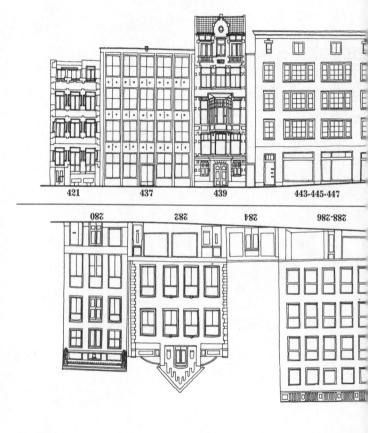

421   437   439   443-445-447

280   282   284   288-286

280 M. early 19thC façade with straight cornice and two consoles; middle window on 3rd floor once had loft-doors; ornamentation in window corners; little changed since.
282 4 window wide façade (most houses 2-4 windows wide) with window frames and straight cornice interrupted by a dormer ±1855.
284 gap in façade wall; became a workshop in 1950.
286-288 newly built in 1963; 'open' *attiek* built in form of a balustrade; no sash work; no wooden window frames.

449 M. late 18thC façade with straight cornice, two consoles, dormer and transverse roof; stoop renovated 20thC.

451 M. early 18thC shop (see wooden street front); earlier gable gone; now a spout gable; restored in 1974; two fan railings. This was the 100th restoration by 'Stadsherstel'.

453 a sharp contrast with its neighbors; this building or what remains of it, was built ±1900.

455 M. 17thC corner house; always a shop; 19thC street front with shop window; wooden street front still there in altered form; predominantly 19thC cornice façade.

457 M. narrow cornice façade predominantly 19thC; wooden street front, (altered later), originally from 17thC (see small door); 'Stadsherstel').

449   451   453   455   457

Berenstraat

Elandsgracht

290 M. predominantly early 19thC façade; straight cornice enclosing windows; finally restored in 1977.

292 newly built ±1915 with ornamented roof cornice interrupted by brick dormer that almost takes the shape of a step-gable.

294 newly built ±1890 with flat-topped roof; façade ornamented with stone blocks (compare 290); cut-away corner with net-formed balcony railings.

459 M. ±1750 building with straight cornice, two consoles and a transverse roof; soon to be restored by 'Stadsherstel'.

461 M. 17thC house as identified by building height; much altered; façade partly 18thC; straight cornice and dormer from beginning 19thC.

463 Jugendstil-like building from ±1905; top reminiscent of a castle; glazed brick.

465-467 ±1890 double house with straight cornice, two dormers, pilasters, window frames and flat-topped roof; street front altered drastically.

469 M. neck-gable built 1713 (date stone below fronton); lower structure altered ±1910 when stoop was removed.

| 459 | 461 | 463 | 465-467 | 469 |

Elandsgracht

| 296 | 298 | 300 | 302 | 304 |

296 M. predominantly ±1850 façade with straight cornice; fan railing.

298 M. façade early 19thC with straight cornice; saddle roof finished with wainscoting (wooden spout-gable).

300 M. remarkably preserved bell-gable with wooden street front from ±1760; above the two doors is a fox with a bird in his mouth; 'Stadsherstel'.*

302 18thC neck-gable rebuilt 1940's; window grouping altered then; stoop gone; new brick.

304 newly built in the 1940's in historical style; straight cornice; hoist beam; door frame.

471 lower structure dating from 1940.

473 cornice façade built 1951; flat roof.

475 late 18thC façade with straight cornice; dormer fitted into a kind of wooden top-gable; 19thC street front.

477 M. built 18thC; once had other top, now straight cornice ±1870; façade stuccoed in same period.

479 M. early 18thC neck gable; ±1870 façade was ornamented with stucco, pilasters and consoles.

481 neck-gable from ±1730; fronton from elsewhere; once had one large door (compare with no. 483).

483 M. ±1765 bell-gable with Louis XV ornamentation at top (asymmetrical); handsomely restored; sash work renovated.

471   473   475   477   479   481   483

306   308   310   312   314

Oude Looiersstraat

Prinsengracht 306-314

306 newly built ±1910 with brick and stone ornamentation at top (trapezoidal-shaped gable); frontal stoop; iron hoist beam.

308 newly built ±1895 with straight cornice interrupted by a dormer with hoist beam; almost flat roof; frontal stoop.

310 newly built 1912 with three balconies; asymmetrical façade.

312 newly built ±1880 with roof cornice and dormer; almost flat roof; white stones above windows; lower structure altered.

314 demolished in 1976; now a gap in the wall of façades.

485 late 19thC cornice façade; hoist beam sticks through straight cornice.
487 late 19thC cornice façade with dormer and almost flat roof; street front rebuilt 1972 in historical style; house does not lean.
489 M. early 18thC neck-gable with unusual semi-circular loft-doors.
491 M. early 17thC warehouse; top slightly altered (ornaments on side missing); little else changed; original construction.
493 ±1860 façade with straight cornice, dormer and almost flat roof; stoop older; earlier only one door; now tiled portal with two doors.
495 ±1880 façade with straight cornice, consoles and dormer.
497 entrance to *hofje* (courtyard) with annexed buildings.
499 M. neck-gable with sculpture of animal in fronton; date stone above hoist beam (1728); handsomely restored in 1976.

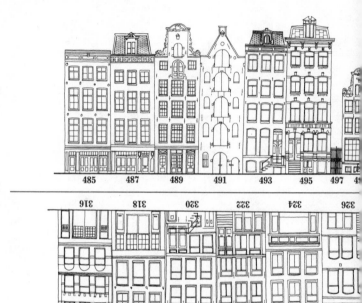

485   487   489   491   493   495   497   4

316   318   320   322   324   326

316 newly built ±1880 with large ornamented dormer.
318 M. predominantly 19thC façade with straight cornice; lower part changed.
320 M. 18thC façade; earlier a genuine bell-gable; sobered into bell-like gable in 19thC; woooden street front.
322 M. early 18thC house; earlier a neck-gable; top sobered into bell-like gable 19thC.
324 M. 18thC façade; earlier a genuine bell-gable; top sobered in 19thC when straight cornice was fitted; 20thC shop front.
326 newly built ±1890 with straight cornice; dormer with round hoist beam.

505 M. ±1640 bell-gable with fronton and shell motif; two corner vases;
gable stone fitted in 1962; 18thC door frame; three doors.
507 ±1740 neck-gable; hardly changed; restored.
509 M. 17thC house; rebuilt considerably; top sobered into spout-gable
19thC; 2nd entrance below stoop; restored in 1977.
525 newly built ±1895; straight cornice with consoles and mansarde roof;
front has no door, side entrance.
527 M. once a neck-gable; door frame from ±1760; top drastically altered
±1910; now straight cornice and flat roof; stoop renovated 1977; 2nd
entrance below stoop.
529 late 19thC cornice façade; earlier wooden street front; 17thC building
height; entrance at street-level (compare with no. 527).
531 - (Runstraat 32) M. ±1730 neck-gable with two corner vases, sculptured
elephant.

Runstraat

505   507   509   525   527   529   531   (32)

328   330   332

Looiersgracht

Prinsengracht 328-332

328 newly built ±1905 with glazed bricks; asymmetrical façade with bay
windows and balcony; Jugendstil.
330 façade with straight cornice, ornamented dormer, and almost flat
roof; ornamented anchors from ±1885; iron hoist beam painted to look
like wood.
332 newly built 1912 (see stone, side façade); asymmetrical façade; brick
dormer with iron hoist beam and mini-dormer; roof cornice; almost flat
roof.

(Runstraat 33) M. side façade of mainly 18thC house with neck-gable; 17thC street front and pothouse; height of door ±1.85 meters (±6 feet).

533 M. ±1760 bell-gable with Louis XV ornamentation on top (asymmetrical); wooden street front from a somewhat later period beginning with Louis XVI.

535 M. lower structure still 18thC; earlier a neck-gable; elevated cornice is from beginning 19thC; *attiek* shutter and hoist beam fitted into this elevation; stoop bench.

537 old building demolished in 1900; replaced soon after with this building; beautiful bay window and balconies; asymmetrical façade; tiled porch.

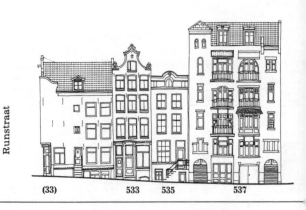

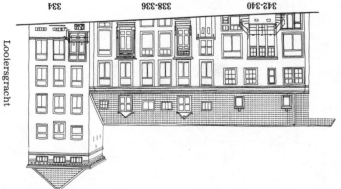

with two turning approaches.
340-342 M. 17thC houses with transverse roof; considerably less altered than nos. 336-338; middle door is entrance to upper floors; double stoop with two turning approaches.

336-338 M. 17thC houses with transverse roof; façades predominantly early 19thC with straight cornices, large windows and large doors; door frame of no. 336, Empire ±1800; frontal stoops.

334 M. 18thC building; floor added 19thC when straight cornice built.

Prinsengracht 334-342

545 late 19thC façade with straight cornice, dormer and flat-topped roof; same size windows on all floors.

547 house built ±1870 with straight cornice, almost flat roof and dormer; lower structure ornamented with brick later.

549 newly built ±1910 with bay window and balcony; flat roof with terrace; street front altered later; door at street-level (compare with no. 551).

551 M. 17thC house as identified by building height, and wooden street front which was later altered; top altered 20thC; now cornice façade with flat roof; frontal stoop.

555 late 19thC cornice façade; little change from original building height; ornamented dormer; beautiful windows; ornamented anchors.

571 M. early 18thC neck-gable with ornamentation in the fronton; lower part of façade stuccoed 19thC; earlier had one door.

545   547   549   551   555   571

344   346   348   350   354-352

Passeerdersstraat

Prinsengracht 344-354

344 ± 1860 façade with straight cornice; frontal stoop; ornamented anchors.

346 M. predominantly early 19thC façade with straight cornice and consoles; house leans (compare nos. 344-348).

348 newly built ±1880 with straight cornice, dormer with hoist beam and almost flat roof; same size windows on all floors (compare with no. 346).

350 since 1950 had a gap (note use of timbers to support neighbours).

332-334 twin cornice façade from ±1880; shop front from same period; straight simple cornice fitted later; iron hoist beam.

573 newly built in 1938 in historical style (spout-like gable); same size windows on all floors; wooden street front; window railings.

575-577 twin cornice façade from ±1849; no. 575 is least altered and still has straight cornice with closed *attiek;* floor added to no. 577 later.

579 newly built ±1905 with step-gable on top; ornamented shop front (lion with arms); Jugendstil ironwork.

581-583 newly built ±1900 with many semi-circular windows; maximum allowed building height on canals is 16 meters (±51 feet); these two are almost 20 meters high (64 feet).

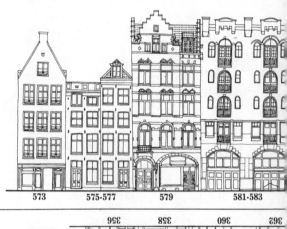

573　　575-577　　579　　581-583

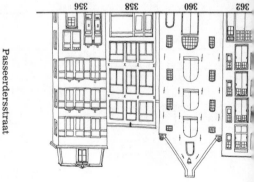

Passeerdersstraat

356 358 360 362

356 newly built ±1890 with roof cornice, dormer and hoist beam; almost flat roof; cut-away corner.

358 19thC façade; much spoiled; lower structure altered.

360 M. early 18thC warehouse with spout-gable; two sandstone volutes; little else changed; hoist beam parallel to building walls.

362 small warehouse built ±1910; the loft-doors show floor to ceiling heights inside; no ornamentation at top.

Prinsengracht 356-362

587 example of adapted architecture from 1975 by De Klerk (also architect of Marriott and Sonesta hotels); façade mainly brick with inward relief which suggest several smaller houses; various window frames used; building perhaps a bit too high and deep (it runs through to the Keizersgracht); stoop built.

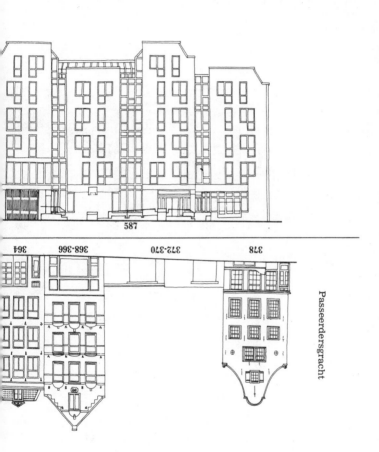

587

Prinsengracht 364-378

364 newly built ±1870 with straight cornice, dormer with hoist beam and ornamented anchors; flat-topped roof; lower structure rebuilt 1930.
366-368 newly built 1892 (see date stone) with spout-gable; façade ornamented with many kinds of stone; shop front renovated 1974.
370-372 three houses were demolished here leaving a large gap.
378 M. early 18thC shop/home withitop sobered in 19thC; once a neck-gable, now resembles a bell-gable; handsome pothouse; round door at corner.

611 M. 17thC warehouse; somewhat rebuilt; old roof gone; straight cornice fitted early 19thC; below cornice two semi-circular windows.

615 M. house built ±1740; earlier neck-gable; roof and top altered beginning 19thC; now transverse roof with dormer; stoop gone.

625 M. 18thC building; floor and straight cornice added 19thC.

627 remarkable house built ±1890 with pointed, ornamented top; handsome iron hoist beam; ornamented anchors; door at street-level (compare no. 625).

629 ±1870 façade with straight cornice, ornamented dormer and wooden street front (altered later); building height 17thC.

645 newly built in 1932 with point-like gable; hoist beam, cross-frame windows.

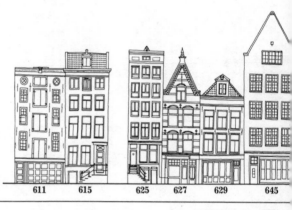

611   615   625   627   629   645

Passeerdersgracht

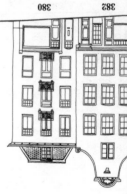

380   382

382 1932 reconstruction of early 18thC bell-gable (see sandstone ornaments at top); new brick used; same size windows on all floors; wooden shop front and door frame.

380 newly built in 1908 with roof cornice, dormer and almost flat roof; three balconies with railing and decoration.

647-649 the two houses that stood here were torn down in 1976; there are plans to fill this gap.

651 late 19thC cornice façade; earlier two houses, 5 windows wide; 17thC building height.

653 newly built with spout-like gable in 1936; same size windows on all floors; wooden street front; entrance at street-level (compare no. 655).

655 M. lower structure is early 18thC; earlier neck-gable; door frame from same period; part with ornamented anchors altered ±1840; 20thC brick, finishing details above.

657 M. façade with straight cornice enclosing *attiek* shutter; ±1850 saddle roof just visible above cornice; door frame from same period.

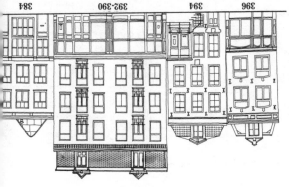

647-649   651   653   655   657

384   392-390   394   396

Prinsengracht 384-396

384 ±1910 cornice façade; saddle roof just visible above straight cornice.

390-392 two identical houses with cornices, dormers with hoist beams and a flat roof built 1897; balconies; wooden shop fronts.

394 M. predominantly ±1840 façade with straight cornice, dormer and mansarde roof; gable stone reminiscent of 17thC façade; door frame from ±1800; two doors.

396 newly built ±1880 with straight cornice, dormer and almost flat roof; natural stone above windows; wooden shop front.

659 M. double warehouse from ±1640; original construction; altered here
and there; part on right with hoist beam and white stone altered least;
lowest door fitted later; tops sobered later into trapeziodal gable.
661 M. early 18thC warehouse with spout-gable; size of loft-doors indicates
height of floors; once had a door for carriages.
663 M. predominantly 19thC corner house; straight cornice and door frame
early 19thC; three lily anchors; frontal stoop.

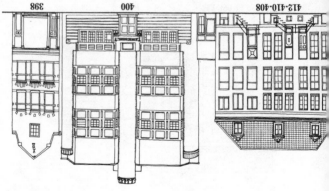

408-410-412 M. three almost identical 18thC houses under one large roof;
the straight cornices date from the early 19thC; windows grow smaller
towards top like in most old Amsterdam houses.

400 newly built in 1925 with Amsterdam School features; outward bending
relief, ornamentation with brick; two sculptured heads near doors; much
use was made of sculpture in this period.

398 newly built in ±1800 with white stone; top later renovated now has
shape of mansarde roof.

(Molenpad 15-17) built 1882; relieving arches above windows on 1st floor. 667 also a part of Leidsegracht 68; see page 282; ±1850 façade with straight cornice; transverse roof; rebuilt beginning 20thC; three dormers and bay window added.

Molenpad

(15-17)   667

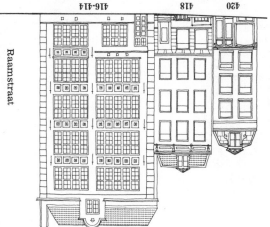

Raamstraat

416-414   418   420

Prinsengracht 414-420

414-416 newly built in 1925; tall with brick dormer and ornamentation at the corners (so-called lisenas); accent is on windows' width (compare with no. 418); ornamentation with brick; ornamented anchors.

418 façade with straight cornice and four consoles; dormer with hoist beam and flat-topped roof from ±1885.

420 M. ±1860 façade with simple straight cornice and ornamented dormer.

(Leidsegracht 68) M. late 17thC corner house (by its building height, pothouse and wooden street front); larger windows fitted into side façade later; has always been a shop (often the case with corner houses); original construction.

(68)

Leidsegracht

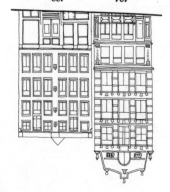

422   424

Leidsegracht

Prinsengracht 422-424

422 two late 18thC façades, possibly with cornices; now soberly finished with straight simple cornice; small windows in middle light staircase well; two fan railings; frontal stoop.

424 newly built in ±1883 (see date stone on right) with white stone on the façade; top has shape of a mansarde roof and is ornamented with pinnacles; wooden shop front.

(Leidsegracht 63) M. side façade of neck-gable built ±1755; oval windows
light staircase well; large windows installed 19thC; top of façade supported
by iron pole.
669 late 19thC façade with straight cornice, dormer with hoist beam, and
mansarde roof; same size windows on all floors; door at street-level
(compare with no. 671).
671 M. neck-gable built ±1660; rebuilt and floor added 19thC; beautiful
door from ±1880; stoop bench; pull-bell.

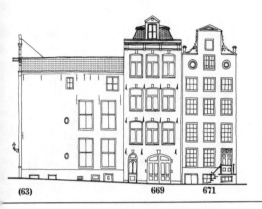

(63)   669   671

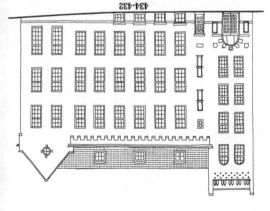

Prinsengracht 432-434

432-434 newly built in 1915; this broad, over-scaled building replaces five
houses; ornamentation in brick below straight roof cornice; above semi-
circular windows (left) a brick balustrade with two crenelles.

673-673a twin cornice façades built ±1860; flat-topped roof; dormers with hoist beam; same size windows on all floors (compare with no. 677).

675 M. 18thC coach house; lower structure unchanged (unusual), though top was altered; old roof barely visible.

677 M. ±1755 bell-gable with early Louis XV ornaments (see crest); one S-shaped bottle baluster; stoop bench.

679 M. early 19thC façade with straight cornice and transverse roof; ashlar street front fitted later; door at street-level (compare nos. 677 and 681).

681 M. see no. 683.

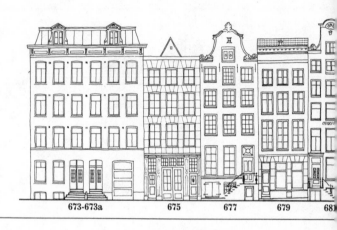

673-673a   675   677   679   681

(681)-683-687-689-691-693 M. seven neck-gables probably built ±1715, dating back to the time of the Republic of United Netherlands when the seven provinces joined; see names of façades; above most of the hoist beams is a fronton with shell motif; the tallest neck-gable, 'Gelderland', has a double stoop which is quite unusual for 3 window wide houses; it also has two corner vases; little else changed.

683-685-687-689-691-693

436

436 M. the Palace of Justice; this kind of large building is rare in this city, better known for its houses; here once stood an orphanage; between 1825 and 1829 it was drastically rebuilt. There are three sections that stand out in relief with Corinthian pilasters; façade is finished with a stone cornice and 'closed' *attiek*, 'open' *attiek* in the form of a balustrade.

695 M. 19thC cornice façade; street front renovated; door gone; hoist beam in unusual place (compare with no. 697); floor added later.

697-699 M. $\pm$1850 façade with straight cornice and window frames; ornamented street fronts; transverse roof.

701 M. 18thC house with top altered later; now 19thC straight cornice with windows; transverse roof; iron door frame.

703-705 newly built in $\pm$1910 with ornamented shop fronts; once a forge (see handsome mosaic).

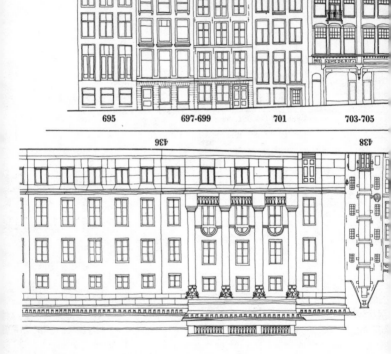

695   697-699   701   703-705

436   438

front.

XIV ornamentation; recently restored; sash work repaired; wooden street

little else changed.

440 M. $\pm$1740 narrow house with elevated cornice and handsome Louis

438 M. 1737 warehouse with spout-gable (see memorial stone); low door;

436 M. see text page 286.

705a M. predominantly 19thC façade; bell-like top with ornamental vases saved from the 17thC house that once stood here; shop front renovated; frontal stoop.

707 · (Leidsestraat 80) newly built in 1917 with balcony and bay window; shop/home with an asymmetrical façade.

Leidsestraat

5a   707

442

Leidsestraat

Prinsengracht 442

442 much reconstruction is done on corners; this building dates from 1926; lower structure ornamented with stone; façade has ornamentation in brick; outward bending relief.

(Leidsestraat 79) late 19thC shop/home with mansarde roof; round corner with convex windows; ashlar shop front added later.
709 late 19thC cornice façade; stuccoed; top and straight cornice removed; shop front added 1922; no door.

(79)   **709**

450 - (Leidsestraat 81) newly built in 1896 (see date stone) with wooden, ornamented shop front and wooden bay windows; small tower on top; three dormers; flat-topped roof.
452 Newly built in 1902 (see year-stone); pointed gable form, with gable stone situated between iron hoist beam and brick *makelaar*.

709-713 newly built in the 1920's with Amsterdam School features (ornamentation in brick and outward bending relief).

715 M. house rebuilt from warehouse that had bell-gable; top front of this gable once on a house at Dam Square; ±1790 vase on top.

717 M. 5 window wide double house with straight cornice; door and semi-circular doorway lintel from ±1810; 2nd entrance below stoop.

719 ±1860 façade with straight cornice, four consoles, dormer, flat-topped roof.

709-713   715   717   719

456-454   458   460   462   464

Prinsengracht 454-464

454-456 M. twin neck-gables from ±1860 with segment-shaped frontons, and oval windows with sandstone sculptured frames (so called bull's-eyes); wooden street fronts (no. 454 dating ±1790).

458 M. ±1760 bell-gable; lower structure altered 20thC.

460 M. façade predominantly from ±1840 with straight cornice; flat-topped dormer from later period; frontal stoop; two handsome, ornate fanlights.

462 ±1880 façade; two window frames, straight cornice, ornamented dormer and flat-topped roof; ashlar street front.

464 newly built ±1875 with straight cornice and ornamented dormer.

721 M. façade with ±1750 elevated cornice and consoles from 19thC; *attiek* shutter in elevation.

723 M. 18thC façade, earlier neck-gable, with early 19thC straight cornice.

725 M. early 18thC façade, once a neck-gable; simple straight cornice, dormer and transverse roof from middle 19thC; door frame.

727 M. early 18thC façade, once a neck-gable; simple straight cornice, dormer and transverse roof from middle 19thC; stoop bench.

729 M. ±1840 cornice façade with wooden street front, two doors and two fanlights.

731 ±1860 façade with straight cornice and four consoles; dormer and unusual roof (something between saddle and flat roof); ornamentation below windows; ornamented anchors; door at street-level (compare no. 727).

466 M. predominantly 19thC façade with straight cornice, ornamented dormer.

468 M. ±1680 neck-gable with triangular fronton, two oval windows, one festoon and pilasters; lower structure altered ±1850.

470 M. predominantly ±1860 façade with straight cornice and ornamented dormer with hoist beam; stucco removed during 1969 restoration.

472 M. built ±1730 with handsome, elevated cornice, open *attiek* named 'Het Lam' (the lamb) rebuilt 1973, with two corner vases, crest.

474 newly built ±1880 with white stone, block straight cornice.

476 ±1860 façade with straight cornice and dormer; T-windows.

733 M. ±1655 warehouse witp spout-gable and sandstone volutes.
735 newly built with simple gable; shop front from ±1910.
737 newly built in 1913 with bay windows; in spite of pointed-gable, a flat roof; ornamentation in brick on façade.
739-741 newly built ±1880; handsome protruding dormer with small tower on top; relief above large doors.

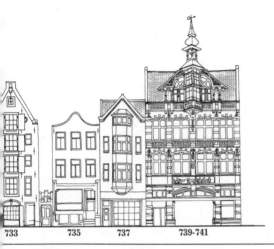

733   735   737   739-741

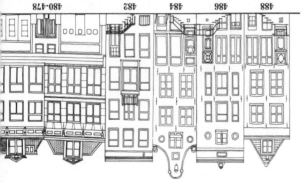

478-480   482   484   486   488

478-480 twin cornice façades dating ±1860; straight cornices with consoles; dormer with hoist beam; no. 480 has a 'contemporary' shop front.
482 ±1900 simple façade with straight cornice, wooden bay window; stoop older; Jugendstil iron work.
484 M. ±1700 house; earlier neck-gable; sobered top.
486 M. early 18thC house; once a neck-gable; rebuilt into cornice façade beginning 19thC; window in straight cornice.
488 M. early 18thC house; once neck-gable twin with no. 484; window grouping altered and straight cornice fitted beginning 19thC; old roof preserved; 18thC door frame.

743-745 M. early 18thC warehouse with spout-gable; no. 743 least altered; lower structure of no. 745 altered; some loft-doors missing.
747-749-751-753-755 M. five neck-gables built 1701 (see top of no. 747); nos. 747-749-751 rebuilt 1961 and are office fronts; at no. 747 stoop restored; no. 753 little changed; no. 755 has handsomely ornamented claw pieces; lower structure altered (entrance at street-level); compare no. 753.

743-745   747-749-751-753-755

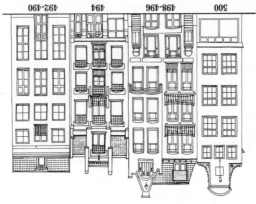

Leidsekruisstraat

492-490   494   498-496   500

Prinsengracht 490-500

490-492 M. early 19thC façade with straight cornice and transverse roof; door in unusual position (most are to the left or right); sash work.
494 newly built in ±1915; brick dormer with baluster, two crenelles and iron hoist beam; flat-topped roof.
496-498 newly built ±1911; no. 596 has spout-like gable, iron hoist beam; no. 498 has balcony, glazed bricks.
500 1936 reconstruction of late 17thC neck-gable; two floors added during reconstruction; stoop not rebuilt.

757 M. 17thC house (building height still 17thC); altered considerably; late 18thC bell-gable; lower structure rebuilt 20thC.
759 this 'modern' building from 1958 is not worthy of the canal on which it stands; too much glass, too little brick.

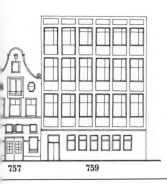

757   **759**

502   **506-504**   **508**

Prinsengracht 502-508

502 M. neck-gable from ±1720; top of gable removed; windows on 1st floor made smaller when street front was fitted in 20thC.
504-506 M. ±1860 façade with straight cornices, dormers with ornamentation and transverse roof; door at street-level (compare with no. 508); gable stone; door frame; stoop posts.
508 M. 18thC double house; altered drastically ±1860; straight cornice with two consoles and three dormers; door with balcony; frontal stoop; two window railings.

769 newly built in 1903; broad, over-scaled with stress on horizontal lines; replaces seven houses; semi-circular windows on 1st and 2nd floors; sandstone entrance.

769

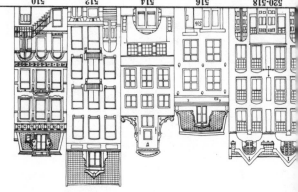

510   512   514   516   520-518

Prinsengracht 510-520

510 newly built in 1880 with straight cornice, richly ornamented dormer and almost flat roof; window frames; stoop older.

512 1891 façade with simple roof cornice, ornamented dormer and transverse roof.

514 M. late 17thC neck-gable with segment-shaped fronton, claw pieces from ±1720; lower structure altered 1922 when stoop was removed.

516 ±1865 façade with straight cornice, ornamented dormer with hoist beam.

518-520 newly built in 1906; brick dormers in shape of pointed-gable; semi-circular windows; three iron hoist beams.

771-773 ±1655 warehouses with spout-gables; remarkably well preserved; original construction; during 1976 restoration these almost 30 meters deep warehouses were rebuilt into offices; name of warehouses fitted on loft-doors.

775 M. ±1760 façade; earlier bell-gable; ±1840 top changed into straight cornice; door in two parts; pull bell.

777 late 19thC reconstruction of warehouse with spout-gable; middle windows once a loft-door.

771-773   775   777

Prinsengracht 522-532

522 M. 17thC house; building height, wooden street front altered later; predominantly 19thC façade with straight cornice; 2nd stoop below entrance.

524 M. ±1710 neck-gable; window grouping altered; hoist beam protrudes through round hole; 19thC door frame.

526-528 newly built in 1895 (see date stone) with straight cornices, ornamented dormers and flat roof; wooden bay window.

530 M. house built 1674 (see date stone); straight cornice, window grouping altered drastically ±1870; stoop bench.

532 M. ±1860 warehouse with unusual, interrupted cornice; stuccoed and painted. Most warehouses were built in 17thC (see no. 534).

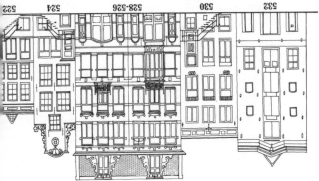

522   524   528-526   530   532

779 building with 1904 date stone; neo-Gothic style (see entrance with pointed arch); hipped roof.
783-785 newly built in 1914; at top an extended dormer in shape of bell-gable; gable stone from elsewhere; street front renovated in 1960's.
787 ±1860 simple cornice façade; 17thC building height; one large door (compare with no. 789).
789 ±1880 façade with straight cornice, dormer and mansarde roof; decorated window tops.

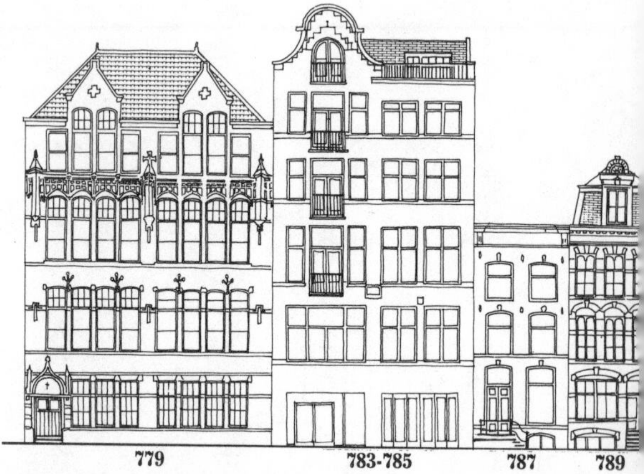
779
783-785
787
789

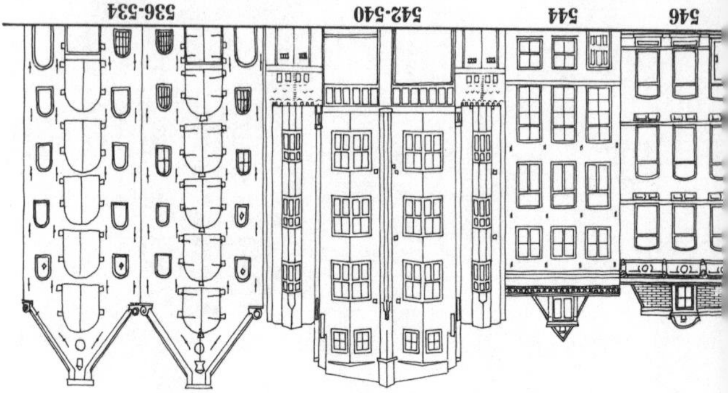
536-534
542-540
544
546

Prinsengracht 534-546

534-536 M. ±1670 remarkably preserved warehouse with spout-gable; semi-circular loft-doors; almost 30 meters deep (96 feet); original construction.
540-542 newly built in 1918 with Amsterdam School features: outward bending relief, ornamentation in brick, window accent on width, handsome wooden shop front.
544 M. ±1855 façade with straight cornice; dormer with hoist beam; old roof barely visible; entrance at street-level.
546 ±1875 façade with straight cornice, four consoles, sculptured heads; dormer with fronton and hoist beam; flat-topped roof; ornamentation below windows; new door.

791 M. early 18thC façade; top somewhat sobered beginning 19thC; sandstone volutes on sides of bell-gable; stoop bench.

793 M. ±1840 cornice façade with mansarde roof and dormer.

795 M. ±1790 façade with straight cornice, handsome Louis XVI consoles and transverse roof; dormer; window railings on 1st floor.

797 late 19thC façade with straight cornice, dormer with hoist beam; bay window.

799 M. 18thC façade drastically altered ±1860; sadlle roof gone; now almost flat roof; straight cornice fitted; ornamented anchors.

801 M. early 18thC house altered considerably ±1860; floor added, straight cornice; flat-topped roof.

803 M. house built ±1655; original construction; wooden street front.

791   **793**   **795**   **797**   **799**   **801**   **803**

548   **550**   **552**   **554**   **556**   **560-558**

Prinsengracht 548-560

548 early 18thC warehouse with spout-gable; little changed; warehouses often quite deep, this one almost 30 meters; Empire door on left.

550 M. neck-gable from ±1703 (see date stone) with triangular frontron; on 1st and 2nd floor, one wide and two narrow windows; 19thC fanlight.

552 M. 1698 neck-gable with frontron; top floor still has original window grouping (one large, two smaller windows).

554 newly built in ±1880 with ornamented straight cornice, festoons, and dormer with frontron and hoist beam; ornamentation below windows.

556 M. house built 1669 (see gable stone); predominantly 18thC façade; earlier bell-gable; changed 19thC into ogee-gable; fronton on top.*

558-560 M. twin cornice façades built ±1820; earlier twin neck-gables; no. 558 has transverse roof; stoop bench.

805-807 shop/home built ±1850; wooden street front with sculptured heads, somewhat altered later (large glass); straight cornice and almost flat roof.
(Nieuwe Spiegelstraat 67) newly built ±1885 with dormer and almost flat roof; wooden bay windows have been fitted at cut-away corner; original shop front.
809 M. ±1660 house with large transverse roof; original construction; façade renovated 18thC; wooden street front from same period; large door gone, now two doors with porch.
811 newly built 20thC in historical style with pilasters, hipped roof and sash work.

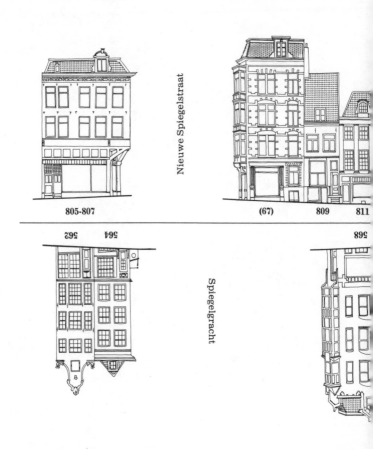

805-807   Nieuwe Spiegelstraat   (67)   809   811

562   564   Spiegelgracht   568

568 newly built 1908 with wooden bay windows on cut-away corner; brick dormer; glazed stones worked into façade.
564 M. 17thC corner house; earlier step-gable; façade predominantly 19thC with straight cornice and same size windows; one floor added; has always been a shop, like many corner houses; restored in 1973 by 'Aristoteles'; together with no. 562 and Spiegelgracht no. 2.
562 M. until 1971 a monstrosity from ±1920 stood here; present bell-gable was restored in 1973 by 'Aristoteles'. The top comes from a ±1755 house demolished in 1963 that used to be on the Nieuwendijk.

813 M. ±1655 house with large transverse roof; 'modernized' ±1735 when cornice and door frame were renovated.

815 M. ±1655 house, that once looked very much like no. 813; floor added in ±1840 resulting in loss of transverse roof.

821 newly built in 1905 (see stone) and topped with a gable, wooden bay window.

823 M. early 18thC neck-gable; rebuilt 1940's; stoop gone.

825 M. early 18thC house (see lower structure); altered beginning 19thC with straight cornice and small windows; door frame.

827 M. house built ±1660; original construction; neck-gable replaced with bell-like gable in 19thC.

829 M. neck-gable built ±1660; fronton with family arms; pull-bell.

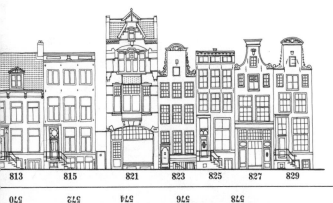

813   815   821   823   825   827   829

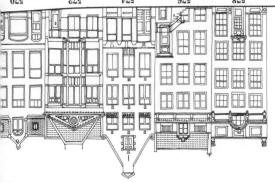

570   572   574   576   578

570 newly built ±1915 with straight roof cornice interrupted by brick dormer with semi-circular window; flat roof.

572 newly built ±1910 built in historical style; wooden bay window.

574 ±1880 façade with spout-gable; white stone above windows; window railings on 3rd floor; iron hoist beam.

576 M. predominantly 18thC façade with straight cornice; four consoles, dormer and 'open' *attiek* with two corner vases dating ±1730; lower structure altered ±1750; gable stone.

578 Primarily 18thC façade; elevated cornice with 4 ornamented consoles and closed *attiek* with 2 corner vases dating ±1730; lower part of façade changed in later period, ±1750; gable stone.

831 M. house built ±1660; once its neck-gable was part of group of six (see no. 833); house was drastically altered in ±1860 when straight cornice was fitted and stoop removed; door in two parts.

833-835-837-839 M four neck-gables built ±1660 with frontons and coat of arms; once a group of six that included nos. 829 and 831; two still have stoops; original construction.*

841 M. early 18thC building; earlier neck-gable; rebuilt ±1850 when straight cornice was fitted; street front altered; stoop gone; 18thC hoist beam.

831   833-835-837-839   841

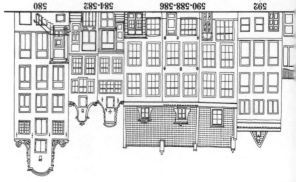

580   582-584   586-588-590   592

580 M. ±1730 neck-gable; door frame from same period; sash work altered on 1st and 2nd floor ±1870.

582-584 two houses built ±1665; original construction; compare building height with no. 580; no. 582 received new façade 100 years later (bell-gable with Louis XV ornamentation).

586-588-590 M. three houses built ±1665 under one large transverse roof; sash work altered in 19thC; original construction.

592 M. early 19thC façade with straight cornice, and sandstone street front; old roof just visible; little changed since.

843 M. early 18thC neck-gable; somewhat altered; ±1870 sash work changed on 1st and 2nd floors.

845 M. early 18thC façade, once a neck-gable, altered 19thC; stoop gone; now straight cornice.

847 M. neck-gable; earlier a twin of no. 845.

849 M. early 18thC neck-gable; once part of group of five neck-gables (nos. 847, 845, 843, 841); lower structure altered most.

851 M. handsome neck-gable with fronton built ±1730; house-number, name of house and occupants, fitted in same style.

853 M. house built ±1690; predominantly ±1850 façade; transverse roof.

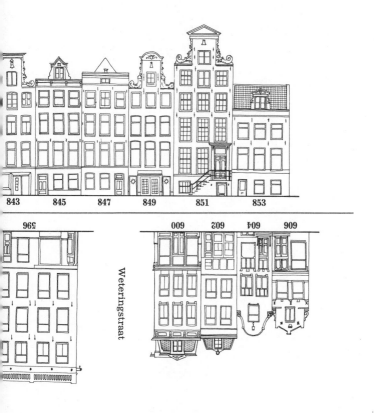

843   845   847   849   851   853

596   600   602   604   606

Weteringstraat

Prinsengracht 596-606

596 newly built 1909 (see commemorative stone) with brick ornamentation at top; brick balustrade instead of wood.

600 newly built ±1890 with straight cornice, dormer with hoist beam and flat-topped roof; ornamented shop front; not classified a monument, yet restored by 'Stadsherstel'.

602 newly built ±1890 with straight cornice, dormer and almost flat roof; street front altered 20thC; not classified a monument, yet restored by 'Stadsherstel'.

604 17thC house as identified by building height; renovated end of 19thC; bell-like gable with two sandstone volutes; frontal stoop.

606 17thC house as identified by building height; predominantly 19thC façade with neck-gable like top; wooden street front.

855·857·897·899 M. façade of the 'Deutzen' poor house built 1695; see date stone above entrance with proverb translated 'Agneta Deutz showed her love and faith as a comfort for the poor and as an exemple to the rich'; two marble cherubs flank this tablet; the chamber of the trustees is above the entrance; coat of arms on festoon; behind the wide façade is the 'hofje' (courtyard) with 20 2-room apartments; earlier only poor women of Reformed faith were permitted to reside here; little changed; original construction.*

855-857   897-899

Prinsengracht 608-612

608 newly built ±1910 with brick top and two pinnacles; adapted advertisement with wrought-iron signboard.

610 M. early 18thC neck-gable; rebuilt early 20thC when sandstone ornaments were added and window grouping was changed; stoop not rebuilt; two fan railings.

612 over-scaled architecture in height as well as width from 1920 replaces six old houses that were demolished in 1917 (compare with nos. 610 and 624).

901-903-905 M. three almost identical neck-gables from ±1705; window grouping unchanged on second floors; 18thC sash work; house numbers fitted in same style.

907 late 19thC façade (17thC building height) with straight cornice, mansarde roof, and dormer; door at street-level (compare with no. 905).

909 M. cornice façade from ±1850; windows become smaller towards top (after 1850 most buildings have same size windows on all floors).

911-915 newly built in 1911 with semi-circular windows on 1st and 2nd floor; four dormers and transverse roof; roof cornice supported by consoles.

901-903-905   907   909   911-915

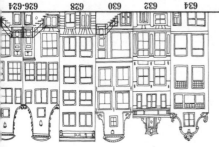

626-624   628   630   632   634

Prinsengracht 624-634

624-626 M. twin bell-gables built ±1665 with segment-shaped fronton; restored 1975; 2nd entrance below stoop; little changed; original construction.

628 M. façade from ±1865; floor added at this time; cornice façade; entrance souterrain level; ornamentation in window corners.

630 M. ±1680 neck-gable with segment-shaped frontom; window grouping altered 19thC; earlier a wooden street front; original construction.

632 M. 17thC house as identified by building height; façade predominantly ±1840; stuccoed; stoop missing; entrance moved to souterrain level.

634 M. 17thC house as identified by building height; top of bell-gable dating ±1760; window grouping altered 19thC; stoop gone.

917-919 newly built in 1926 with ornamented street front including four statues above door; transverse roof; same size windows on 1st and 2nd floor; beautiful door.

921 richly ornate façade from ±1890 with bay window, supported by two consoles; dormer; handsome entrance on street-level (compare no. 923).

923 M. ±1690 neck-gable with fronton and shell motif, two corner vases; window grouping altered ±1750 (unique ornamentation above windows).

925 M. ±1690 neck-gable with fronton and two corner vases; handsome window railing; 2nd entrance below stoop; original construction.

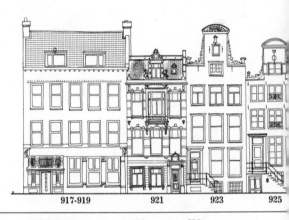

917-919   921   923   925

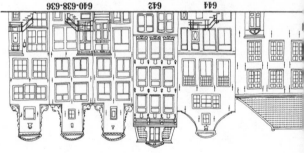

636-638-640   642   644

Prinsengracht 636-644a

636-638-640 M. neck-gable triplets built ±1680; no. 636 retains its large door and door frame (±1760) and an early 19thC window grouping; window grouping of nos. 638 and 640 altered 19thC; no. 640 has 19thC frontal stoop; original construction.

642 newly built in 1884 (see top) with straight cornice supported by four consoles; ornamented dormer and mansarde roof; ornamented anchors.

644 M. 17thC house (building height and wooden street front altered later); top sobered 19thC into bell-like gable; fronton reminiscent of late 17thC neck-gable; door in two parts.

644a see 644b.

927 newly built ±1870 with neo-Renaissance features including relieving arches.
(Vijzelstraat 68-78) most controversial modern building in old city; dating 1967; opened 1973; designed by Prof. Duintjer (see Keizersgracht 648); Vijzelgracht filled 1937 (almost an extension of Vijzelstraat).

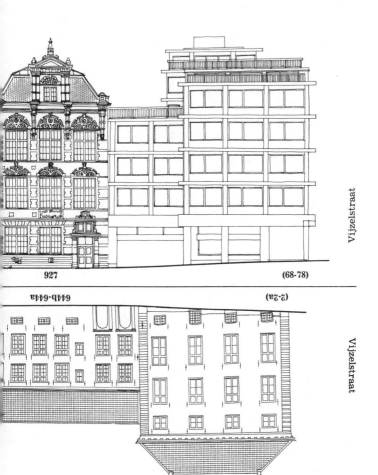

927   (68-78)

Vijzelstraat

644b-644a   (2-2a)

Vijzelstraat

large hipped roof; brick ornamentation in relief at corners (so-called built 1669-1671 from a design by Adrian Portsman; straight cornice and
(Vijzelgracht 2-2a) M. side façade of former 'Walenweeshuis' (orphanage);
(orphanage); straight cornice; large transverse roof; original construction.
644a-644b M. these houses were part of the late 17thC 'Walenweeshuis'

Prinsengracht 644a-644b

(Vijzelgracht 137) newly built ±1870; shop/home with cut-away corner and flat-topped roof; same size windows on all floors; dormer with hoist beam; so-called T-windows.

Vijzelstraat

(137)

Vijzelstraat

(I)

(Vijzelgracht I) M. late 17thC façade with 19thC shop front; gable stone. Nos. 1, 3 and 5 Vijzelgracht and nos. 646 and 648 Prinsengracht formed an important corner in the city but by the time of the 1960's what little was left was demolished, leaving an ugly gap; in 1971 the spectacular restoration by 'Stadsherstel' was realized; eleven homes reinforced the function of the inner city; the restored complex, designed by architect G. Prins, houses two shops and a bar/restaurant.

Prinsengracht

955 newly built in 1906 with Ionic pilasters, bay window and balcony; old stoop preserved; narrow door; two chimneys.

959-961 M. twin neck-gables built ±1691; original construction; rebuilt 18thC; gate added ±1870; gable stone from 1963.

963 M. ±1800 façade with straight cornice, dormer and hipped roof; sash work and door frame from same period; little else changed.

965 M. house built ±1690; altered considerably; straight cornice with two consoles fitted ±1800; also one floor added; frontal stoop.

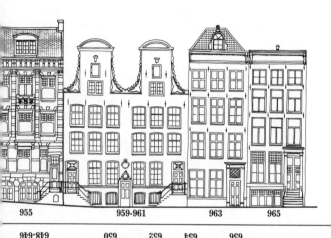

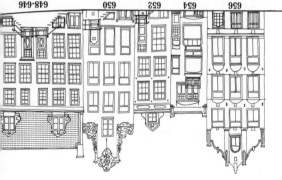

646-648 M. (see also Vijzelgracht no. 1) late 17thC houses underneath large transverse roof; door frame of no. 646 fitted in 19thC; ornamented dormer; straight roof cornice; fan railings.

650 M. neck-gable from 1725 (see top) with richly ornamented claw pieces.

632 M. 17thC house (see building height); façade from ±1860 with straight cornice and dormer with hoist beam; ornamented anchors.

634 newly built ±1915; wooden bay window and balcony; asymmetrical façade; 17thC building height.

656 M. ±1850 façade; remarkable top with unusual type of pilasters; stoop missing (compare with no. 658); entrance at souterrain level.

967 newly built ±1910 with bay windows, balcony; flat roof; stoop.
969 M. ±1690 neck-gable; fronton on top missing; middle window on 2nd floor once had loft-door.
971 M. ±1690 bell-gable with segment-shaped fronton and shell motif; rebuilt 19thC when floor was added (compare with no. 973).
973 M. ±1690 bell-gable with segment-shaped fronton and shell motif; rebuilt 19thC when stoop disappeared; original construction.
975 M. house built ±1690; altered considerably; predominantly 19thC façade with straight cornice and dormer; entrance at souterrain level.

967   969   971   973   975

658   660   662   664   666   668

658 M. late 17thC house under transverse roof ornamented; straight cornice fitted 18thC; original construction.
660 M. late 17thC house (see building height); predominantly ±1840 façade with straight cornice, two consoles and semi-circular dormer.
662 newly built in historical style 1937 (see commemorative stone); hoist beam; sash work; straight cornice.
664 late 17thC house window grouping altered 19thC when straight cornice was fitted; 2nd entrance below stoop; stoop bench.
666 M. early 19thC façade with straight cornice; windows become smaller towards top as in most old houses; stoop bench.
668 M. ±1680 bell-gable with fronton, shell motif and two corner vases; circular window below hoist beam; original construction.

977-979 M. twin bell-gables built ±1680 with segment-shaped frontons and clustered fruit motif on sides (both late 17thC features); no. 979 still has original window grouping; door frame from ±1750; no. 977 altered more, stoop gone; original construction.

981 late 19thC façade with ornamented street front; window frames; straight cornice with consoles and mansarde roof from ±1895; house does not lean like no. 979.

983-985 ±1680 large house under transverse roof (unusual for Amsterdam; most had saddle roofs; see nos. 977 and 979); altered ±1800 when straight cornice and door frame were fitted.

987 ±1860 façade with straight cornice and new ashlar street front; entrance at souterrain level; new door.

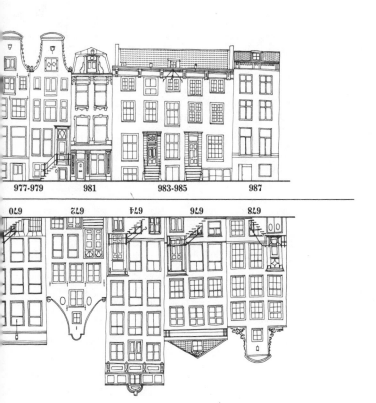

977-979   981   983-985   987

670   672   674   676   678

670 19thC cornice façade, rebuilt 1920's.

672 M. 17thC house (see building height); once a step-gable; sobered into bell-like gable in 19thC; frontal stoop.

674 M. ±1730 façade with elevated cornice, *attiek* shutter; middle window on top floor once had loft-doors.

676 M. late 17thC house; altered considerably; upper part and window grouping altered ±1840 when straight cornice was fitted.

678 M. ±1675 neck-gable with segment-shaped fronton; hardly altered; handsome stoop railing; stoop bench; original construction.

989 late 19thC façade with 'bent' cornice and three pairs of consoles.
991 M. ±1680 bell-gable with segment-shaped fronton; little else changed.
993 M. late 17thC house (building height); façade from ±100 years later
(compare with no. 991); bell-gable with Louis XV ornamentation.
995 predominantly 19thC façade; 17thC building height; top altered ±1910
when fronton was fitted.
997 façade from ±1750, once a bell-gable; floor added and finished with
straight cornice 19thC; door frame 18thC.
999 M. ±1680 warehouse with spout-gable; most warehouses 17thC were
built with spout-gables.

Prinsengracht 680-692

680 M. ±1865 cornice façade with straight cornice and consoles; semi-
circular dormer; windows somewhat arched (compare with no. 682).
682 ±1750 façade with unusual wooden cornice, *attiek* shutter within; late
18thC door frame.
684 M. ±1865 cornice façade with mansarde roof; same size windows.
686 M. late 17thC façade, once a genuine bell-gable; sobered into bell-like
gable (straight cornice on top) in 19thC; stoop gone.
688 newly built in 1930 with Amsterdam School features.
690 M. ±1865 façade with straight cornice; three consoles with sculptured
lion heads and dormer; saddle roof (compare with no. 688).
692 M. restored late 17thC bell-gable with fronton and clustered fruit.

1001-1003-1005-1007-1009 M. once a group of five neck-gables dating from ±1680; no. 1003 is the most altered, a straight cornice was fitted ±1800, its slightly altered roof is just visible; the other four preserved their frontons and late 17thC claw pieces; five stoops, some with stoop benches; 2nd entrance below stoops; original construction.

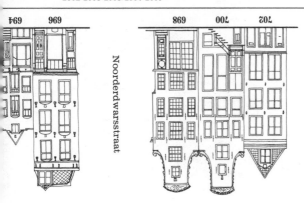

1001-1003-1005-1007-1009

Noorderdwarsstraat

Prinsengracht 694-702

694 ±1900 façade with Jugendstil ornaments (see the two doors); frontal stoop; 17thC building height remains unchanged.

696 corner house with straight cornice, dormer and flat-topped roof from 1900 (see commemorative stone).

698 M. ±1680 bell-gable with fronton and shell motif; wooden street front altered later; original construction, little else changed.

700 M. ±1680 bell-gable with fronton; upper window grouping (two narrow windows next to large one) dating from same period; clustered fruit motif.

702 M. ±1850 façade with straight cornice, dormer and saddle roof; ornamented anchors; two doors.

1011-1013-1015-1017 complex built ±1860; the idea of individual homes does not exist here; broad over-scaling; 1st floor center windows accentuated; four dormers with hoist beam; frontal stoops; nos. 1011 and 1017 have mansarde roofs.

1011-1013-1015-1017

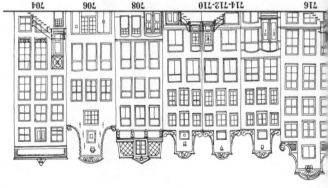

716   **714-712-710**   **708**   **706**   **704**

704 M. early 17thC façade with straight cornice; saddle roof just visible; sash work; door and window railing from ±1800.

706 M. ±1860 bell-gable with segment-shaped fronton and shell motif; façade and window grouping altered 19thC; wooden street front.

708 ±1890 façade with straight cornice and four consoles; dormer with hoist beam and almost flat roof; entrance at street-level (compare no. 710).

710-712-714 M. ±1730 neck-gable triplets; upper window grouping with three windows side-by-side, dating from same period; lower structure altered 19thC; at no. 714's large door removed in 19thC.

716 M. large neck-gable with unusual claw pieces from ±1735.

1019-1019a twin cornice façades from 1883 (see commemorative stone) with dormers and flat-topped roof; same size windows all floors (compare with no. 1021); door frame witp Ionic pilasters.
1021 M. house built ±1680, once a bell-gable; straight cornice and door frame early 19thC; 2nd entrance below stoop.
1023 M. cornice façade; once a bell-gable ±1745; floor added after 1800.
1025 M. ±1740 bell-gable with unique top; iron rod by hoist beam to ease transport of goods.

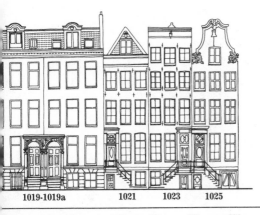

| 1019-1019a | 1021 | 1023 | 1025 |

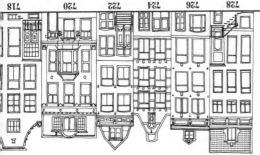

718 M. late 17thC bell-gable, rebuilt 19thC; fronton replaced with simple, straight cornice; doors restored.
720 newly built ±1910 with straight cornice, dormer and almost flat roof.
722 façade with ornate straight cornice and dormer; frontal stoop from ±1870; ornamented ashlar street front.
724 newly built in shape of spout-gable from 1880; ornamented façade.
726 façade with straight cornice and three consoles; dormer with hoist beam; key stone above arched windows; ornamented ashlar street front.
728 M. 18thC house under transverse roof with straight cornice and door frame; stoop bench; 2nd below stoop.

1029-1031 M. complex built ±1680 under large hipped roof; well preserved warehouse runs through to Kerkstraat (backside); lower structure still has cross-frames windows which once had leaded glass); lower structure on right altered; original construction.

1035 M. ±1730 warehouse with spout-gable; hardly altered; many warehouses like this were built on the Prinsengracht.

1037-1039-1041 M. neck-gable triplets built ±1710 with fronton; no. 1037 still has original window grouping (compare with no. 1039) and stoop; in 1976 the fronton was restored at no. 1041.

1029-1031   1035   1037-1039

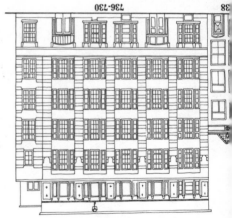

730-736 four houses were demolished for this 'modern' building from 1929; over-scaling in width and depth; variations in brick color; on front red and yellow.

738 M. predominantly ±1840 façade; straight, ornate, cornice with ornamented, ashlar street front from same period.

1041 M. see nos. 1037 and 1039.

1043 M. late 17thC façade, once a neck-gable; top altered into straight cornice with consoles and ornamented dormer ±1850; ornamented anchors.

1045 M. ±1740 neck-gable with vase at top; late 18thC sash work; stoop bench; little else changed.

1047 M. ±1750 façade, 3 meters wide, with wooden street front; sobered in 19thC; houses close to corners usually not very deep, this one ±3 meters (28 feet) deep, and usually have a blind backwall (no windows); frontal stoop.

(Reguliersgracht 92) M. shop/home from ±1675; original construction; saddle roof just visible from side; top of house supported by an iron rod; fine long pothouse; sculptured top at corner above wooden street front; façade leans slightly.

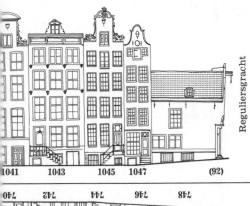

740 M. late 17thC house, once a genuine bell-gable; top sobered into bell-like gable 19thC; triangular fronton.

742 ±1880 tall house with straight cornice, interrupted by ornamented dormer; stoop older; 2nd entrance below stoop.

744 M. earlier a neck-gable, now a cornice façade; altered into straight cornice with flat roof 19thC; stoop bench.

746 M. ±1680 bell-gable with segment-shaped fronton; once a wooden street front; top sobered in 19thC; 18thC window grouping altered.

748 newly built ±1910 with asymmetrical façade.

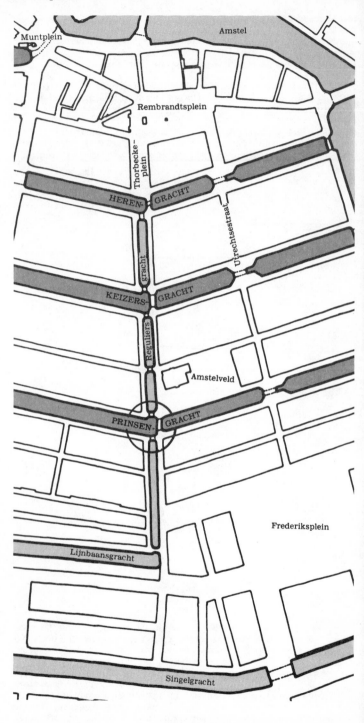

Amstelkerk built 1670, probably from design by Daniël Stalpaert; intended as wooden 'sermon barn' to serve as temporary church; a permanent church was to be constructed on the Amstelveld by that never occured; somewhat altered in 1892 by W. Springer.

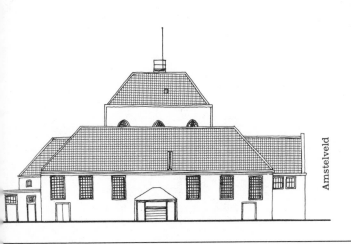

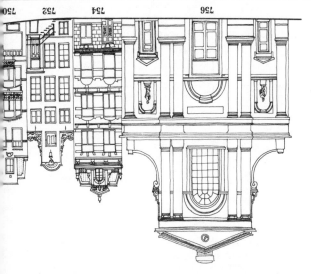

Prinsengracht 750-756

750 newly built in 1909 with two balconies and brick dormer.
752 M. ±1725 neck-gable with fronton and shell motif.
734 M. newly built ±1890 with straight cornice and ornamented dormer; recently classified a monument.
756 M. neo-Classic building from 1857 designed by Th. Molkenboer; named 'De Duif' (the pigeon).

Amstelveld

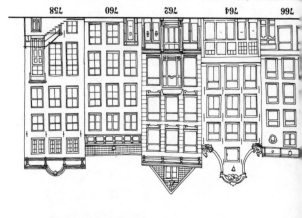

738 760 762 764 766

Prinsengracht 758-766

758 M. predominantly ±1750 façade with elevated cornice and ornamented consoles; door frame from same period; 2nd entrance below stoop.
760 M. ±1800 façade with straight cornice and triglyphs; transverse roof; door at street-level (compare with no. 758); little else changed.
762 M. ±1870 façade with straight cornice and four ornamented consoles; bay window.
764 M. 1770 bell-gable (see top ornaments); lower structure altered drastically 20thC when stoop was removed; wooden shop front.
766 M. predominantly 19thC façade with straight cornice and consoles; two circular windows next to *attiek* shutter; ashlar street front.

Amstelveld

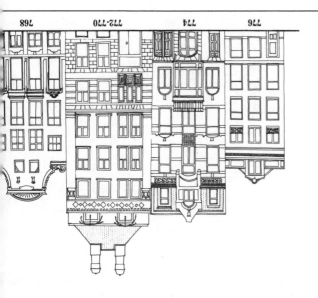

768   772-770   774   776

Prinsengracht 768-776

768 M. 4 window wide bell-gable from ±1740; most old houses are 2-3
windows wide; two hoist beams; window frames from ±1870.
770-772 newly built in 1922 with brick and stone ornamentation.
774 newly built ±1910; wooden bay window.
776 M. predominantly ±1870 façade; straight cornice.

Prinsengracht 778-788

778 M. ±1870 unusual ashlar façade with straight cornice and 'closed' *attiek*; once the twin of no. 776.

780 M. 1975 reconstruction of 18thC bell-gable; top sobered 19thC; two fan railings.

782 newly built in the 1970's; frontal stoop.

784-786 newly built in the 1950's with 4 window wide façade, straight cornice, two hoist beams and hipped roof; sash work.

788 newly built ±1885 with straight cornice, three consoles, dormer and almost flat roof; lower structure altered 1970's.

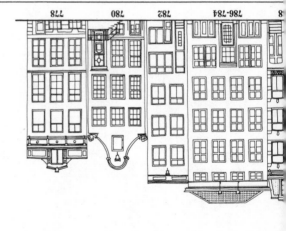

Amstelveld

1047a · **(Amstelveld 21)** complex built ±1860 underneath hipped roof with two chimneys; straight cornice; dormer with hoist beam; door at street-level (compare with no. 1049).
1049 lower part is the oldest (18thC); bay windows fitted ±1900; stuccoed façade; flat-topped roof; frontal stoop; straight cornice interrupted by dormer with hoist beam.

Amstelveld

(21)   1047a   1049

790   792   794   796   798   800

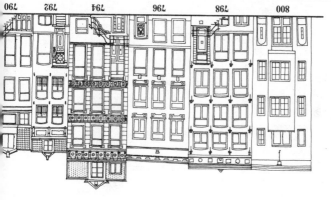

Prinsengracht 790-800

790 M. late 17thC house with straight cornice and transverse roof, brick *attiek*; original construction; altered and stuccoed in 19thC.
792 M. earlier a house with transverse roof (see no. 790); façade predominantly ±1870 with straight cornice and consoles; frontal stoop.
794 M. 18thC house (see stoop); façade drastically altered 19thC.
796 M. predominantly ±1860 façade, stuccoed and ornamented below windows; straight cornice; stoop gone (compare with no. 794).
798 M. 18thC house (door frame); much altered 19thC.
800 newly built 1940 in historical style with straight cornice at the hoist beam; brick bay windows.

1051 M. ±1760 bell-gable with handsome Louis XV ornamentation on top (asymmetrical); window on 1st floor enlarged; frontal stoop.
1053 M. ±1740 façade, earlier a neck-gable; top altered into bell-gable 19thC; fronton on top.
1055 newly built ±1890 with bay windows and ornamented shop front.
1055a - (Utrechtsestraat 102) shop/home built 1890 (see commemorative stone); brick bay windows with ornamentations; cut-away corner with small tower.

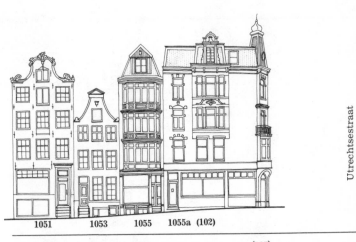

1051 1053 1055 1055a (102)

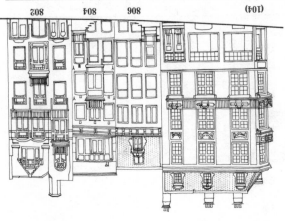

802 804 806 (104)

802 newly built ±1905; asymmetrical façade; remarkably big small tower; unusual sash work; Jugendstil elements (see doors).
804 once a twin with no. 806 (see); windows enlarged at end of 19thC; wooden bay window and large dormer.
806 M. house built ±1725 with ornate straight cornice; new door.
(Utrechtsestraat 104) shop/home from ±1915 with historical elements including festoons, straight roof cornice, three dormers and three chimneys.

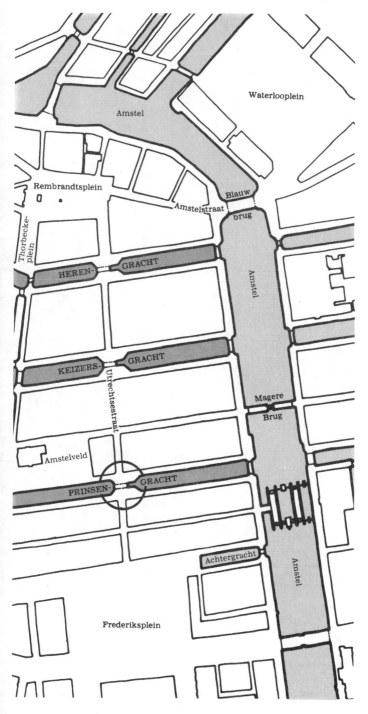

1055b · (Utrechtsestraat 117) shop/home built 1918; cut-away corner; same size windows on all floors; flat roof.
1057 newly built ±1915 with bay window; 17thC building height retained; dormer with hoist beam.

Utrechtsestraat

(117)   1055b   1057

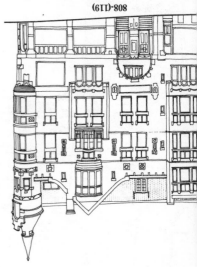

808·(119)

Utrechtsestraat

intersection.
Corners are often rebuilt. Note dates for all 4 corner houses at this
corner; richly ornamented façade (tiled tableau).
808 · (Utrechtsestraat 119) shop/home built 1906 with circular tower at

1059 ±1885 cornice façade with relieving arches and tiles.
1061 M. ±1690 neck-gable; rebuilt; fronton gone; lower structure altered end 19thC; original construction.
1063 unusual façade from ±1870; frontal stoop; ornamented anchors.
1065 ±1885 façade with relieving arches; a kind of cross-breed between a spout- and step-gable; ornamented anchors and iron hoist beam.
1067 ±1860 façade with natural stone above windows; dormers; flat roof.
1075 M. ±1690 warehouse with spout-gable; original construction; top sobered later; *pui* beam; property of 'Stadsherstel'.

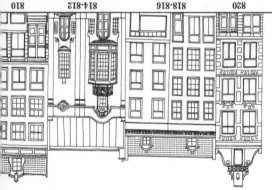

1059   1061   1063   1065   1067   1075

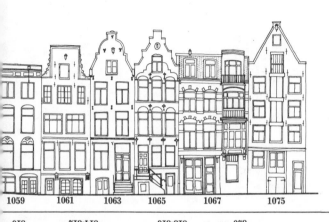

810   814-812   818-816   820

Prinsengracht 810-820

810 M. ±1800 façade with straight cornice, ornamented dormer and transverse roof; wooden street front; frontal stoop.
812-814 two houses once stood here; now church built ±1910 with bay window, balcony and frontal stoop.
816-818 early 19thC cornice façade twins under one large transverse roof; semi-circular dormers; at no. 816 window grouping altered end 19thC; shop front 20thC.
820 newly built ±1885 with ornamented top; façade ornaments in white stone (compare with no. 818).

1077 newly built ±1905 with Jugendstil-like ornaments (top).
1079 M. 18thC house with transverse roof and dormer with hoist beam;
19thC door frame; straight cornice renovated 19thC; handsome fanlight.
1081 M. early 18thC neck-gable with ornamented fronton; probably original
construction; hardly altered.
1083 M. lower structure is early 18thC; door frame from same period; floor
added ±1900, also flat roof.
1085-1087 M. bell-gable twins from ±1740; earlier had ornaments above
hoist beam; no. 1087 least altered.

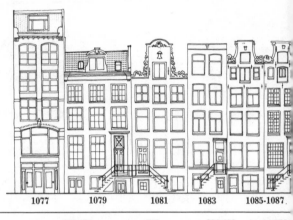

1077 1079 1081 1083 1085-1087

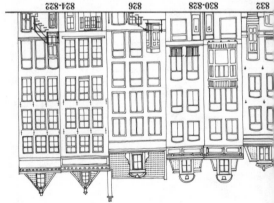

832 newly built ±1890 with straight cornice, dormer, flat-topped roof.
and flat-topped roof; at no. 830 bay window fitted 1920's.
828-830 late 19thC cornice façade twins with dormer, hoist beam, fronton
door.
dormer; stoop older; window frames with round corners; earlier only one
826 M. predominantly ±1870 façade with straight cornice and ornamented
822 preserved its stoop and handsome door.
822-824 M. 18thC houses; floor added and straight cornice fitted 19thC; no.

1089-1091-1093-1095 M. group of four neck-gables from ±1770; oval windows with sculptured, sandstone frames; hardly altered; no. 1095 without fronton; in 1904 (see gable stone, top) saddle roofs of nos. 1089 and 1091 since removed, note joining constructions above.

1097 late 19thC cornice façade; ornamentation in brick and stone on façade; stoop older.

1099 M. rare bell-gable with handsome crest from ±1745; usually bell-gables have ornamentan running down both sides of top; 3rd floor has 'leefluiken' (loft-doors with glass); little changed.

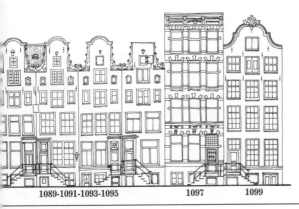

1089-1091-1093-1095   1097   1099

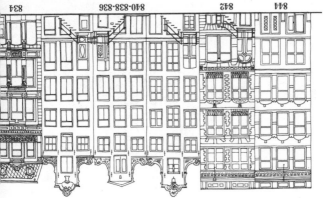

834   836-838-840   842   844

Prinsengracht 834-844

834 ±1890 unusual façade with pilasters, window frames and two oval windows, ornamented frames.

836-838-840 M. neck-gable triplets from ±1740; no. 838 lost its Louis XV style crest; no. 836 preserved its large door and doorway lintel from ±1800; 2nd entrance below stoops.

842 newly built ±1910 with straight cornice and 'closed', *attiek*; two sculptured girls' heads and two sculptured lion heads; stoop older.

844 newly built ±1910 with straight cornice and 'closed', *attiek*; lowest part altered later when cross-frame windows were fitted.

1101 M. ±1695 house with transverse roof; original construction; unusual asymmetrical window grouping; late 19thC straight cornice.
1103 once identical to no. 1101; façade renewed ±1890; richly ornamented (compare simple façade of no. 1101).
1105 M. ±1690 bell-gable with triangular windows next to attic shutter; top sobered 19thC (ornaments removed).
1107 M. 18thC façade, once neck-gable top; renovated 19thC; now ogee-gable (S-curved profile) with straight cornice on top; only 20 ogee-gables in Amsterdam.
1109 ±1850 façade with hipped roof, once a coach house.

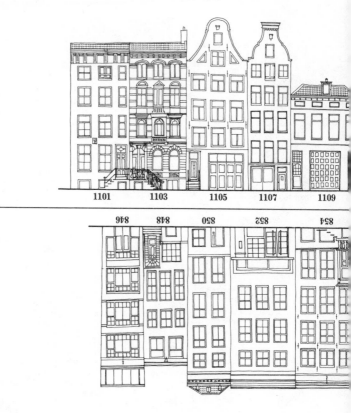

1101	1103	1105	1107	1109
846	848	850	852	854

846 newly built ±1915 with three large window units and straight cornice with iron hoist beam; flat roof; does not lean like no. 848.
848 M. house built 1667; original construction; much altered; middle part 18thC; floor added end 19thC and straight cornice fitted; house number in same style.
850 M. ±1800 façade with straight cornice; two hoist beams and hipped roof; windows become smaller towards top as in most houses.
852 early 19thC cornice façade; lower structure altered 1928.
854 M. 18thC house, once a bell-gable; 'modernized' ±1860 into cornice façade; door frame with two consoles from same period.

1111 M. early 18thC house, once a warehouse with spout-gable; semi-circular loft-door below hoist beam; street front altered 20thC.

1113 predominantly ±1860 façade with straight cornice interrupted by dormer; stoop older; two smaller doors replace large single door.

1115-1117 M. twin neck-gables from ±1730; stoops removed; earlier doors changed into windows; entrance moved to souterrain.

1119 newly built ±1915 spout-like gable with bay window and high, glass street front; house does not lean like nos. 1123 and 1117.

1123 M. late 18thC bell-gable; top sobered 19thC; handsome door frame with ±1790 Louis XVI ornaments; glass door.

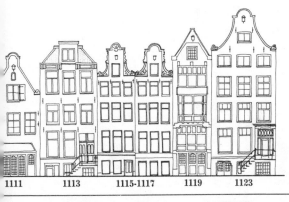

1111   **1113**   **1115-1117**   **1119**   **1123**

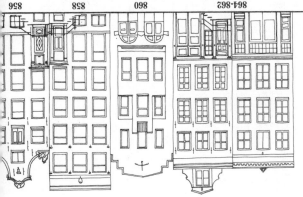

856   **858**   **860**   **862-864**

856 M. ±1760 bell-gable; in this period most bell-gables built; door frame; cushion door and doorway lintel from ±1800; house number above doorway lintel; little else changed.

858 M. 18thC house, once twin with no. 856; floor added and straight cornice fitted in 19thC; late 18thC door frame.

860 newly built in the 1920's with ornamentation in brick at top; brick bay window (Amsterdam School).

862-864 M. cornice façade twins from early 19thC; no. 864 altered least, its old roof preserved; wooden street front from same period; once a coach house; frontal stoop.

1125-1127 ±1880 façade with much stone work; two dormers; same size windows on all floors (compare with no. 1123).

1129 ±1910 façade with bay windows and balcony; stoop older; iron hoist beam not centered.

1131 M. house built ±1690; wooden street front still present in altered form; saddle roof removed late 19thC when straight cornice and flat roof were fitted; two early 19thC doors.

(Amstel 284) M. side façade of a house dating 1769 (see gable stone at front); two oval windows above the low door with sculptured, sandstone frames (bull's-eyes); ornamented dormer with loft-shutters; pothouse; 2nd entrance below stoop.

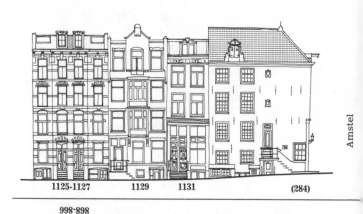

| 1125-1127 | 1129 | 1131 | (284) | Amstel |

866-868 newly built in 1920 with Amsterdam School features (e.g. decorations in brick at top); iron hoist beam.

870 demolished 1963.
872 demolished 1963.
874 demolished 1945.
876 demolished 1963.
878 demolished 1963.
880 demolished 1963 with final result, the notorious gap by the Amstel. This kind of development is unusual along the canals fortunately.

998-898

Amstel

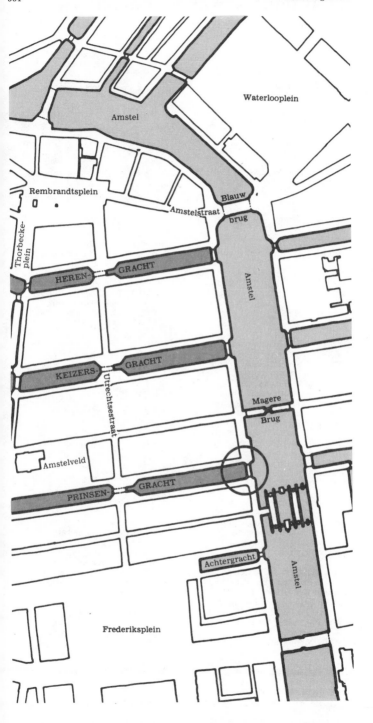

A few houses in greater detail

houses, the windows grow smaller towards the top. Instead of being painted the usual canal-green, the doors have been varnished. The second entrance underneath the stoop was once the servants' entrance. The sash work on no. 66 is early 19th century. Both houses have had very little alteration.

Singel 2-2a M.   Most step-gables in Amsterdam were built between ± 1600 and ± 1665. This double house is one of the widest and oldest in the city, built in 1603 as a combination of home and warehouse. The gable stone, between the two loft-doors, represents a wheel barrow due to the fact that the name of one of the first occupants' was called Cruywagen (wheel barrow). In the 19th century the windows were enlarged and the wooden street front (the *pui)* was altered. During a restoration in the 1950's, the wooden street front, the window-grouping and the sash work were all repaired. Relieving arches were built above the windows and the hoist beam was roofed over.

Singel 66-68 M.   Their height identifies these twins as typical 18th century houses. The brick façades have elevated cornices that include Louis XV ornaments from 1760. Below the hoist beam, an *attiek* shutter is incorporated into the cornice and the small windows on either side of the loft-doors admit light into the *attiek.* The middle windows on the second and third floors of no. 68 once had loft-shutters and these windows are somewhat taller for easier handling of goods. As in most old Amsterdam

Singel 104-106 M.   For 18th century houses, these twin bell-gables are a bit too high. Both of these 3 window wide merchants' houses date from ± 1740. The handsome tops have ornamentation around the hoist beam and vases above. The top floors were once used for storage. The windows grow smaller towards the top as in most old houses. No. 106 has a 19th century fanlight and there is a second entrance underneath the stoop. Little else was changed on these houses.

Singel 140-142 M.   These twin step-gables with roll ornaments called 'De Dolphijn' (the dolphin),

date from ± 1605 and were designed by Hendrick de Keyser, one of the 17th century's best known architects who also designed the Westerkerk and the Zuiderkerk. The twin on the right, rebuilt into a cornice façade in the 19th century, was restored to its original form in 1967.

Before the restoration

Reconstruction became possible when the original designs were found. The original

cross-frame windows with shutters, however, were not reconstructed. At the front of the house on the red escutcheon, one can read that Frans Banningh, the central figure in Rembrandt's famous 'Nightwatch', lived here between 1605 and 1655.

Singel 288 M. Most old Amsterdam façades are brick, but this one is made of sandstone. The top has been finished with a sculptured, elevated cornice. The ornaments, in Louis XV style, date from ± 1755, the construction period. The shamrock-shaped *attiek* shutter is surrounded by branch-shaped ornaments. Below the top ornament, called the crest, is the hoist beam which has been worked into a sculptured dolphin's head. The stoop is ornamented with three Louis XIV bottle-shaped balusters and a small stoop bench. This 3 window wide canal house was restored in 1963 and is now part of the Amster Center hotel.

Singel 377-379 These twin neck-gables were built in 1730. The dates are to be found just under the sandstone claw pieces and vases. The house on the left retains its original window grouping (one wide and two narrow) and is altered the least. The window grouping at no. 379, as well as the shop fronts, were altered in the 19th century. Probably both have always been shop fronts. The low door in the middle is the entrance to the living quarters above. Both houses were restored in 1976. The house number and the

Before the restoration

form. Today, this one-time merchant's home has been divided into flats.

Singel 432 M. This neck-gable, with a hoist beam that sticks out through a cartouche, dates from the beginning of the 18th century when most neck-gables were built. The claw pieces that fill the in-steps are made of sandstone. The small oval windows with sculptured, sandstone frames are called 'bull's-eyes'. Until recently this building was used as a warehouse. Around 1900 a shop front was fitted which did not harmonize with the rest of the façade (horizontal over-scaling) and further, was once combined with no. 430. During the 1973 restoration, the lower structure was reconstructed in period style.

occupant's name of no. 377 are in period style and the house still has two pull bells.

Singel 430 M. This house, with its straight cornice and two consoles, is typical of many houses built at the end of the 18th century when the era of cornice façades began. The hipped roof dates from ± 1795, the time of construction. The middle window on the top floors once had a loft-door. Around 1900 the lower structure was altered into a shop front together with no. 432, but they did not harmonize with their surroundings. In 1973 however, the lower structure and stoop were restored to their original

Singel 460 M. This neck-gable from 1662 (see date-stone) was built from a design by Philip Vingboons (1607-1678). Together

with his brother Justus, this architect built many houses in the 17th century especially in Amsterdam. The front is ornamented with festoons and two transversely fitted oval windows framed in sculptured sandstone. The hoist beam sticks out through a cartouche. There was once a sculptured lamb on the segment-shaped fronton and the claw pieces are finished with cluster ornaments. The middle windows on the top floors once had loft-doors. Little else was altered on this merchant's house, although the cross-frame windows and the stoop have since disappeared. The door has been 'sunk' to street level. The house has an Empire concert-hall inside from ± 1830 when the older gable stone 'Nurenberg' was changed to read 'Odeon'.

Herengracht 81 M. This part of the canal dates from 1585. This house was built in 1590 and acquired its step-gable in ± 1620. The house itself has already been restored twice in the 20th century. It was 'consolidated' in the 1950's and the lower part was reconstructed in 1975, the 'Monument Year'. At reconstruction, the window on the left was replaced by the present door and the stoop rebuilt. The 17th century cross-frame windows with lower shutters were refitted. Relieving arches were built into the façade above the windows. The upper or lower part of the two-piece door can be opened separately.

There is a small stoop bench on the left side of the door.

Herengracht 281-283 M. These so-called *elevated* neck-gables are unusual. Next to each larger claw piece is a small 'wing-piece'. Elevated neck-gables always date from the 17th century and from ± 1650. The houses are a bit over six meters wide. The top is ornamented with a segment-shaped fronton and a festoon is fitted around the hoist beam. No. 283 has oval windows with sculptured, sandstone frames (bull's eyes). The street front of no. 281 was altered in the 18th century and the house was restored in 1957. The 3 window wide brick façade of no. 283 was hardly altered. Doors and windows are more often subject to change and here they were renovated in the 19th century.

Herengracht 361-363-365-367-369 M. This row of houses clearly shows several types of gables. No. 361 is the oldest, dating from ± 1655 and is called 'De Sonnenberg' (see gable stone). Drastic alterations in the 18th and 19th centuries included a cornice façade and left little of the original step-gable. 'Stadsherstel' bought the house in 1959 for ƒ 7000 and reconstructed the original façade in 1962 with G. Prins as the architect. The plaque, from 'Stadsherstel' (right of the door), was fitted after the restoration. No. 363 is the most common type of façade, a cornice. Like this one, most cornice façades date from the 19th century. The house on the backside however, is older. The building height and the wooden street front are reminiscent of the 17th century

361   363   365   367   369

house that once stood here. The restoration was completed in 1964.

No. 365: although the building height and street front are typical of the 17th century, this small bell-gable actually dates from ± 1760 when most bell-gables were built. This type was no longer built after 1790. The upper window groupings are from a 19th century alteration and the *attiek* shutter now has glass.

No. 367: this tall, narrow house has a bell-gable dating from ± 1750. Its wooden street front was replaced in the 18th century and the house itself was restored in 1971. The house number and the occupant's name are in period style.

No. 369: concerning its height, this is a typical 18th century house. The neck-gable with sandstone claw pieces in Louis XIV style dates from ± 1735. Although the street front was altered in the 19th century, this house has probably always been a combination of shop and home. There is still a pothouse on the side.

Herengracht 427-429 M. These early 18th century twin neck-gables have ornaments above the hoist beams. The claw pieces

are made of sandstone. The *attiek* shutters were not altered but the windows below were once loft-doors. These twins once had one wide and two narrow windows but the window grouping was probably altered at the end of the 18th century. This conclusion was made from drawings of these houses found in the 'Grachtenboek' (canal book) by Caspar Philips written in ± 1770. Like most old Amsterdam houses, these twins

have a single stoop. The reason for this was that the ground-water level was so high (0,40 meters) that the souterrain or the cellar had to be on a higher level than in most cities. Because of this high cellar level, the first floor is not at street-level: therefore the stoop. Both houses were restored in 1966.

Herengracht 476 M. This house, one of the most beautiful double houses on the Herengracht, was built in ± 1740. Its 17th century character is preserved in the sandstone, Corinthian pilasters and festoons in fruit motif. The house has a sculptured *attiek* in the form of a balustrade with coat of arms, two reliefs with merchants' goods, the mace of Mercury, a globe, Jacob's staff, ornate vases and a sculptured eagle. The double stoop was rebuilt during the restoration of 1938. It had been removed during a late 18th century reconstruction. The fanlight has a lantern. In addition to a handsome interior, the house has an early 18th century garden house. The house itself is one of the show-pieces of 'Hendrick de Keyser' which received this 5 window wide classic as a gift in 1953.

Herengracht 539 M. This kind of house one sees primarily on the Herengracht. Mostly they are 5 windows wide and, like this one, the façade is made of sandstone. The straight cornice with triglyphs, ornate consoles, small windows and sculptured fish are all also made of sandstone. An *attiek* is fitted on top of the cornice in the form of a balustrade and in its center is a coat of arms with a bust and two statues. Along the sides are the so-called corner lisenas in slight relief. There is a second entrance underneath the stoop which was once a servants' entrance. The balcony is supported by two sculptured figures of women. Balconies are a rarity on the canals. The present stoop, the fanlight and the balcony railing date from ± 1830. This palace was restored in the early 1960's and ceiling paintings from the original construction period were found during the restoration. The foundation was renovated as well.

Keizersgracht 62-64 M. As identified by its height, no. 62 is a typical 17th century house. This neck-gable with segment-shaped fronton and two corner vases was built around 1660. Fruit motifs have been worked into the claw pieces and the brick façade is ornamented with four pilasters. The house is about 5.50 meters wide. Building height identifies no. 64 as a typically 18th century house, 5.50 meters wide, with a neck-gable richly ornamented top that includes two sculptured figures of children. It dates from 1738. The top ornamentation is executed in Louis XIV style. The middle windows on the three top floors

were once loft-doors. The larger part of the façade has been reconstructed, possibly by making use of the 'Grachtenboek' (Canal Book) by Caspar Philips, who made drawings of all the houses on the Herengracht and the Keizersgracht in the 18th century. 'Stadsherstel' bought these houses in 1962 and they became the largest and most expensive restoration in its history. It was completed in 1973 and afterwards, as usual, the 'Stadsherstel' plaques with the three crosses of Amsterdam fitted on the houses.

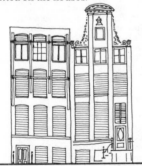

Before the restoration

The buildings, as well as the monumental garden house that comes from elsewhere but was rebuilt on this site, accommodate the 'Muzieklyceum' (school of music). The interiors of both buildings are also worth seeing.

Keizersgracht 194-196 M. No. 194 has a sandstone, elevated cornice in the form of a bell and dates from ± 1760. The top is ornamented with an

asymmetrical crest in Louis XIV style and the hoist beam is fitted above the loft-door. Most old houses have similar hoist beams. The stoop railing dates from the beginning of the 19th century. At no. 196 the brick façade is 4.95 meters wide and has a richly ornamented cornice in the form of a bell. The two corner vases as well as the door date from ± 1730, the original construction period. The sash work has been altered but little else was changed on the rest of the façade. The house still has a pull bell.

Keizersgracht 244-246 M. These two identical façades have cornices and the 5.50 meter wide houses date from ± 1750. The tops have been ornamented with an 'open' *attiek* in the form of a balustrade. An iron pole was fitted on the hoist beam for easier handling of goods and an ornate vase was fixed above. The cornice with two consoles is arched to accommodate the loft-door (now with glass) which is surrounded by ornaments in Louis XIV style. The original sash work was not reconstructed during restoration. The so-called T-windows date from ± 1870 and have been preserved. The door frames date from the original construction period. At no. 246, the traditional large door was replaced by two smaller doors.

Keizersgracht 319 M. 17th century elevated neck-gables

upper or lower part of the two-piece door can be opened separately. A second entrance underneath the stoop was once a servants' entrance. The house still has a pull bell.

Keizersgracht 387 M. This 7.50 meter wide, elevated neck-gable with a segment-shaped fronton was built in 1668. The date-stone is underneath the loft-door. The

have two pairs of claw pieces, the smaller ones are sometimes called 'wing pieces', as opposed to the single pair common to the *normal* neck-gable that was built later. This, over 8 meter wide, sandstone façade was built in 1639 from a design by Philip Vingboons. The façade has two rows of Doric pilasters and two frontons fitted above windows that grow smaller towards the top. There is also a triangular fronton on the top, two oval windows with sculptured frames above, and a festoon next to the loft-doors. The gateway behind the second entrance underneath the stoop is decorated with about 3.000 antique tiles. The construction is original and has been altered little. The house was restored in 1958.

house owes its name 'De vergulde ster' (the gilded star) to a gable stone which can be found on a gate just left of the house. Two oval windows with sculptured frames are fitted on both sides of a loft door that has festoons underneath. The house is an original construction and the sandstone façade is remarkably unaltered. It became property of 'Hendrick de Keyser' in 1955 and was thoroughly restored in 1967. The foundation's bronze plaque with its name is fitted just left of the door frame.

Keizersgracht 322 M. This 5.50 meter wide bell-gable with Louis XV, asymmetrical, sandstone ornaments dates from ± 1750. As in most old houses, the windows grow smaller towards the top. The middle, 3rd floor window of this merchant's home was once a loft-door. The door frame below also has asymmetrical ornaments. The

Keizersgracht 546 M. This home, ornamented in Louis XV style and built ± 1760, is one of the most beautiful in Amsterdam. The hoist beam is framed in an ornamentation. The top floor retained its loft door although it was later altered into windows. The middle window is a little

wider than the windows on either side and the sash work is early 19th century. The steps of the stoop are ornamented in Louis XV style (see ornamentation next to the door underneath the stoop). This nearly 5 meter wide home has undergone little alteration since its construction.

Keizersgracht 606-608 M.   These are the largest twin neck-gables in Amsterdam. Built in 1730, they are about 7.50 meters wide and were once the homes of merchants. The hoist beam projects out through a cartouche and a crest in Louis XIV style is fitted above. The top merely serves as ornamentation and is supported by iron poles on the backside (visible from the bridge near the Nieuwe Spiegelstraat).

The windows grow smaller towards the top. At no. 608, the early 19th century sash work on the ground floor has disappeared. No. 606 has an early 19th century door as well as a stoop-bench. Coach-houses that can be reached via the Kerkstraat (on the backside) belong to these houses. There is a second entrance underneath the stoops. Before ± 1790 when no. 610 was sobered into a cornice façade, the three gables were identical.

Keizersgracht 672-674 M.   These 5 window wide sandstone façades were built in 1671 from a design by Adriaan Dortsman who built houses after a classic pattern. An identical façade stood at no. 676 until 1856. These façades are finished with a straight cornice with triglyphs. In between, small windows were fitted. No. 672 has, on the right side, a small door worked into the cornice with a small hoist beam on top. An open *attiek* is fitted on top of the cornice with four statutes of Greek gods: Athena (war), Ares (also war), Hephaitos (fire) and Demeter (earth). In the middle of the *attiek* is a coat of arms with the date of construction. Both houses were built just after the digging of the canal so the construction is original. The restoration (1964-73) was executed by a private party who was awarded for it in 1975. The restoration not only included the exterior but especially the interior. The house, with its predominantly 18th century interior, may be viewed. The coach-house, annexed to the garden house, also dates from 1671. One of the first tenants was the then already well known painter, Ferdinand

Garden and coachhouse annex

Bol who lived here until 1680. The present occupant lives in the old servants' quarters on the *attiek* floor; they can now be reached by elevator.

Prinsengracht 2-4 M. With the exception of a few wooden houses sprinkled here and there, step-gables were prominant in Amsterdam until 1665. Prinsengracht 2 is a combination shop and home that dates from 1641. Instead of one step-gable, it has two; one on each side of the corner. A small pilaster, supported by a console with a sculptured girl's head as an ornamentation, is fitted above the loft-door. The windows once had cross-frames and vary in width which is unusual. The wooden street front with supporting *pui* beam was hardly altered. The stoop and pothouse double up and there is a pull bell beside the narrow door. The house was bought in 1918 by 'Hendrick de Keyser', the same year the foundation was established. At one time the tops were altered into spout-gables. The present step-gables on the front and the side façade were reconstructed during a thorough restoration in 1955.
Prinsengracht 4 is unusually tall for a house dating 1656 (see date stone). Until ± 1755 it had a step-gable. During that period the façade was 'modernized' into a bell-gable. This house is now also a property of 'Hendrick de Keyser' (see plaque, left of door).

Prinsengracht 36 M. This elevated neck-gable with triangular fronton and four Ionic pilasters dates from 1650 (see date stone). A festoon is fitted below the loft door. Oval windows are set in sandstone frames that feature the sculptured head of a girl. The frames are next to small claw pieces with a fruit motif. The gable stone illustrates a bag full of feathers, hence the name 'De Veersack'. This house was bought in 1918 by 'Hendrick de Keyser', the year it was established (see plaque right of door). The house, with its unusual floor plan, was restored in 1967. Once there was a shop behind the high wooden street front. As with most old houses, this one was built leaning out over the street. There are several theories for this 'leaning'. Among them: aesthetical considerations (perhaps it was considered to improve visual impact), protection from snow and rain; and easier transport of goods to the upper floors. However, they all remain just theories.

Prinsengracht 124-126 M. Until recently these were the showpieces of 'Diogenes' which owns about 85 buildings. This foundation buys old houses that are let to artists after restoration. No. 124 is late 18th century with a straight cornice, two consoles and a hipped roof. The wooden shop front dates from ± 1790, the construction period. The windows are somewhat arched and the 18th century sash work

was repaired during the restoration in 1969. No. 126 is from ± 1755. The asymmetrical wooden crest above the elevated cornice is executed in Louis XV style. Two corner vases complete the ornamentation. There is a loft-door in the elevation and four consoles. A sculptured head of a man is fitted above the hoist beam. Due to the wooden street fronts and lack of stoops, each house was probably a combination of shop and home before as well as after restoration. Both houses share a unique view of the Leliegracht.

also for its warehouses, most of which can be found on the Brouwersgracht and the Prinsengracht. During the city-planning of 1613 this 'last' canal was used primarily for commercial purposes, hence the great number of warehouses on the Prinsengracht. Most of them have retained their 17th century spout-gables. These four date from ± 1690 and have sandstone volutes, small cornice-details and white-painted blocks around arched loft-doors. Because warehouses almost never had another function other than storage (for which they were built), they were seldom altered; as soon as they lost their only function, they were torn down. Next to this row stood another identical row of warehouses with spout-gables dating from ± 1620. They remained until 1938 when, despite protest, they were demolished. The remaining warehouses have hardly been altered on the outside although the interiors of nos. 215 and 217 have been rebuilt by the University of Amsterdam.

Prinsengracht 300 M. Since 1957, this house has been the property of 'Stadsherstel', an Amsterdam society founded in 1956. 'Stadsherstel' owns 220 buildings, making it the largest building restoration society in the Netherlands. So far, 140 of their buildings have been restored. This remarkably well preserved bell-gable dates from ± 1760. The top is merely ornamentation and supported by iron rods on its backside. The wooden street front with doors from the original construction period is unique with its ornamented *puibalk* (horizontal beam supporting the brick work).

Prinsengracht 211-213-215-217 M. Amsterdam is not only well-known for its private homes but

A sculptured fox with a bird in its mouth is fitted above the doors which are topped with Louis XV ornamentation. 'Stadsherstel's plaque can be found next to the door on the right. The combination shop and home was restored in 1961 and leans out over the street as do many old Amsterdam houses.

Prinsengracht 556

Prinsengracht 349 M.   Most warehouses have a spout-gable but this exception dating from ± 1650 has a bell-gable with cluster ornaments and a segment-shaped fronton. Since there has been little alteration, this warehouse is probably an original construction. It is nearly 30 meters deep which is not unusual for many old warehouses. The small door on the left is no higher than 1.80 meters.

Prinsengracht 556 M.   This house dates from 1699 and has the lowest fitted gable stone in Amsterdam that shows its date and a ship. The predominantly 18th century façade once had a bell-gable with a fronton. This type of ogee-gable is easily recognized by its S-curve profile. There is a second entrance underneath the stoop and a stoop bench above. About 20 ogee-gables are left in the city and another ogee-gable can be found around the corner at Spiegelgracht no. 30.

Prinsengracht 833-835-837-839 M.   This group of four neck-gables dates from ± 1660. Each has segment-shaped frontons ornamented with a coat of arms. The claw pieces have fruit and flower motifs. The hoist beams

above the loft doors can still be used. The middle, somewhat wider windows on the second floors were also once loft doors. The entrance doors of the houses are framed. Prinsengracht no. 837 has a stoop bench, a pull bell and a door in two pieces which can be opened separately. The house number as well as the occupants' name are fitted in period style. Together with nos. 829 and 831, these houses once formed a group of six. These four are an original construction - meaning no other houses were built before on this site. There has been little alteration.

Foundation

Eén, twee, drie
Haal op die hei!
Al in de Mei
Al in de grond
Daar staat ie pront
Fris en gezond ...

heiblok

Heien: earlier

Most of the houses in Amsterdam stand on piles. The driving of the piles
into the ground is called *heien* (pronounced 'hay-in'). Drawings from over
300 years ago show that the basic idea of hammering a long pile into the
ground with a heavy *heiblok* has changed very little since.
Three tall, poles are set up in a tripod which supports two more, parallel
poles vertically in the center. One end of a rope is passed up through a
pulley in the top of the tripod and attached to the heavy hammering block
called the *heiblok*. The *heiblok* is free to slide up and down along the two
parallel poles between which the pile is held. The other end of the rope
is split into 30 to 40 separate ends - one for each of so many men. By
pulling and releasing at the same time the men could lift and drop blocks
weighing as much as 500 kilograms (over half a ton). Depending on how
many men there were, the last time the pulley was oiled, and how good
his friends were feeling, each man would pull between 5 and 10 kilos (11
and 22 lbs). One man standing nearby, the *heibaas* directs and sets the
tempo. There were specific chants sung by the men, one line for each
blow of the hammer (see above).
In one old engraving there are some suspicious looking barrels near the
heibaas. With working days longer than they are today and work that can
not be called inspiring, it is a safe guess that the contents of the barrels
were alcoholic.
In the beginning there must have been a certain element of guesswork
in determining how many piles there should be and how long. The sand
layers underneath differ in depth and thickness and there was no way of
knowing how much without trying. What worked for other buildings in
the neighborhood would have been the best starting point. If the first pile
was made just a little extra long the exact depth was sure to be found.
Further checks could be made in much the same way as they are today
simply by seeing how much weight each pile can support before it starts
to sink. Upon reaching a sand layer the driving would go noticeably slower.
Among other things, it depended on how much money was available, but
findings have shown that a safety margin of 40% was not uncommon in
the foundations. But it is more difficult to say how much was actually
intended by the early builder who had a more limited scientific knowledge
of the forces involved than is available today.
Nevertheless, one of the few differences between the old way and the way
it is often still done is that the singing probably sounded better than the
steam and diesel driven hammers of today.

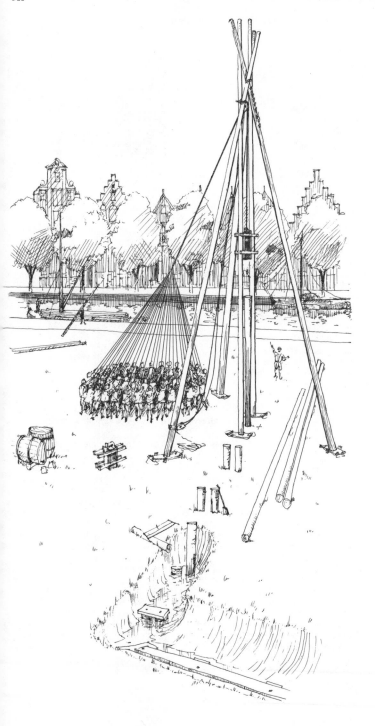

The development of the foundation

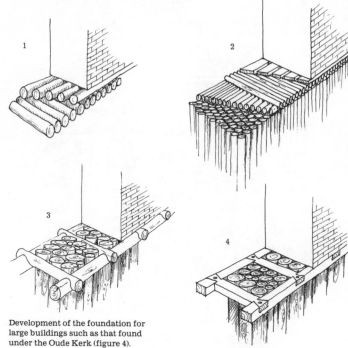

Development of the foundation for
large buildings such as that found
under the Oude Kerk (figure 4).

Because the ground is so soft, the Amsterdam house is supported on piles
reaching down to one of the relatively hard layers of sand that lie from 7
to 20 meters below the surface.

The early Frisians in the north of Holland built their houses on raised
mounds of earth called 'terps'. Trial and error would have guided a large
part of the later experimentation with actual foundations. Poor design
had a built-in self-destruct mechanism. What remained standing set an
example for the next building.

Costs would always have been a consideration, especially for the private
individual. Larger public buildings and churches provided opportunities
to work with more resources and better materials (figs. 1-4).

By $\pm$ 1750, however, the foundation system for the private house had
evolved into a form which has changed very little since (figs. 5-8). Piles
are driven at certain intervals along the lines of what will become the
walls. The piles usually $\pm$ 15 meters long, are arranged in pairs, side by
side (b). After driving, the piles are cut off just below the ground water
level (a). A short plank, the 'kesp' (c), is laid across and fastened to the tops
of the piles. Two long planks (d) are then laid side by side in the direction
of the wall, and a third 'key' plank (e) is laid between the first two so that
it sticks up above the others which helps prevent the masonry from sliding
off to the side. By using pairs instead of single piles, a much wider, more
stable connection can be made between the masonry and the wood below.
The number of piles depends on how heavy the building is, but one way
to build in a safety margin was to drive an extra, single pile in between
the paired piling (dotted circles).

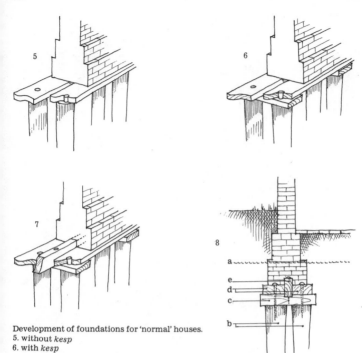

Development of foundations for 'normal' houses.
5. without *kesp*
6. with *kesp*
7. with key plank
8. stage of development reached by $\pm$ 1750

$\pm$ 1750

On the other hand it could also be a way to stretch materials and cheat on costs if it was done when no one was looking and covered up fast enough.

If all the wooden parts of the foundation are kept below the water level the problem of rot is minimised. Exposure to oxygen and drying out, however, will allow the wood to rot very quickly. A drop in the water level would have major consequences throughout the city.

One of the problems with this type of foundation for the early builder would have been how to keep the water level artificially low while the mortar in the foundation was allowed to set. Modern pumps do it today but exactly how it was done earlier is not well documented. Nevertheless people who were already using windpower to dry out entire polders, should have had little difficulty in mastering this problem.

(Source: H. J. Zantkuyl, Bouwen in Amsterdam, part 7).

What goes wrong?

Underground

A cracked or sagging wall is often a sign that something is wrong with the foundation underneath. If it appears serious enough, the unfortunate houseowner may receive a *'missive'* from the building inspector requiring him to make the necessary repairs. This can easily become a very expensive affair.

In most cases a research hole is first dug around the suspect area. If the problem lies at the upper end of the pile, it may be easily seen and perhaps relatively easily repaired. If not, it is possible to make a test. A section of pile is cut away and a type of jack is placed in between. By measuring how much push is needed to drive the pile deeper, a calculation can be made about the condition of the ground below. There are other machines designed especially for testing the ground which will print out 'maps' of the layers below.

Shown above are symptoms of various types of foundation problems:

(a) the kesp piece splits;
(b) one or a pair of piles sink more than the others;
(c) one or more piles sink on one side and the wall slides off;
(d) one or more piles do not sink as fast as the others;
(e) one of the long planks breaks;
(f) the wood simply rots away.

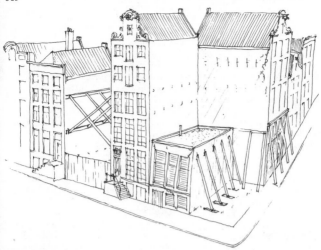

Above ground

There is another destructive factor above the ground which can also be seen as a kind of rot, but on a much larger scale. Corner buildings are the most susceptable. Gravity pushes the buildings out as well as down. In the middle of a block the pressure on each side is equalized, but the corner building is pushed from two different directions and has nothing to push back against. Once the sides of a corner building start leaning further out over the street than orginally intended, it is only a matter of time before the building is torn down if nothing is done to stop it. One often sees heavy columns bracing weak walls but these are only temporary measures. Sometimes it is already too late and the top of the house must be 'amputated'; but even so, the same problem remains for the next house in line. If not properly stopped this kind of corner rot will begin a domino process that can destroy much of an entire block. The same forces exist in the middle of a block. If one house is torn down, especially if the walls were shared with the neighbors, it is necessary to brace the remaining houses against each other to keep them from being pushed into the same hole and starting a chain reaction.

Various stages of this type of 'rot' are to be found on:
page 264 (Prinsengracht 254);
page 269 (Prinsengracht 453);
page 207 (Keizersgracht 539-543);
page 306 (the corner of Prinsengracht and Vijzelgracht has been completely rebuilt);
page 330 (Prinsengracht 870-880);
page 275 (Prinsengracht 350 where one can see the wooden *stutten* (supports) used in the middle of a block).

An innovation

How to make a foundation when the building is already there.
Until only recently there was very little to be done once something went
wrong with the foundation. And the vibration caused by heavy traffic
only helps the building to topple even faster. The big problem was how
to drive new piles under when the walls were already standing on top.
A modern solution for this problem is to slowly push the pile into the
ground using hydraulic jacks. This system, named after the innovator
J.A. De Waal is widely used today by the De Waalpaal B.V. (pronounced
'vahl-pahl'). *Paal* is the Dutch word for pile.
First, preparations are made to cast a thick, heavily reinforced slab of
concrete which will become the new floor - usually the basement floor.
In addition to the steel reinforcing bars, wooden molds are positioned
within the floor wherever there will be a new pile. When the concrete
dries these molds, pyramidal in form, become holes that are smaller
on the top than at the bottom. Also cast into the floor around the holes
are steel anchor bolts which will later serve to fasten the hydraulic jacks
firmly to the floor. But before pouring the concrete additionel holes,
kassen, are cut into the existing wall at the same level as the new floor so
that when the concrete sets, it locks itself into the old walls. Since the
floor is made extra strong, the jacks may use the weight of the building
itself to drive the piles into the ground through the pyramidal-shaped
holes. The piles, made of hollow concrete pipe, come in sections of one
or two meters depending on how high the ceiling is.
Each section has a steel pipe in one end that fits into the end of the next
section as the pile is driven down. When the right depth is reached, a ram
can be dropped through the hollow part to make ball-shaped 'foot' at the
bottom which is filled with concrete. When all the hollow is filled with
concrete the pyramid form at the top acts to lock the pile against the floor.
The rest is hardly more than cutting off the anchor bolts and rolling out
the carpet.

This system, begun only 65 years ago, has had a major impact on the city,
for it solves several problems at one time. First and most importantly, it
provides a way to support a heavy wall without having to get under it.
Second, its short sections of piles means that it can be used in a low space
without having to remove the floor above. And third, it avoid the vibrations
of the hammer technique which can damage nearby walls.
The system also contributes to the very high cost of restoration work. But
on the other hand it is also responsible for having given a second life to
many old monuments.

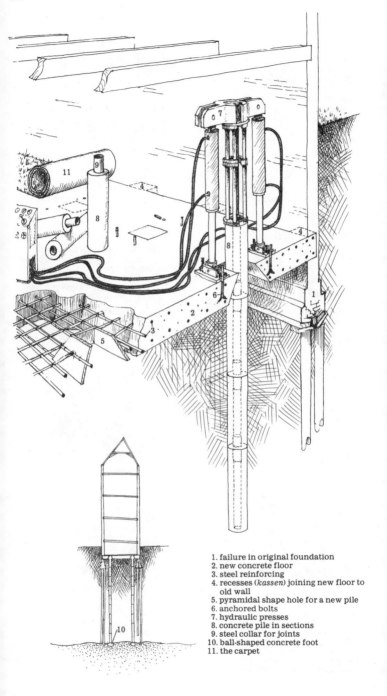

1. failure in original foundation
2. new concrete floor
3. steel reinforcing
4. recesses (*kassen*) joining new floor to old wall
5. pyramidal shape hole for a new pile
6. anchored bolts
7. hydraulic presses
8. concrete pile in sections
9. steel collar for joints
10. ball-shaped concrete foot
11. the carpet

List of terms

(S = Singel; H = Herengracht;
K = Keizersgracht;
P = Prinsengracht)

adapted architecture: a new construction in a historical setting which through its material, color, height and other characteristics, blends in with its neighbors. (e.g. S428 and P421)

ashlar: stone masonry made of rectangular blocks which may vary in finish from smooth to rough-cut; often sandstone or limestone.

alliance shield: coats of arms from families bound together by marriage, mounted up on the façade by the houseowner. (e.g. H543)

Amsterdamse School: a building style from the 1920's that first developed in Amsterdam. The term was first used in 1916. The style is recognized by the frequent use of brick for ornamentation and there is usually relief in the façade. The windows accentuate width rather than height. (e.g. S46-48 and P400)

anchor: a metal fastener that prevents the outer walls from coming loose from the floor beams inside; sometimes ornamented.

arched windows: windows that are slightly arched across the top rather than completely straight. (e.g. H151 and K286)

'Aristoteles': an organization founded in early 1970. The purpose of the foundation is to administer and manage, with or without compensation, houses of which it remains the legal owner. The occupant is the financial owner. Often the house is split into several separate living units. The foundation is housed in one of the 64 buildings of which it is the legal owner, H43, (tel . 020-22 14 28).

attiek: (Dutch; the 2nd syllable is pronounced 'teak'; not to be confused with the Eng. word 'attic'): the ornamental surface at the top of a façade that runs above the cornice and hides the roof from the street: used primarily in the 18th century (e.g. K244-246); may be found in 'open' form, often a balustrade, or 'closed' form (e.g. K317).

baluster: a small column supporting a railing; often a handrail; may range from simple to ornate.

bay window: a window structure that protrudes out from the façade; usually wood; rarely used on the canals. (e.g. S458 and 504)

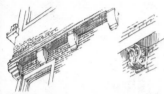

beam-ends: the outer ends of the floor beams that transverse the building; in the case of corner buildings they are seen along the side façade. (e.g. S410 and 412)

bel-etage (Dutch: last syllable rhymes with the last in 'massage'): the floor above the souterrain, higher than street-level, reached via a stoop.

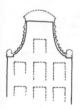

bell-gable: a brick façade with upper ornamentation usually from sandstone; the top has the silhouette of a bell; built ±1660-±1790; most are 2 or 3 windows wide. (e.g. P300 and K716)

Berlage, H.P.: one of the most well-known Dutch architects of this century; designed several entire areas in south Amsterdam; most important design is the Beurs (stock-exchange) on the Damrak, built 1903. (See also e.g. H184)

bull's-eye: small, oval windows often used in the top of a façade with sandstone framing; predominantly 17th century; also called by its french name *oeil-de-boeuf*. (e.g. S432)

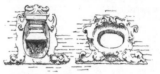

cartouche: ornamental sandstone framing often applied around the hoist-beam, small rounded window or yearstone. (e.g. S460)

city-forming: a crowding out of the living functions by the construction of large roads, metros, or office buildings. See buildings along the Vijzelstraat.

claw piece: literal translation of Dutch word *klauwstuk* referring to the ornamented sandstone that fills the in-step on a neck-gable. (e.g. H508-510)

cluster ornamentation: 17th century sandstone ornamentation with fruit or flower motif used on the upper sides of neck- and bell-gables. (e.g. S434-436)

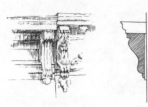

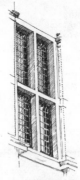

console: a bracket, often ornamented, used to support e.g. a cornice.

consolidation: a restoration whereby the starting point is the period style the building is in at the outset of the restoration. Reconstructions from later periods are left intact; not to be confused with the more common meaning to put together.

corner lisena: lisena along the sides of a building; see lisena.

cornice: a molded projection often crowning a façade and frequently ornamented; may also be found over doors or window fronts; usually wood but sometimes sandstone. (e.g. K317 and H166)

crenelle, crenellation: an element of or the use of the squared-off tooth motif of battlements.

crest: an 18th century ornament applied to the top of a façade, primarily neck- and bell-gables. (e.g. K546 and P993)

cross-frame windows: window casing in the form of a cross that divides the window into 4 parts; often furnished with shutters. (e.g. H81 and K123)

cushion-door: a door with pillow-shaped forms in slight relief; applied primarily in the 19th century. (e.g. H325)

'Diogenes': founded in 1960. The foundation often buys delapidated houses in neighborhoods less attractive to other private buyers. After restoration, these houses are leased to artists. The foundation presently owns 87 buildings and is housed in a 1643 ferrymans house, Sloterkade 21 (tel. 020-17 27 35).

door framing: used here to identify the casing around the outside of the entrance; usually ornamented; often used in the 18th century. (e.g. S390 and P527)

Doric: one of the classical orders; see pilaster.

dormer: a window projecting out of the roof, often above a straight cornice; mainly used in the 19th century. (e.g. H3)

double house: instead of two, a single house built on two lots; often 5 windows wide. (e.g. H576 and H457)

elevated cornice: an 18th century crowning of the façade with a straight cornice interrupted by an elevation in the middle where loft-shutters may be placed for easier access to the hoist beam; often richly ornamented. (e.g. K244-246)

elevated neck-gable: a 17th century gable type with a brick façade that has two pairs of in-steps and claw-pieces rather than the single pair; often seen with pilasters. (e.g. K453)

Empire: name of a period in art history from 1800 to 1830 when there was little built except reconstructions, especially doorways; much use made of motifs with Egyptian origin such as rosettes and sphinxes. (e.g. K743)

fanlight: the window over the front door lighting the entrance; often finely ornamented. (e.g. H218-220)

fan railing: an iron fence in the shape of a fan sometimes seen around entrance to souterrain.

festoon: an ornament on the façade in the form of a garland, usually with fruit and flower motifs; primarily 17th century. (e.g. S460)

floor, 1st: in Europe, the 1st floor is the one above the ground floor.

frontal stoop: stairs in front of a house in which the steps are parallel to the façade; not very common in Amsterdam. (e.g. K56)

fronton: a piece, often triangular but sometimes rounded, that crowns the façade; occasionally seen over windows; primarily used in the 17th century. (e.g. P1039-1041)

gable: technically just the part of the wall that covers the triangular end of the roof, but used here to mean the upper part of the façade or sometimes, like the Dutch word *gevel*, to refer to the entire façade.

gable stone: a sculptured, stone tablet embedded in the façade which acted like a house number; primarily used in the 17th century. There are still about 600 gable stones left in Amsterdam. (e.g. 'De Sonnenburg' on H361)

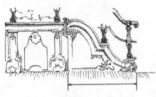

harp piece: a stone element that hides the view of the treads on a stoop from the side. (e.g. H402)

'Hendrick de Keyser': the oldest restoration group in Holland, founded in 1918 and named after the 17th century architect Hendrick de Keyser. The society buys houses whose interiors and exteriors are of historical art value and therefore its real-estate portfolio, including ± 200 buildings of which ± 70 are in Amsterdam, is unique. Houses belonging to the society are recognized by the small bronze plaque with its initials. The offices are housed in one of the society's own buildings, Herengracht 284 (tel. 020-23 33 34).

hipped roof: a roof in which the two ends have a slope as well as the sides.

hoist beam: The beam sticking out through the top of a façade from which block and tackle can be hung for the purpose of hauling goods in and out of the upper floors.

Ionic: one of the classical orders; see pilaster.

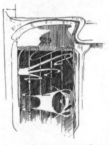

Jugendstil: name of a period in art history, ± 1895 to ± 1910 recognized by its characteristic organic lines. (e.g. K329)

Keyser, Hendrick de (1565-1621): a Dutch architect known primarily for his churches (Zuiderkerk and Westerkerk). He also built private houses among which are Herengracht 170-172, Keizersgracht 123 and Singel 140-142.

lintel: the horizontal beam over a window or door which in the latter case separates the door from the fanlight above and is sometimes ornamented.

lisena: an ornamental, masonry column applied to the façade, often with horizontal banding or grooves.

loft: 1. the uppermost space within the attick 2. unpartitioned space on any floor used for storage.

loft-doors, loft-shutters: large and small openings respectively, used in place of windows to facilitate the transport of goods in and out of the loft spaces.

Louis XIV: a style named after the French king who reigned from 1643 to 1715. By 1700 the style had reached Holland where its characteristics could be found in the sandstone ornamentation on the façades. Acanthus leaves are one of the leaf motifs often employed until 1740 when this style went out of fashion. (e.g. H166)

Louis XV: reigned in France from 1715 to 1774; by ± 1740 the style named after him reached Holland, where it is recognized by its exuberant, curled, asymmetrical ornamentation, most commonly used on bell-gables. (e.g. K546)

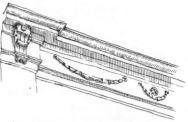

Louis XVI: reigned in France from 1774 to 1792; the style reached Holland in about 1770; characterized by garlands and vases. (e.g. K590 and S145)

makelaar (Dutch): the middle piece in a wooden roof that act as the backbone joint for the rafters; sometimes with pointed ornamentation.

Mansarde roof: a roof with a double slope on each side; named after 17th century architect Mansarde; used primarily towards the end of the 19th century. (e.g. P907 and P981)

monument: 'a building at least 50 years old and of such historical or aesthetic value that it needs protection' (1961 Monument Law). There are almost 7,000 houses built before ± 1850 on the Monument List in Amsterdam. This means that in practice, demolition is (almost) impossible. Government, province and municipality subsidize the restoration of these buildings. The Municipal Bureau for Monument Care gives advice and applies for subsidies. In 1973, a total of 81 buildings all built around the turn of the century were put on the Monument List in a catagory sometimes called 'Young Monuments'.

neck-gable: this type of façade has a higher middle part, the 'neck', with two 90 degree in-steps on the 'shoulders', in which sit the so-called claw pieces. The first neck-gable dates from 1636 (H168), most were built, between 1700 and 1750 (e.g. K634 through 646); and the last in ± 1780. Most neck-gables are 3 or 4 windows wide.

newly built: as opposed to 'original construction'; see term below.

oeil-de-boeuf (French): see 'bull's-eye'.

ogee-gable: an unusual 19th century gable type. The silhouette of the top is distinguished by two S-formed lines. the upper parts concave and the lower parts convex (e.g. P 556 and K 157).

original construction: as used here, a building that has stood on a given spot since the land was parceled out.

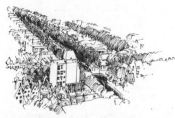

over-scaling: Amsterdam is divided up into basic units of one plot. When more than one plot is used for a single building, the construction is termed here 'over-scaled'. (e.g. H293-305)

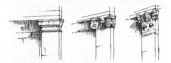

pilaster: a flattened column in the form of a pillar projected just slightly from the façade; may have a decorative and/or structurel function; often ornamented with elements from the classical orders; Doric, Ionic and Corinthian.

pinnacle: a ball- or spire-shaped ornament, usually made from sandstone and placed often on top of the façade.

pothouse: an extension of the kitchen, often used for storage of pots; later used by handycrafts people. (e.g. H77 and P378)

pui (Dutch; pronounced 'pow'): the lower part of the façade, the street-front. It is usually made from wood or sandstone. (e.g. S310). The horizontal beam that

runs across the top and supports the masonry work above, is called the *pui* beam; a cornice there would be the *pui* cornice.

pull-bell: an old-fashioned doorbell pulled manually.

putto: an ornament in the form of a sculptured infant. (e.g. K401)

relieving arch a masonry arch incorporated into the wall above windows and doors used to divert the weight of the wall from the top of the opening.

Renaissance: a period in Amsterdam's art history ± 1550

to ± 1650 when the classical styles were revived. Building in this period consisted mostly of step-gables which included the characteristic features of the period: an accent on horizontals with much use of arches and ornamentation. Towards the end of the 19th century this same style revived again in the so-called neo-Renaissance. (e.g. S31)

roll ornamentation (also called fractables): a sandstone coping in a rolling motif; used mostly between ± 1550 and ± 1610 and there seen only rarely in Amsterdam today. (e.g. S423 and 140-142)

row line: legally the line along the street between private and public ground; in practice it is used to refer to the line formed by the façades.

saddle roof: the most common roof form in Amsterdam, built primarily up until ±1860.

sash window: a window with a wooden framework supporting smaller glass panes; also called a double-hung window if it slides vertically to open.

sash work: the wooden framework within the window which holds the glass.

sobering: used to describe the architectural process begun in the 19th century when the use of lavish ornamentation on the façade declined, and many older gables were 'modernised' into cornice façades. (e.g. P847)

souterrain (French): The space in a house that lies under street-level and often reached via a door under the stoop. Due to the high groundwater level in Amsterdam the souterrain is slightly higher than the normal cellar.

spout-gable: a brick gable with sandstone ornamentation on the top; silhouette similar to upside-down spout; most 17th century warehouses have spout-gables. (e.g. P211-217)

'Stadsherstel': short for Amsterdamse Maatschappij tot Stadsherstel N.V.; (the word *stadsherstel* means city-restoration) founded in 1956; since become the biggest restoration group in Holland owning 220 buildings of which 140 are restored. They buy deteriorating buildings, which are restored and then leased. The small plaque (with the three Amsterdam crosses combined as a column) near the door identifies a house that 'Stadsherstel' has restored. (e.g. P646-648 and H 361). Present address: Keizersgracht 462 (tel. 020-22 07 74).

step-gable: a gable with small steps climbing up along the top; often occurs with a wooden street front below; built between ± 1600 and ± 1665. (e.g. H81)

stoop: the stone steps in front of a building leading up to the entrance. The high groundwater level and therefore high basements and 'ground' floors necessitate such stoops under which there is often a second entrance to the basement used in earlier times for the servants. Most stoops rise across the façade as opposed to a frontal approach, and some have a small bench built into the railing.

transverse roof: a roof whose peak is parallel to the front façade (e.g. P809), whereas most Amsterdam houses have the common saddle roof.

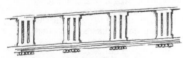

triglyph: an ornament with two or three vertical grooves; often used under the cornice.

tympan: a larger version of the triangular fronton used on top of a façade. (e.g. K324 and P235)

Vingboons, Philip (1608-1675): a well-known architect of the 17th century, who designed e.g. H168 (the first neck-gable) and S460; his brother Justus was also an architect.

volute: the spiral or scroll-form element in a claw piece or on the 'shoulder' of a gable; also refers to the ornamentation on the top of Ionic or Corinthian columns (see pilaster).

warehouse: built along the canals for convenient storage of goods; primarily in the 17th century with spout-gables. (e.g. P771-773)

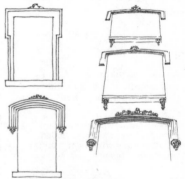

window framing: used here to describe the ornamentation that frames and accentuates a window.

window railing: iron railings used in front of windows; primarily 19th century. (e.g. P925)

wing piece: a smaller version of a claw piece (see claw piece).

Important dates from Amsterdam's history

1275 First recorded reference to the city, then called Amstelledamme: a toll-tax exemption for the inhabitants granted by Floris V.

1309 The Oude Kerk (Old Church), the oldest building in the city, is begun; many enlargements followed. The steeple dates from 1565. Restoration begun 1955.

1421, 1452 Two large fires; much of the wooden architecture destroyed.

1488 The Waag (weigh-house) is built on the Nieuwmarkt employing the oldest gable stone in the city. Together with the Munt it once formed part of the 15th century city walls.

1568 Beginning of the 80 Years War; the Dutch fight to throw off the Spanish yoke.

1578 Amsterdam joins in the fight against Spain. Roman Catholic church services are forbidden.

1585 The fall of Antwerp (to the Spanish) sends a stream of refugees to Amsterdam.

1613 Beginning of the first phase of the 17th century expansion which employed planners for the first time. The three concentric canals were dug according to a plan by Staets, the city carpenter, and Oetgens the mayor. In 1658 the second phase begins extending the canal girdle from Leidsegracht to the Amstel.

1614 The Zuiderkerk (South Church) is built from plans by Hendrick de Keyser.

1648 The beginning of the construction of the townhall from a classical design by Jacob van Campen. Since 1808 it has been used as a palace..

1795-1813 Holland is annexed by France; very little is built in the city.

1798 The guilds are discontinued resulting in a sobering of the building arts: much less or no ornamentation at all on the façades.

1839 First rail laid, between Amsterdam and Haarlem.

1875 Introduction of present system of house numbers.

1876 The North Sea Canal opens; a big factor in the city's economic revival.

1889 Central Station, a design by P.J.H. Cuypers, is opened, thus blocking the view of the IJ (pronounced like the Eng. letter 'A') from the Dam.

1894 Opening of the Stadsschouwburg (city theater).

1895 The first city 'break-through': Raadhuisstraat is extended, and houses on both the Herengracht and the Keizersgracht have to be torn down for it.

1903 The Beurs (stock-exchange) by architect Berlage is opened and a new era in the city's architectural history is begun.

1917 Vijzelstraat, once just as narrow as Leidsestraat, is widened from ± 7 meters (±30 feet) to 22 meters wide (± 72 feet). One side of the street is completely torn-down.

1953 Establishment of the Municipal Bureau for Monument Care which gives advice and restoration subsidies for the almost 7,000 protected houses.

1975 Amsterdam celebrates its 700th Anniversery.

Statistics about Amsterdam

± 740,000 inhabitants
± 90,000 people living in the inner-city
± 500,000 bicyclists
± 120,000 elderly
± 22,000 students
± 540 professors
± 290,000 dwelling units
± 250,000 telephone lines
± 200,000 trees
± 230,000 square meters of office space still available for rent
± 30,000 people looking for living space
± 25,000 moves (to a new address) per year
± 7,000 buildings classified monuments
± 700 buildings owned by foundations and other non-profit groups
± 600 gable stones
± 240 restorations per year

± 100 kilometers of canals (± 62 miles)
± 1.6 million foreign tourists per year
± 1.4 million visitors to the Rijksmuseum per year
± 150,000 pedestrians through the Kalverstraat per day
± 8,100 parkingmeters
± 4,000 wrongly parked cars per day
± 2,850 police officers
± 65 cars towed away per day
± 2,800 houseboats
± 1,250 cafés
± 1,200 bridges
± 600 taxis
± 30 movie theaters

Sources: Centraal Bureau voor de Statistiek; several newspapers, magazines, brochures and other publications

Filled-in canals

The canal 'girdle' formed by the four major canals and the Jordaan area were part of an expansion begun in the early 1600's and finished in the late 1600's. It would enlarge the city by 400 percent. There were no further expansions until 1870 and no changes in the canals and street plan until 1856 when the first of many canals was filled in:

year filled	old name	new name
1856	Goudsbloemgracht	Willemstraat
1861	Anjeliersgracht	Westerstraat
1865	Begijnensloot	Gedempte Begijnensloot
1867	N.Z. Achterburgwal	Spuistraat
1870	Achtergracht (partially)	Falckstraat
1870	Kattegat	
1872	Nieuwe Looierssloot	Fokke Simonszstraat
1882	Houtgracht	Waterlooplein
1882	Leprozengracht	Waterlooplein
1882	Spui	
1883	Damrak (partially)	
1884	N.Z. Voorburgwal, (Martelaarsgracht)	
1889	Rozengracht	
1891	Elandsgracht	
1895	Warmoesgracht	Raadhuisstraat
1895	Lindengracht, Palmgracht	
1902	Overtoom	
1909	Lijnbaansgracht (partially)	Kleine Gartmanplantsoen
1934	Vijzelgracht	
1936	Rokin (partially)	
1968	Houtkopersburgwal	

Identifying buildings

Is there still a stoop?

Houses with stoops were no longer built after ± 1850

Is there still a pothouse?

Pothouses are 17th century building elements.

Is there still a gable stone?

Gable stones are 17th century building elements.

Does the façade lean out over the street?

If so, the house is from the 17th or 18th century. After ± 1850 the façades were built without any lean.

Do the windows have cross-frames?

The smaller the panes of glass, the older the window style. The T-windows were introduced ± 1870.

Do the upper windows get progressively smaller?

If so, the house was built before ± 1800, after which time it was no longer done.

How much sash work is there?

If so, the house is from the 17th century. The (sliding) sash window was introduced around 1700.

Are there festoons on the façade?
Is there a fronton on top?
Is there a fruit and/or flower motif worked into the sandstone ornaments?

These are all 17th century characteristics.

Are there pilasters on the façade?

Pilasters were used in the middle of the 17th century.

Does the house have a saddle roof?

Until ± 1850, most houses had the pointed, saddle roof.

Does the façade have sandstone ornamentation on top?

If so, it dates from the 17th or 18th century. The practice of using sandstone ornaments ceased, for the most part, after ± 1800.

How many floors are there?

A house with a bel-etage, 1st floor, *attiek, attiek* loft, and roof beginning just above the 1st floor ceiling dates from the 17th century. If there are more than two floors above the bel-etage, the house is from the end of the 17th century or later.

Books about Amsterdam

Allings, H.W. *Amsterdamse hofjes* (1965).

'Amstelodamum'. Publication from the Genootschap Amstelodamum, 1900-up to now.

Amsterdam omstreeks 1800 (1965).

Amsterdam omstreeks 1900 (1940).

Amsterdam 1900-1940. Commemorative book on the 40th anniversary of the Genootschap Amstelodamum (1940).

Amsterdam door de bank genomen (1967).

Annual reports from the Vereniging 'Hendrick de Keyser', 1918-up to now.

Annual reports from the Amsterdamse Maatschappij tot Stadherstel N.V., 1965-up to now.

Annual reports from 'Aristoteles', 1970-up to now.

Annual reports from the Amsterdam Municipality.

Bewaard in het hart. A publication of the Municipal Bureau of Monument Care (1965).

Brinkgreve, G. (ed.), *Alarm in Amsterdam. Het lot der oude binnensteden* (1965).

'De Lamp'. A publication from the Vrienden van de Amsterdamse Binnenstad, 1960-up to now.

De vroegste foto's van Amsterdam (1974).

Farber, J.B., *Groot Amsterdams Boek* (1975).

Grachtenboek. Verzaameling van alle huizen en prachtige gebouwen langs de Keizersgracht en Heerengracht der Stadt Amsteldam, beginnende van den Binnen Amstel en eindigende aan de Brouwersgracht; bestaande in ruim 1400 prachtige en trotsche gebouwen, origineel van huis tot huis geteekend en op kunstige koopere plaaten afgebeeld door Caspar Philips Jzn. (1768-1771). Reprinted in 1962 with text from E. van Houten.

'Heemschut'. Periodical from the Bond Heemschut.

Hoek-Ostende, J.H. van den, *Amsterdam vroeger en nu* (1969).

Hofker, W.G., and T. Koot, *Langs de Amsterdamse grachten* (1973).

Houten, E. van, *Amsterdamse merkwaardigheden* (1942).

Kok, A.A., *Amsterdamse woonhuizen* (1941).

Kok, A.A., *De historische schoonheid van Amsterdam* (1940).

Koot, T., *En nu Amsterdam in. Zwerftochten langs de beschermde monumenten* (1975).

Koot, T., *Help! Ze verpesten ons land* (1973).

Kruizinga, J.H., *Amsterdam – stad der duizend bruggen* (1973).

Meischke, R., *Het Nederlandse woonhuis van 1300-1800. Vijftig jaar Vereniging 'Hendrick de Keyser'* (1969).

Monument Lists of Amsterdam, 1928-1969.

Olie, J., *Amsterdam gefotografeerd (1860-1905)* (1973).

'Ons Amsterdam', 1949-up to now.

Quarles van Ufford, C.C.G., *Amsterdam voor 't eerst gefotografeerd.*

Rapport inzake de demping van stadswateren.

Roy van Zuydewijn, H.J.F. de, *Amsterdamse bouwkunst 1815-1940* (1969).

Schade van Westrum, L.C., *Groeten uit Amsterdam, Briefkaarten uit grootvaders album* (1964).

Swigchem, C.A. van, *Afbraak of restauratie. Monumentenzorg in Nederland* (1968).

Tien jaar Diogenes, 1960-1970 (1970).

Willema, J.A.C., *Geschiedenis Monumentenzorg 1875-1975* (1976).

Kamp, W., *Monumentenjaar 1975, behoud van historisch gegroeide verscheidenheid.*

'Werk in uitvoering', monthly from the Amsterdam Publics Works (1975).

Vier eeuwen Herengracht. Het nieuwe Amsterdamse Grachtenboek (1975).

Wattjes, J.G., and F.A. Warners, *Amsterdams bouwkunst en stedeschoon* (1975).

Winckebach, L.W.R., *Oud-Amsterdam. 100 stadsgezichten* (1907).

Witkuyl, H.J., *Restaureren.* Brochure (1974).

Witkuyl, H.J., *Bouwen in Amsterdam. Periode sinds 1973.*

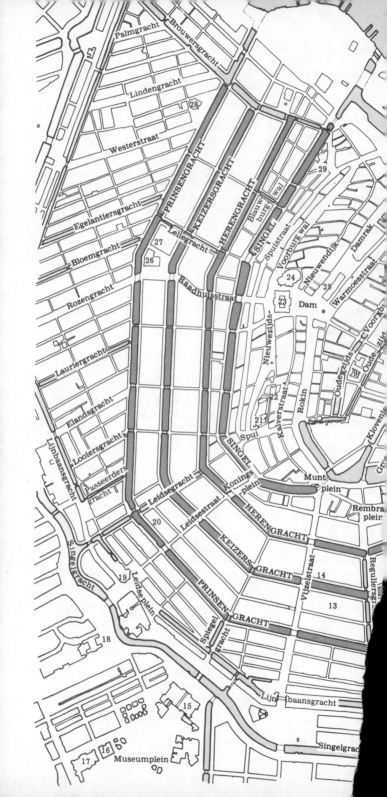